Somme Offensive

Somme Offensive

March 1918

Andrew Rawson

Pen & Sword
MILITARY

First published in Great Britain in 2018 by
PEN & SWORD MILITARY
an imprint of
Pen & Sword Books Ltd
47 Church Street
Barnsley
South Yorkshire S70 2AS

ISBN 978 1 52672 332 1

A CIP catalogue record for this book is available from the British Library.

Printed and bound in England by
TJ International Ltd, Padstow, Cornwall.

Pen & Sword Books Limited incorporates the imprints of
Atlas, Archaeology, Aviation, Discovery, Family History, Fiction,
History, Maritime, Military, Military Classics, Politics, Select,
Transport, True Crime, Air World, Frontline Publishing, Leo Cooper,
Remember When, Seaforth Publishing, The Praetorian Press,
Wharncliffe Local History, Wharncliffe Transport,
Wharncliffe True Crime and White Owl.

For a complete list of Pen & Sword titles please contact
Pen and Sword Books Limited
47 Church Street, Barnsley, South Yorkshire, S70 2AS, England
E-mail: enquiries@pen-and-sword.co.uk
Website: www.pen-and-sword.co.uk

Contents

Regiments

Regiments in Alphabetical Order	Abbreviations Used
Argyll & Sutherland Highlanders Regiment	Argylls
Bedfordshire Regiment	Bedfords
Black Watch Regiment	Black Watch
Border Regiment	Borders
Buffs (East Kent) Regiment	Buffs
Cambridgeshire Regiment	Cambridgeshire
Cameron Highlanders Regiment	Camerons
Cameronians (Scottish Rifles) Regiment	Scottish Rifles
Cheshire Regiment	Cheshires
Coldstream Guards	Coldstreamers
Connaught Rangers	Connaughts
Devonshire Regiment	Devons
Dorsetshire Regiment	Dorsets
Duke of Cornwall's Light Infantry	DCLI
Duke of Wellington's (West Riding) Regiment	Duke's
Durham Light Infantry	Durhams
East Lancashire Regiment	East Lancashires
East Surrey Regiment	East Surreys
East Yorkshire Regiment	East Yorkshires
Essex Regiment	Essex
Gloucestershire Regiment	Gloucesters
Gordon Highlanders	Gordons
Green Howards (Yorkshire) Regiment	Green Howards
Grenadier Guards	Grenadiers
Hampshire Regiment	Hampshires
Herefordshire Regiment	Herefords
Hertfordshire Regiment	Hertfords
Highland Light Infantry	HLI
Honourable Artillery Company	HAC
Irish Guards	Irish Guards
King's (Liverpool) Regiment	King's

King's Own (Royal Lancaster) Regiment	King's Own
King's Own Scottish Borderers	KOSBs
King's (Shropshire Light Infantry) Regiment	Shropshires
King's Own (Yorkshire Light Infantry) Regiment	KOYLIs
King's Royal Rifle Corps	KRRC
Lancashire Fusiliers	Lancashire Fusiliers
Leicestershire Regiment	Leicesters
Leinster Regiment	Leinsters
Lincolnshire Regiment	Lincolns
London Regiment	Londoners
Loyal North Lancashire Regiment	Loyals
Manchester Regiment	Manchesters
Middlesex Regiment	Middlesex
Monmouthshire Regiment	Monmouths
Norfolk Regiment	Norfolks
Northamptonshire Regiment	Northants
North Staffordshire Regiment	North Staffords
Northumberland Fusiliers	Northumberland Fusiliers
Oxford and Buckinghamshire Light Infantry	Ox and Bucks
Queen's (Royal West Surrey) Regiment	Queen's
Queen's Own (Royal West Kent) Regiment	Queen's Own
Rifle Brigade	Rifle Brigade
Royal Berkshire Regiment	Berkshires
Royal Dublin Fusiliers	Dublin Fusiliers
Royal Fusiliers	Royal Fusiliers
Royal Inniskilling Fusiliers	Inniskilling Fusiliers
Royal Irish Fusiliers	Irish Fusiliers
Royal Irish Regiment	Irish Regiment
Royal Irish Rifles	Irish Rifles
Royal Munster Fusiliers	Munsters
Royal Scots Fusiliers	Scots Fusiliers
Royal Scots Regiment	Royal Scots
Royal Sussex Regiment	Sussex
Royal Warwickshire Regiment	Warwicks
Royal Welsh Fusiliers	Welsh Fusiliers
Scots Guards	Scots Guards
Seaforth Highlanders	Seaforths
Sherwood Foresters (Notts and Derbyshire)	Sherwoods
Somerset Light Infantry	Somersets
South Lancashire Regiment	South Lancashires
South Staffordshire Regiment	South Staffords

South Wales Borderers	SWBs or Borderers
Suffolk Regiment	Suffolks
Welsh Guards	Welsh Guards
Welsh Regiment	Welsh
West Yorkshire Regiment	West Yorkshires
Wiltshire Regiment	Wiltshires
Worcestershire Regiment	Worcesters
York and Lancaster Regiment	York and Lancasters

Introduction

This book focuses on the British army's traumatic experience during the German offensive on the Somme between 21 March and 5 April 1918 and many sources have been used to create it. The backbone of the story comes from the two military operations in France and Belgium which belong to the twenty-eight volume series of Official Histories on the Great War. The compiler, Brigadier General James Edmonds, found that record-keeping during the battle was often less than satisfactory and many documents were missing. This is hardly surprising, considering how fast battalions were moving and how often units were surrounded or overrun. Lieutenant General Launcelot Kiggell interviewed many officers to try and fill in the gaps but the end result is an uninspiring and bland record of what were very exciting and dangerous times.

A lot of information comes from the divisional and regimental histories published in the years after the Great War. The quality of information these published histories give varies tremendously. Some are taken from the unit war diaries while others give the bare details. But they all add something to the Official History account. They always explain the successes and disasters although they do tend to blame the actions of others rather than their own unit. But they are all good at describing the heroic exploits of brave men in their regiment or division.

Many of the divisional and regimental histories can be accessed for a small fee at militaryarchive.co.uk. You are also able to look at medal rolls, army orders, army lists and get help with locating biographical information, awards and photographs of individuals. Joining the archive has given me annual access to these resources for the same cost as a day in the London archives.

Some of the information comes from the war diaries held in the National Archives at Kew, London. They are the original source material of a unit's battle experiences; however, they are of mixed quality during the hectic retreat. The diarists were often fully occupied fighting and in many cases the battalion records were destroyed so they would not be captured. Material was sometimes removed or lost after the war, making this source of information patchy at best. The war diaries can be accessed through ancestry.co.uk and other websites, again for a reasonable fee.

I had to judge at what level of detail to pitch the story. There is little new to learn if the level is too shallow but it becomes overwhelming if there is too much information. This is not an exhaustive account of the retreat across the Somme but it is a comprehensive look at the British Expeditionary Force's testing experiences in the spring of 1918.

A comprehensive account of the campaign would be at least twice the length of this book, so some things have had to be left out. There is only the minimum of information on the liaison between the War Cabinet, the Chief of the Imperial General Staff and the BEF's General Headquarters. The same goes for the formation of and the meetings of the Supreme War Council. The meetings between British and the French politicians and generals are explained in brief as are the consequences of the events on the Eastern Front. There is some information on the movement of troops from east to west and the preparations for the offensive, as well as British defensive preparations. There is some information on the German tactics used, particularly at the start of the offensive. However, the detail of German units involved does not go below army level and discussion of German strategic decisions is kept to a minimum.

There are few details of casualties in the narrative unless they were disproportionately high. Records are incomplete and they often changed as men returned to their units or were reported as prisoners. Casualties were always very high and both sides suffered. Units were often reduced to a few dozen weary men which must have had a tremendous impact on the survivors. I do not use personal diaries, which usually follow a depressing theme of mud and blood. Instead the quotes used demonstrate the men's pride in their spirit and achievements during extremely adverse conditions. Sometimes their dark humour illustrates a situation perfectly.

So what will you find in the book? There is the planning behind the German attack and how they assembled so many men and such vast amounts of material. The attack against each corps is considered in turn from north to south and day by day. There are the reasons behind the successes and failures of each attack. Often the men who led the attacks or who stopped the counter-attacks are mentioned; so are all the men who were awarded the Victoria Cross.

The British army faced many tactical problems as they fought their first defensive battle in the open since the beginning of the war. Time and again men fought until their ammunition ran low and then withdrew to fight another day. Sometimes they could not escape and fought to the last round before surrendering. Casualties were horrendous but morale never broke and while the line was often bent, it was never broken. The cadre of survivors kept fighting and teaching the replacements sent up to replace casualties what to do.

Many military books rely on a few small-scale maps to support the text. I think they do little to help the reader understand the events described. The saying is 'a picture is worth a thousand words' and I believe the same applies to maps. There are over sixty tactical maps included in this book to help the reader understand the different stages of the campaign. Typically there is one for each corps on each day it was engaged. Plenty of detailed maps has been a feature of all the books in this series.

My inspiration for this series was Noah Trudeau's *A Testing of Courage*, a book about the 1863 epic battle of Gettysburg in the American Civil War. I was left baffled after reading several books on this three-day engagement but Trudeau's book explained it clearly. He uses large-scale maps every few pages, each illustrating the developments across the battlefield. It helped me understand the unfolding battle when I visited Gettysburg. I wanted to do the same for the events across the Somme in March and April 1918.

The Official History maps are sometimes cited as good examples, but, while the level of detail is high on the March 1918 maps, it often muddles the information to the point of distraction. There is never any definition between what ground was lost in battle and what was given up by a planned withdrawal either. This book uses trench map extracts, which are well known to anyone with an interest in the First World War, for the topographical background. Their grid system is 1,000 yards (914 metres) for each large square and 100 yards (91 metres) for each minor graduation. The terrain has changed little – contours, roads, rivers, woods and villages have rarely altered; only towns have expanded a lot. It means these maps can be used to help locate places on the battlefield.

The map symbols have been kept as simple as possible. The front lines before the battle started are marked by solid lines but only the British morning line is marked after that. Any ground captured, either by the Germans or the Allies, is marked by a dashed line. Any ground given up by a planned withdrawal, and this was often far more than that captured, is marked by a line of dots. Corps boundaries are marked by a line of dashes and dots.

Arrows are sometimes used to clarify the direction of an advance or a retreat. Each division, brigade or composite force is marked with its number. Battalions moved around so often that it would be impossible to chart their progress without obscuring too much topographical information (which is what the Official History maps do). But it is quite easy to estimate a battalion's movements by checking the text and the maps together.

I have also bucked the army convention of describing events from right to left. We read text and look at maps from left to right, so I have written the narrative the same way. On a few occasions the sequence of events dictates it is best to describe another way.

This is the seventh book in a ten-book series on the British Expeditionary Forces' campaigns on the Western Front in the Great War. I first visited the Somme area in detail in the early 1990s and like most visitors I focused on the 1916 campaign. That fateful year was what most of the books were about and that is still the case thirty years later. It is also the area where most of the cemeteries and memorials are located because the fighting was so concentrated and prolonged. A detailed study of the ground in 2015 followed up by several months of reading and research has increased my understanding of the March 1918 campaign. I have enjoyed writing about the 'Retreat Across the Somme', learning how the British, Irish and Empire soldiers showed their mettle fighting in the open under the most difficult of circumstances and I hope you enjoy reading about them too.

I stayed at No 56 Bed and Breakfast in La Boisselle, close to the 1916 front line. David and Julie Thomson have looked after me many times at their 'Oasis on the Somme' during my battlefield research trips.

Andrew Rawson 2017

Chapter 1

Beat the Germans and the Rest will Follow

1917 Comes to a Close

The Germans started 1917 by withdrawing back to the Hindenburg Line. The Allies then went on the offensive, starting with a combined effort in the spring at Arras and on the Aisne. The failure of the French offensive resulted in a mutiny, leaving the BEF to make the major effort on the Western Front for the rest of the year. It attacked in Flanders between June and November but there was still no breakthrough.

There had been, however, important developments on the Eastern Front, where the Russian army was in a state of collapse. It started with a revolution in Petrograd in March (February in the Russian calendar), followed by the formation of a Provisional Government and the abdication of Tsar Nicholas II. In May, the Chief of the Imperial General Staff, General Sir William Robertson, explained how the Germans could transfer dozens of divisions and hundreds of heavy guns to the Western Front. He also warned that Great Britain 'must keep her troops as near to England as possible and the maximum number must be made available to assist in holding the Western Front, so that the Russian defection may not be followed by the collapse of France'. The War Cabinet did not reply.

Russian and Romanian troops started the Kerensky Offensive in Galicia on 1 July but the counter-offensive drove them back over 150 miles. It was the beginning of the end for the Russian armies. The French, British, Italians and Americans discussed plans at the Inter-Allied Conferences in Paris at the end of July. The first looked at how the Allies could help Russia while the second studied what the Allies had to do if Russia sued for peace. The worry was the Germans would concentrate on the Western Front and they had to defend the Western Front until the American Expeditionary Force was ready. They were sensible suggestions but Prime Minister David Lloyd George still wanted to attack the Austrians on the Italian Front.

The failure of the Kerensky Offensive and the anti-war demonstrations that followed in Petrograd led Robertson to tell the War Cabinet that they could not rely on Russia any more. All they could do was continue the battle in Flanders to relieve the pressure on them. Minister-Chairman Alexander Kerensky finally proclaimed Russia would be a Republic on 15 September, unsure how it could maintain its obligation to the Allies. The nation was in a state of disorder while the army was disintegrating as around two million men deserted in protest at the war.

Britain and France thought they could hold on until the Americans arrived but the British had to maintain pressure until the French army had recovered. Their best hope was to find extra shipping to speed up the deployment of American divisions to the Western Front. The Royal Navy also had to continue using its 'Convoy System' to reduce losses from the U-Boat campaign.

The German armies had suffered terribly, the Austro-Hungarian armies were incapable of offensive action and food rationing was undermining morale at home. The huge territories captured in the east did not provide enough resources to make their occupation worthwhile. The new Chancellor, Georg Michaelis, knew Germany was in economic difficulties but he had been chosen by the military and it was still running the Empire. The Reichstag passed a peace resolution calling for 'an honourable peace without annexations and by means of understanding' on 19 July but it was ignored by both the German High Command and the Allies.

On 25 September Lloyd George and Paul Painlevé met at Boulogne accompanied by their Chiefs of Staff, Robertson and Foch. The British delegation agreed to take over more line from the French but Haig was against the idea because he was committed to the ongoing battle in the Ypres Salient. Lloyd George and Robertson also asked what the BEF would do if the Russians dropped out of the war. Haig said he would have to go over to the defensive but he doubted if the French could stop a concerted attack. He wanted his divisions brought up to strength while as many others as possible were sent from Macedonia, Egypt, Palestine and India to the Western Front. The Allies could then consider going on the offensive again because he wanted to 'beat the Germans and the rest will follow… Success on the Western Front is the only alternative to an unsatisfactory peace.' He certainly did not want to take over more line from the French.

General Paul Pétain asked Haig in person if he could take over a six-division sector facing St Quentin on 18 October. He said the BEF was fully committed to the Flanders campaign and to do so meant he would have to stop all offensive action. They also discussed the consequences of a peace on the Eastern Front and how to coordinate their efforts. They could start with small attacks in the spring with the main battle starting in August, while the Americans would join the final effort. Pétain insisted the British take over the St Quentin area and Haig reported the request to Robertson on 23 October. Everything changed the following day when the German and Austrian divisions broke the Italian line near Caporetto. There was a catastrophic retreat during which 265,000 men and over 3,000 guns were captured; in places the front line moved over 90 miles in less than three weeks.

Italy was in danger of being knocked out of the war, so the British and French governments promised to send divisions and heavy artillery to support it. All the Allied prime ministers met at Rapallo in north-east Italy, on 5 November. They confirmed they would continue sending divisions to the Italian Front, prompting Haig to call off offensive activity in Flanders. But he still planned to launch a tank-led attack at Cambrai for 20 November, with the aim of distracting attention from Italy.

On 19 November, Robertson told the War Cabinet that the Allies could attack on the Western Front if Russia and Italy recovered. But he thought the Allies had to go on the defensive until the Americans were ready if Russia got a separate peace deal. The problem was that waiting on the defensive for a long time would be bad for morale. There was a brief period of elation after the tanks broke through the Hindenburg Line on 20 November but Russia asked for a separate treaty the following day. The Cambrai campaign ended in disappointment when the Germans counter-attacked on 30 November.

Allied strategy was in the hands of the Supreme War Council and they were waiting for the military representatives to complete their study. As the battle of Cambrai came to an end, Haig told his army commanders to make their defensive plans and prepare to be attacked in the spring.

The Balance of Power Changes

Meanwhile, events had been moving fast on the Eastern Front. Vladimir Lenin had signed a Decree of Peace, calling 'upon all the belligerent nations and their governments to start immediate negotiations for peace' on 26 October. The Bolsheviks rebelled against the Provisional Government in Petrograd on 7 November and captured the Winter Palace. The monarchists and liberals organised the White Army and counter-attacked in what became the Russian Civil War. Lenin's new Russian Soviet Federative Socialist Republic asked the Central Powers for an armistice on 21 November and one was signed on 15 December. Negotiations opened in Brest-Litovsk a week later and the peace treaty of the same name would be signed on 3 March 1918.

The armistice meant that Germany could move divisions to the Eastern Front, leaving enough behind to police the captured territories. Estimates believed ten divisions could be transferred every month, increasing the number on the Western Front from 160 to 195 by the end of March. That was nearly 250,000 rifles; a large number of artillery pieces would also be moved.

Preparing the Defences
On 14 December, GHQ declared it wanted three defensive zones, each 1 to 2 miles deep. Each army commander was instructed to produce a defensive scheme and the corps and divisional commanders were asked in turn to draw up their own plans. They had to consider a range of issues including the layout of the defences, artillery plans, deployment of reserves, allocation of labour, anti-aircraft and anti-gas measures. They had to consider the management of the railheads, the distribution of supplies, traffic control, casualty and refugee evacuation. Staff also had to consider the different ways the enemy might attack and then work out how to defend against each danger. Comprehensive instructions and deployment plans were issued to all combat and support arms and they were handed over when a division was relieved.

The Forward Zone would be improved so the soldiers could 'do all in their power to maintain their ground against every attack'. But the front line was often where an offensive had ended or in front of the Hindenburg Line, leaving the trenches vulnerable. The men had to work under fire while a combination of shell fire and bad weather left them repairing existing trenches rather than digging new ones. The British experience of offensives was that it was impossible to hold the first two or three trenches during a sustained assault. So a brigade typically placed one battalion in a line of outposts and supporting positions, expecting it to be overwhelmed. A third line had artillery positions covering the gaps in between redoubts.

The Battle Zone was 1 or 2 miles to the rear, where the terrain favoured the defence. The main fighting was expected to take place in the Battle Zone where the brigades deployed their remaining two battalions and where the corps reserve would deploy. Two out of three guns deployed in the Battle Zone would hit enemy batteries and troop concentrations while the enemy was in the Forward Zone. They would switch to close support when the enemy closed in. The Rear Zone was the last line of defence, some 4 to 8 miles behind. It was where the division's third brigade could deploy and rally any troops falling back. Work on the Forward Zone took priority and while progress on the Battle Zone was patchy, hardly anything was done on the Rear Zone. There was some wire but the trenches were just marked by cutting the turf, a procedure known as spit-locking.

On 17 December, Haig and Pétain arranged for their staff to meet regularly, to coordinate their defensive plans. They believed the Germans would make small attacks before launching a big offensive when an opportunity presented itself. They told their army commanders to reduce trench activity, expecting the Germans to do the same, but they did not and the men at the front had to stay on their guard rather than dig in.

On 3 January, GHQ submitted a disturbing progress report on progress to the War Office. Fourth Army reported that the Flanders defences were in a fair condition; First Army reported the Lys area varied from fair to strong; Third Army reported the Arras area to be strong but the Cambrai front was only fair; Fifth Army reported some areas around St Quentin as poor.

Extending the British Sector

The French had again asked the British to take over the St Quentin sector when the battle of Cambrai ended. Haig objected on the grounds that the BEF had taken over the northern part of the Ypres Salient from the French and it had also sent divisions to the Italian Front. But the War Office reported that the new French Prime Minister, Georges Clémenceau, was threatening to resign over the matter after only a month in office. So Haig agreed to extend the BEF's front to St Quentin by mid-January and the River Oise a couple of weeks later. The French said the Oise marshes were impassable and while they might have been in wet weather, they could be crossed when it was dry. General Erich Ludendorff even believed the St Quentin sector was the weakest part of the line 'because the ground offered no difficulties and it was passible in all seasons'.

It took time to make reliefs and there was universal dismay at the state of the French trenches. Trenches needed shoring up, wire had to be erected and dugouts required digging. The Forward Zone needed improving while there was no Battle Zone or Rear Zone. The combination of a longer line and manpower being stretched even further left Fifth Army with a lot of extra work and no one to carry it out.

Reorganising the BEF

On 3 November the War Office had told Haig there were no more reinforcements because of commitments to industry, shipping and other theatres. Haig said that meant he would have to break up one in four of the divisions in France on 24 November so Robertson told him to wait. The Minister of National Service recommended disbanding cavalry units or finding men from rear area units. He also suggested reducing the number

Nieuport

Ghent

Dunkirk

BELGIAN ARMY

Ypres

SECOND ARMY

Schelde

Armentières

Bethune

FIRST ARMY

Arras

THIRD ARMY

Cambrai

Bapaume

Albert

AMIENS

Somme

Péronne

Oise

St. Quentin

FIFTH ARMY

Somme

Oise

Laon

Ailette

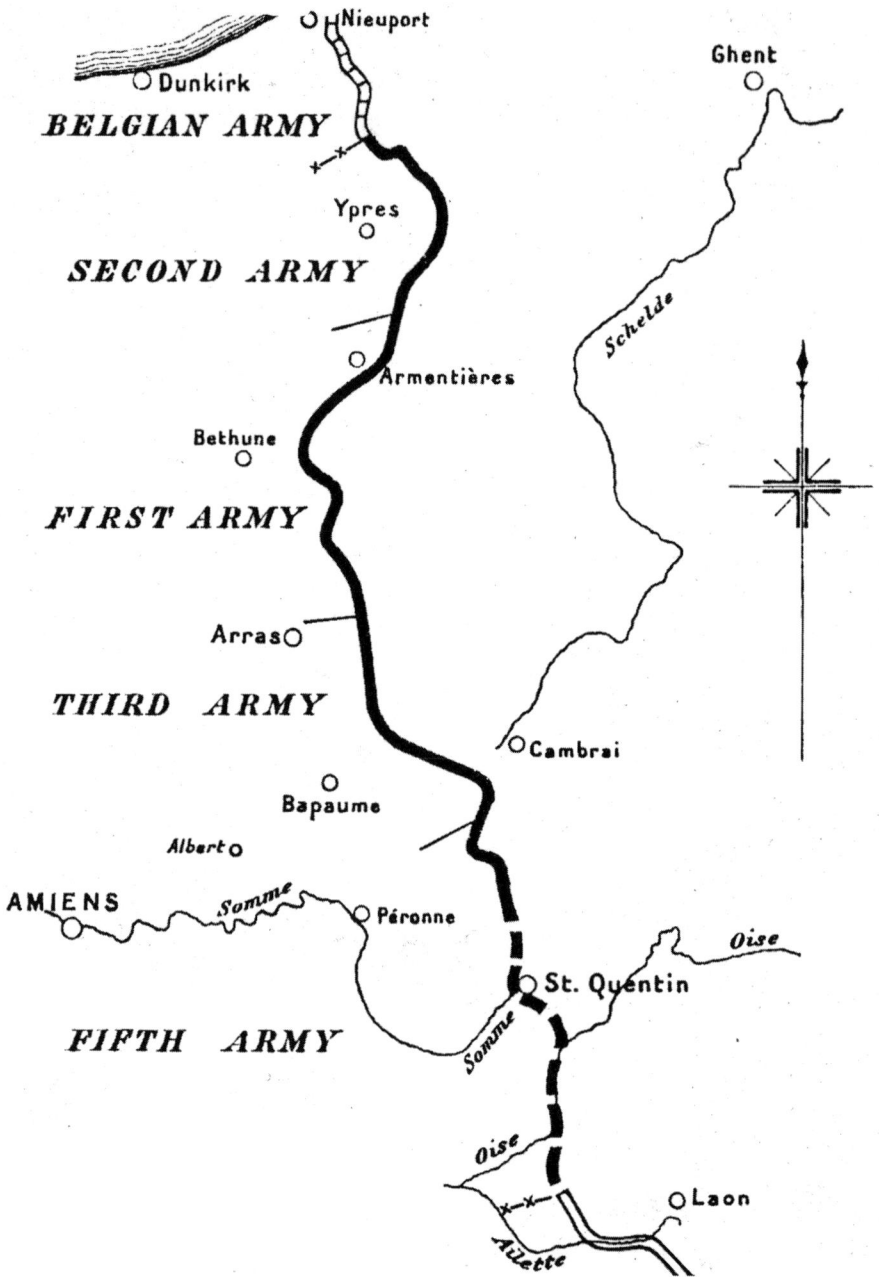

The BEF's sector between Ypres and St Quentin and the extension of the line beyond the Oise.

of infantry battalions in each division from twelve to nine, as the French and Germans had done.

The Cabinet Committee told the Army Council about the increasing pressures on manpower at the beginning of January. Industry and commerce had to remain at maximum output while the Merchant Navy had to stay at full strength, to keep the country fed and to keep shipping American troops to France. It meant the Ministry of National Service would only be able to provide 100,000 men rather than the 600,000 Haig wanted during 1918. The Army Council warned that 'the acceptance of the recommendations in the draft report, was taking an unreasonably grave risk of losing the War and sacrificing to no purpose the British Army on the Western Front.' The warning fell on deaf ears and the War Office issued the appropriate instructions on 10 January.

Haig reported how the BEF would be organised on 18 January and there were protests from many quarters. The regular army battalions were safe but many Territorial battalions would be merged and many new army battalions disbanded. The exceptions were the Canadian, Australian and New Zealand divisions which retained the twelve-battalion structure.

The reorganisation started on 29 January and took until 4 March to complete. Altogether, 115 battalions ceased to exist, 38 were merged and 7 were converted into pioneers. As one diarist recorded, 'it was a heart breaking business.'

Chapter 2

The Closest and
Most Effective Cooperation

Determining Military Policy

Lloyd George discussed forming a war council to coordinate allied military policies with General Foch and the French politician Henry Franklin-Bouillon on 14 October. The idea was for a group of military representatives to advise their governments on all aspects of strategy. Lloyd George got Prime Minister Painlevé's agreement on 30 October and Versailles was chosen as the meeting place. Diplomacy and economic committees would meet at the same place while a naval committee would go to London.

Representatives from Britain, France and Italy agreed there would be a new council of war at Rapallo, in Italy, on 5 November. The new Superior War Council (it would be renamed the Supreme War Council) would be assisted by military representatives and they agreed it would meet at Versailles on 1 December. They then got down to business.

The new French Prime Minister, Georges Clémenceau, chaired and the questions came thick and fast. What should they expect now Russia had collapsed? How fast would the Americans be able to deploy? How long would the British and French troops have to stay on the Italian Front? What were the chances of Turkey and Austria suing for a separate peace? There were no immediate answers.

On 1 December 1917, the Supreme War Council asked the Military Representatives to examine the current situation and make recommendations on what to do next. The problem was they would not meet for another two months and a lot could happen in that time.

In London, the War Cabinet was deciding military policy based on the information given by their own advisers and that coming from the Military Representatives. The consensus was to stay on the defensive on all fronts. Robertson told the War Cabinet that the Germans would stage a large spring offensive, aiming to knockout the Allies before the Americans arrived in large numbers. They would either drive through the French to

Paris or through the British to the English Channel. They could even look for another Caporetto-style success on the Italian Front.

The War Cabinet also asked if 'the prospects of final success justify the sacrifice involved in a continuation of the struggle?' Robertson replied, 'we can win if we determine to do so and if we act accordingly.' They had to find every possible man to stop the offensive, every possible ship to transport the American troops and work at maximum output to provide the arms and supplies the soldiers needed.

In January 1918, Haig twice told the War Cabinet that the BEF could hold on if it was immediately given 100,000 replacements. He thought the German armies would continue to increase in size and that the Supreme Army Command, or *Oberste Heeresleitung* (OHL), would be looking to take advantage of their superiority before the Americans were ready. But he also believed a failed offensive on the Western Front could precipitate a defeat on the German home front because the Allied blockade was undermining the morale of the German people.

The Americans are Coming

Washington DC said five American divisions would reach France by the summer. They were twice the size of the British and French divisions but they needed three months of training to be ready for the trenches. Both Haig and Pétain wanted General John Pershing to hand over men but the Secretary of State for War, Newton Baker, had told him to group the US divisions into an independent American Expeditionary Force. The logistics route through the ports and along the railways meant it made sense to take over part of the French line.

Robertson suggested finding extra ships to carry 12,000 soldiers a month across the Atlantic. The British and French would provide the artillery and ammunition so men could be shipped at five times the rate. It meant there would be 150 American battalions in France by the summer. His argument was that the Americans had to get their battalions into trenches as fast as possible. Pershing still refused to have his battalions added to British infantry brigades but he would let them train behind the BEF's line.

A Combined Strategy

On 21 January, the Military Representatives reported that the Allies needed to treat the Western Front as one sector, rather than two national sectors, to increase their chances of stopping an offensive. They had to improve the trenches, increase the amount of artillery and improve the rail systems to weather the storm. Only then would they be ready to go over to the offensive with American help in 1919. The War Cabinet welcomed the information, forgetting that the French were still recovering from their mutiny while the BEF was about to disband a quarter of its battalions. It was down to Robertson to remind them about the manpower shortage and advised against offensive action in Turkey.

The Military Representatives suggested creating a combined allied reserve which could deal with threats without having to refer to the national commanders-in-chief. Robertson knew the BEF did not have enough divisions to fulfil its current obligations, never mind hand any over for a reserve. On 24 January both Haig and Pétain said they were unable to create an independent reserve but that they had promised to give each other mutual support.

Pershing protested about a lack of shipping, delays at the ports and a train shortage when Haig and Pétain suggested adding American divisions to the reserve. He also complained his troops were being supplied with obsolete equipment, munitions and aeroplanes while there were problems due to a lack of interpreters. It was the first time an annoyed Foch had heard about the American issues.

Robertson wanted to focus on planning the defensive. Foch wanted a counter-attack plan for when they had stopped the German offensive. Haig wanted some of the divisions back from Salonika so the BEF could attack. So the discussion ended in standoff.

A network of civilian spies had been reporting German train movements to agents who took the information to England via neutral Holland. The reports noted a steady movement from east to west but they also indicated that the Germans were recalling divisions from the Italian Front, reducing the risk to that front. The number on the Western Front had risen to 170 by the end of January while Eastern divisions were being used to hold the quiet sectors, releasing divisions for training in offensive tactics. The winter weather also allowed the front line to be thinned out, so even more divisions could rest and practise. Everything was pointing towards an offensive in March, when the weather was better.

The Third Supreme War Council
Prime Minster Clémenceau opened the third Supreme War Council on 30 January 1918. Both Haig and Pétain complained that they had insufficient troops and that they were both about to reorganise all their divisions because of the lack of men. Everyone agreed General Pershing's insistence on creating an independent American Expeditionary Force was a problem because its inexperienced divisions had to be given a quiet sector. The conference agreed they had to plan a coordinated defensive

and counter-offensive action on the Western Front but they could not agree how to organise them. Lloyd George then argued that British losses had been higher since July 1916, while Foch answered that Great Britain was not doing enough.

Lloyd George wanted to defeat one of Germany's allies and they considered Turkey, Salonika, Palestine and Mesopotamia in turn. Robertson said it 'was not a practical plan and to attempt it would be very dangerous and detrimental to the prospects of winning the war'. Lloyd George reluctantly agreed the logistics would put an impossible strain on the BEF, the Royal Navy and the Merchant Navy.

A discussion concluded that everyone wanted a 'General Reserve' but no one had the means to create one. Foch asked the military representatives how to raise it and while they settled on thirty divisions (thirteen French, ten British and seven Italian), no one had any to spare. Haig would not learn about the plans for a 'General Reserve' until 27 February while the War Cabinet did not know he and Pétain had agreed mutual support for each other up to as many as seven divisions.

The Council overruled Lloyd George's objections to the British takeover of a French sector and it was left to Pétain and Haig to sort out the details. Chief of the General Staff, General Sir Henry Wilson then wanted to talk about the 'elephant in the room': the German offensive on the Western Front. They discussed the numbers of Allied and German divisions per month and concluded that they would be equal in June. Wilson concluded that the best time for an Allied attack was at the beginning of May.

The next question was where would the Germans attack? Wilson said they could attack on a front of thirty miles, either in one place or split between several. The suspected places were north-east of Arras, east of Reims or east of Nancy. He doubted they would advance across the 1916 battlefield or the area devastated during the retreat to the Hindenburg Line in the spring of 1917. While Wilson's suggestions were pragmatic, they were not discussed.

Instead, the Council made a joint declaration against the Central Powers' offer to make peace and declared the Allies would continue the war 'with the utmost vigour and in the closest and most effective co-operation'. The Supreme War Council also renamed the Executive Committee the Executive War Board, proving they were the quintessential committee.

The Supreme War Council met again in London on 14 March and they all agreed a large attack was imminent. They postponed forming a reserve but continued to talk about having one. In fact there was a lot of talk about what could be done but no instructions were issued. Foch went as far as to say the Executive War Board was all talk and that they might as well disband it. The Supreme War Council, the Military Representatives, Executive War Board and Committee of General Officers had contributed little or nothing to the preparations for the imminent German offensive. Despite all the conferences, the Allies never formed a General Reserve while the Executive War Board never issued orders for military operations.

A New Chief of the Imperial Staff

Lloyd George wanted to replace General Sir William Robertson with someone more receptive to his ideas. Robertson had been the BEF's Quartermaster General during the battles of 1914 before serving as Field Marshal Sir John French's Chief of the General Staff throughout 1915. His next post was in London where he acted as the CIGS, balancing the requirement of all the theatres while acting as the mediator between the commanders-in-chief and the War Cabinet. By the end of the gruelling campaigns of 1916 and 1917, he had gained a reputation for backing the generals against the politicians. But when it came down to it, Robertson was a soldier's soldier who had risen from the rank of private.

Lloyd George felt that Robertson supported Haig more than him but Edward Stanley, Lord Derby, said he would resign as Secretary of State for War if either Robertson or Haig were removed. So Lloyd George went about undermining Robertson's position to get his way.

Lloyd George wanted the Executive Board to issue orders through their Military Representatives. It meant the British representative, General Sir Henry Wilson, would be issuing instructions even though he was not responsible for the conduct or the safety of the BEF. The War Office complained that the new arrangement would bypass the legal and constitutional role of the Army Council. So Lloyd George invited Haig to London on 9 February, only to learn that he thought only a senior Field Marshal or the Army Council could give him orders through Robertson.

Lloyd George suggested sending Robertson to Versailles, to act as the Military Representative, and recalling Wilson to London to be the new CIGS. Haig was against the move. Wilson might have been able to charm Lloyd George and the French but Haig distrusted him. Lloyd George then suggested basing Haig in London in a new role in charge of all the British Forces. Haig again disagreed, saying the threat of attack made it a bad time to be changing GHQ's staff.

So Lloyd George considered a compromise under which Wilson would discuss strategies with the other Military Representatives and then report back to Robertson. The Military Representative would also be made a member of the Army Council. Robertson would still be the War Cabinet's chief military adviser but he would no longer be issuing orders relating to military operations.

The complicated arrangement also involved Robertson and Wilson exchanging places. Lord Alfred Milner would be appointed the Secretary of State for War while Lord Derby would be sent to Paris to be an ambassador. No one was happy with the plan and Robertson refused to have Wilson work as his deputy.

Lloyd George felt he had exhausted all reasonable suggestions so he resorted to an unreasonable one. The Official Press Bureau announced that His Majesty's Government had accepted Robertson's resignation on 16 February. It was the first that Robertson knew he had been sacked. Wilson was appointed CIGS and Robertson was given Wilson's old Eastern Command in England to add to the insult.

General Sir Henry Rawlinson was appointed the Military Representative in Versailles. His place at Second (temporarily called the Fourth) Army was taken by its old commander, General Sir Herbert Plumer.

The Final Considerations

By the end of January, Haig knew the War Cabinet was not going to send enough men while the Supreme War Council refused to send any divisions from the Eastern theatres. All the divisions withdrawn from Italy would be placed in the new General Reserve and he also had to find another six divisions to add to it. Haig needed to keep the line north of Arras strong, where the Channel ports were only fifty miles behind the front. He knew the clay of the low-lying Lys plain always stayed wet for longer, making the Somme's chalk downs more attractive for spring operations. He also knew there was more space to fall back south of Arras but the BEF had to keep in contact with the French and hold the important rail centre of Amiens.

Both Robertson and Haig believed the first attack would be made in March around St Quentin. But they wondered if it would be designed to pull the British reserves south, so a second attack in Flanders would then drive towards the coast. Fifth Army had just taken over the St Quentin sector and Lieutenant General Hubert Gough reported there was a lot of work to be done on 1 February. His divisions were spread thin leaving too few men to improve existing defences or build new ones.

On 9 February, Haig told General Hubert Gough that Fifth Army would have to conduct fighting withdrawals and that he could not afford to squander his reserves if he was attacked. It was better for him to fall back so the Germans exposed their flank to Third Army's counter-attacks. Fifth Army was to make the River Somme, south of Péronne, its last line of defence but it also had to hold the Crozat Canal, to maintain contact with the French.

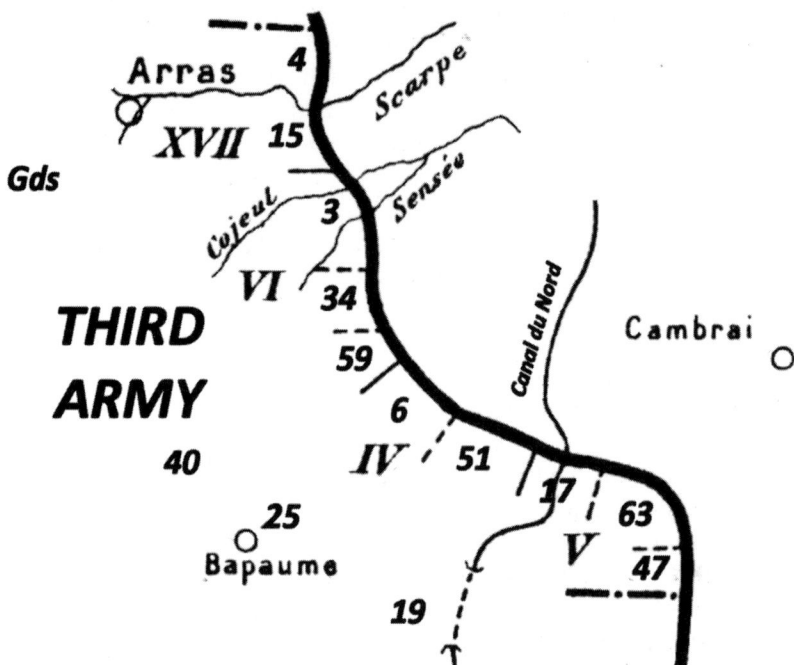

Third Army's sector between Arras and the Flesquières salient.

The number of men working behind Fifth Army's front was soon doubled to nearly 50,000 but it was still not enough. Most were employed on maintaining roads, leaving only 10,000 to work on the Battle Zone; nothing was done on the Rear Zone. Lieutenant General Alexander Hamilton Gordon and General Louis Humbert agreed that French divisions would have to detrain behind the British right flank before engaging the enemy, a plan approved by both Haig and Pétain.

Intelligence Summaries

Brigadier General Cox, head of GHQ's Intelligence (a) section A, produced regular 'Summaries of Information' which listed more detailed information of use to the generals. On 14 January, the French reported that General Oskar von Hutier's Eighth Army headquarters had entered the line opposite Fifth Army, after helping to topple the Russian army. On 16 February, Haig told his army commanders that 'the enemy will attack; he will attack soon; he will attack on the Western Front.' Early signs were it would be between the Scarpe and Oise rivers with an attack in Flanders or against Béthune's coal fields early in April. It was an accurate prediction. On 1 March Cox's report indicated that General Otto von Below's Fourteenth Army had moved into line opposite Third Army. He was 'the best commander in the German army', a recommendation stemming from his success at Caporetto in Italy.

There were also plenty of physical signs like the build-up of troops and artillery registration taking place. The army commanders' conference on 2 March reported, 'there are strong indications that the enemy intends to attack on the Third and Fifth Army fronts, with the object of cutting off the Cambrai salient and drawing in our reserves.' Again it was accurate.

Poor weather made it difficult for the Royal Flying Corps to conduct reconnaissance flights but those that flew saw plenty. Craters along the front line were being converted into mortar pits, military roads were being built right up to the trenches and 'huge convoys of lorries and horse transport' filled the roads. They reported extra airfields and thousands of oblong shapes hidden under camouflage netting which turned out to be a 'remarkable' number of ammunition dumps.

The RFC was told to interfere with enemy preparations the best they could. Some located and reported on targets for the artillery while others carried out strafing and bombing raids. The plan was for the corps squadrons to locate the enemy artillery batteries and the infantry reinforcements when the attack started. The army squadrons would try to drive the enemy planes from the skies.

By March 1918 thirty-nine divisions, or 350,000 men, had moved west. Another 200,000 young and fit men had been transferred across to France. The Western Front had also been thinned out, allowing over fifty divisions to be given at least three weeks training.

On 8 March, the Danish General Staff reported that an attack between Cambrai and St Quentin was imminent; the Germans were just waiting for a favourable wind, so they could use gas. Three days later the Summary of Information hit the nail on the head. It stated that a large offensive would strike between Arras and Cambrai with a secondary attack to follow between Armentières and Neuve Chapelle. It had described Operation Michael and Operation George perfectly.

Brigadier General Cox had done everything he could and all that was needed was the exact date. A captured German pilot revealed the attack would be on 20 or 21 March. Then on 19 March several prisoners reported an offensive was imminent. Two deserters from a trench mortar company even suggested to their interrogators in 36th Division that 'the enemy had fixed 21 March as his Zero day'. Fifth Army Intelligence Summary stated, 'Indications of a more than usually definite nature point to the fact that the

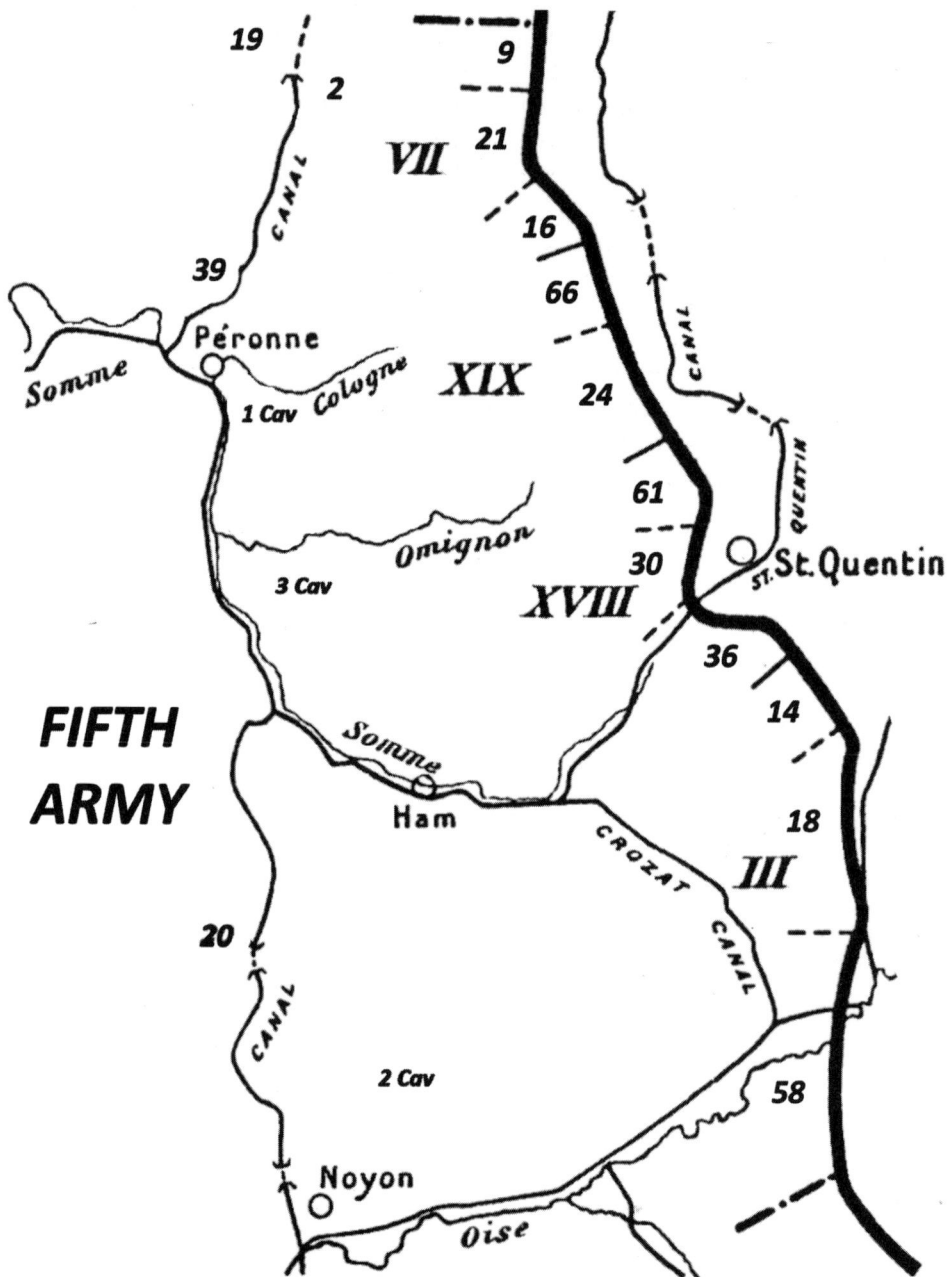

Fifth Army's sector between the Flesquières salient and the River Oise.

enemy's preparations are practically complete.' Gough even wrote to his wife to tell her he expected the attack to start on 21 March.

Operation Michael would hit Third Army's right and the whole of Fifth Army. Third Army was deployed east of Arras and Bapaume while the Flesquières salient would be evacuated if it was threatened. General Sir Julian Byng had fourteen divisions and four tank battalions to hold twenty-eight miles of front. They were backed up by over 1,100 guns and howitzers; around 40 per mile.

Meanwhile, Fifth Army held 42 miles of front east of Péronne and facing St Quentin. Gough only had 12 infantry and 3 cavalry divisions to hold the sector; he also had 3 tank battalions. They were backed up by nearly 1,700 guns and howitzers; again around 40 per mile. GHQ had placed 2 divisions behind each army meaning the BEF had only 13 per cent of its men in reserve; the French had 40 per cent.

Chapter 3

They are Coming at Last, Good Business

German Preparations

General Erich von Falkenhayn had advocated a decisive campaign on the Western Front when he was the OHL's Chief of Staff. A report in the spring of 1915 concluded the Germans should attack at two points. One offensive would hit the junction of the British and French Armies, which was around Arras at the time. The second offensive would drive the British back towards the Channel ports. Therein were the seeds of Operations Michael and George.

General Hermann von Kuhl, Chief of the Staff of the First Army, preferred a knockout blow against the French on the Aisne. But Colonel Hans von Seeckt, Chief of the Staff of the Eleventh Army, suggested an attack between Arras and the Somme. The left wing would hold back the French while the right wing and the reserves pushed the British back to the Channel. This plan had developed the ideas which would be adopted in March 1918.

The problem was, OHL never had enough divisions to conduct a large effort on the Western Front because of its commitments on the Eastern Front. The initial success at Verdun in the spring of 1916 could not be converted into victory because Germany did not have enough resources. They then saw the British and French repeatedly attack with too few resources in a battle of attrition on the Somme in the summer and autumn.

OHL then decided to build a new defensive position out of reach of the Allied guns. A slow withdrawal began in January 1917 with a rapid rearward move in mid-March. The Allies had been monitoring the construction work but the withdrawal to the Hindenburg Line took them by surprise. It shortened the line by thirty miles and placed the Germans behind a purpose-built position but it also increased the size of both the German and the Allies' reserve.

The BEF failed to break through during the battle of Arras, while the Nivelle offensive on the Aisne reduced the French army to a state of mutiny. After the tactical success at Messines in June, the attack in Flanders rumbled on and the Germans were becoming worried when the rains saved them in October.

A report by the Operations Section of the Supreme Command on 23 October 1917 concluded that 'the decision lies in the Western theatre'. Germany needed the British and French to send divisions to Italy and the attack at Caporetto the following day made them do just that. Germany also needed Russia out of the war and three days later Lenin signed the Decree of Peace.

On 11 November 1917, Ludendorff asked the chiefs of staff of both Crown Prince Rupprecht of Bavaria's and the German Crown Prince's Groups of Armies where and when they should attack. General von Kuhl advocated an attack against the British in Flanders but the Ypres Salient was a crater field while the Lys valley would be too wet until April. Meanwhile, Colonel Friedrich von der Schulenberg wanted to attack around Verdun and then wait for Britain to sue for peace when the French capitulated. Ludendorff was interested in advancing west between the Scarpe and the Oise Rivers. Then 'operations could be carried further in a north-westerly direction, with the left flank resting on the Somme, and lead to the rolling up of the-British front.'

On 12 December, the head of OHL's Operations Section, Lieutenant Colonel Georg Wetzell, produced a report summarising the imminent situation on the Western Front. He believed it would be impossible to prepare one huge attack in secret and that it would not be enough to win the war. Instead he advocated several attacks, one after another. Wetzell thought an attack around Verdun would worry the French the most. He did not think an attack around St Quentin would be decisive against the British but it would draw the BEF's reserves south making it easier to launch a second attack across the Lys plain towards the important rail centre of Hazebrouck.

Ludendorff met the chiefs of the staffs on 27 December to discuss three operations: Michael around St Quentin, Mars towards Arras and George near Armentières. There could also be a fourth, George II at Ypres. The final decision was made on 21 January 1918. They would launch Michael first because George needed April's drier weather; British and Canadian observers on Vimy Ridge would make Mars difficult to carry out. The first of three orders to begin preparations was issued three days later.

Other attack plans did not get beyond the conference table. Operation Archangel was planned south of the Oise while Operations Hector, Achilles and Roland were planned east of Reims. Operations Castor and Pollux around Verdun were forgotten about at an early stage.

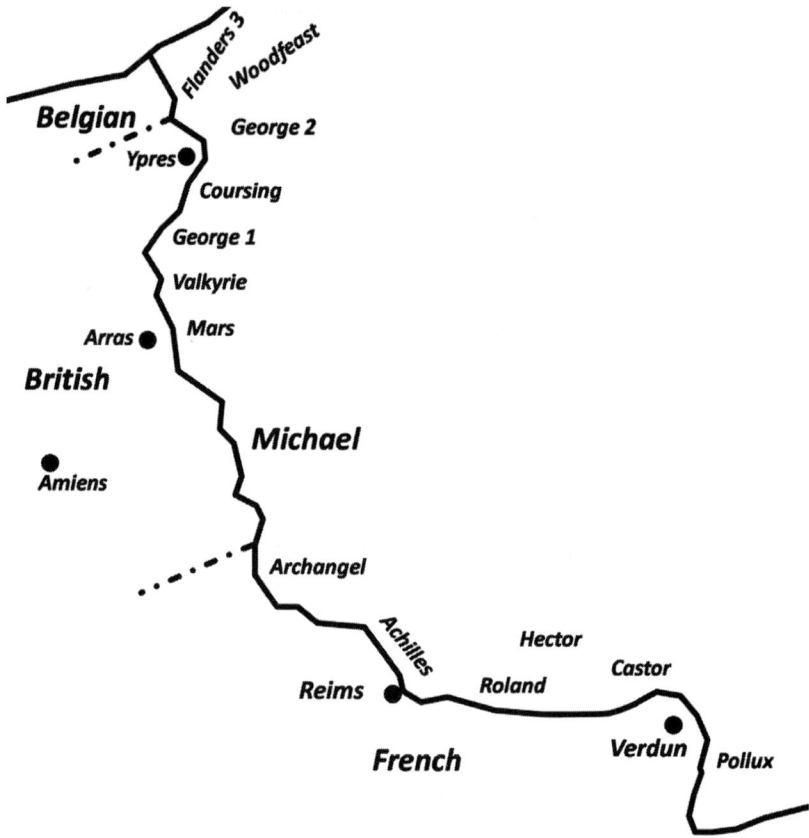

Many operations were considered but some did not get beyond the drawing board.

Ludendorff issued instructions to start planning in earnest on 8 February. Mars and Archangel would widen out Michael if it stalled, followed by George and Roland if all was going well. The extension of the British front as far south as the Oise suited the Germans because it allowed them to advance deeper into British-held territory before the French mobilised reserves.

OHL wanted to make the British think they were safe while making the French think they were threatened. A combination of rumours, misleading information and false battle arrangements climaxed just before the attack. Attack preparations would be made on the Lys front and south of the Oise for three days before Z-Day while there were bombardments on the George and Archangel fronts.

Meanwhile, steps were taken to stop the German troops giving away information. Censorship was introduced but it became harder to keep such a massive attack a secret. All the signs were there, down to officers, maps in hand, seen studying the British trenches from across no man's land. Reports also tell how 'prisoners captured by patrols spoke freely of the next day's attack. They told how their trenches were filling fast with the troops brought up to form the first wave of stormers while the villages behind the line were crowded with troops waiting to pass through to complete the expected success.'

On 10 March, OHL set Z-Day for 21 March and zero hour for 9.40 am, allowing time for observed artillery fire before the attack began. The plan was for Seventeenth Army to advance between Arras and the Cambrai Salient while Second Army made its attack south of the salient. Crown Prince Rupprecht was hoping the pincer attack would trap many men in the salient. Meanwhile, Eighteenth Army would cover the south flank along the Oise and deal with the French reinforcements sent to help the British. Detailed instructions were issued to all three armies a few days later.

General Otto von Below had wanted Seventeenth Army to attack east of Arras but OHL and Rupprecht's Group thought it would be too difficult. Instead they would widen the scope of the attack once Operation Michael was well underway.

The Artillery Deploys

The first batteries started entering emplacements on 11 March and more deployed in camouflaged positions a few days later. The final groups of guns were moved up on the night before the battle, ready to follow the infantry forward. They were all deployed well forward, so the gunners could support the infantry for as long as possible before having to advance.

There were 55 super-heavy batteries, 701 heavy batteries and 950 field batteries. Over 10,000 guns and howitzers would fire at distant targets while 3,500 trench mortars hit nearby ones. A huge amount of ammunition was required and it had all been delivered to camouflaged dumps before 15 March.

OHL had decided that 'a laboured artillery preparation was out of the question' because it would give the British time to move reserves into the area; it would also require a huge amount of ammunition.' Instead, the artillery expert Oberst Georg Bruchmüller had devised an intense five-hour bombardment. The batteries opposite Fifth Army went as far as forfeiting registration, to keep their positions a secret. Instead they would use predicted shooting (or map firing) to begin with and then rely on aerial observers to report targets to them.

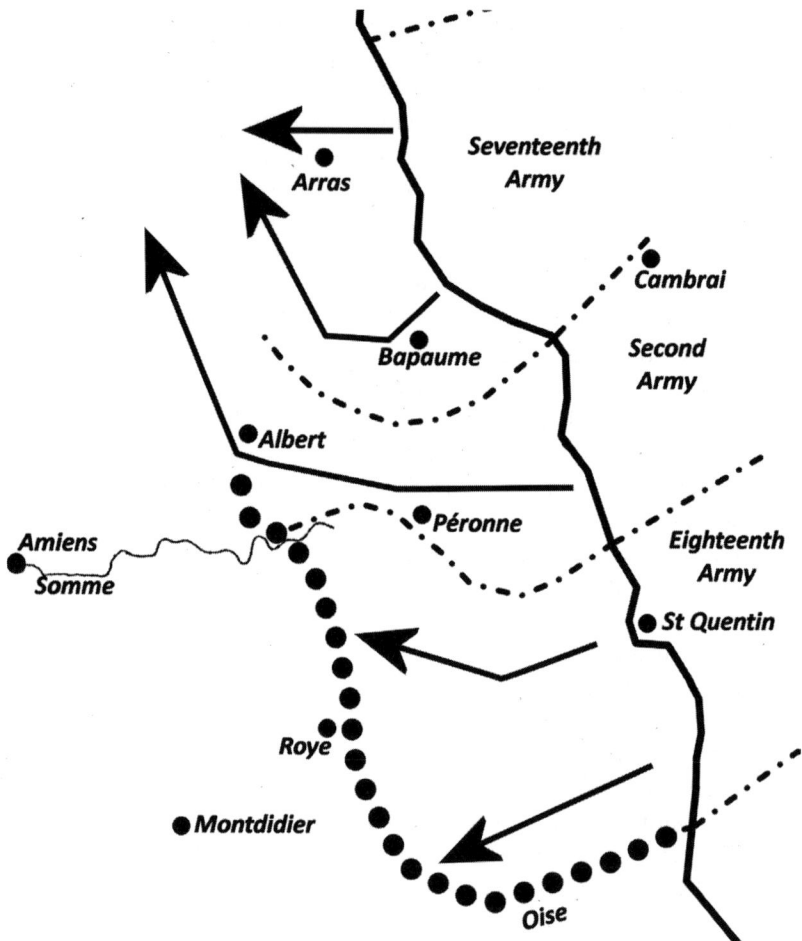

The plan was for Seventeenth and Second Armies to swing north behind Arras while Eighteenth Army held the south flank.

The Infantry Deploys

The British may have known that an attack was coming but the infantry development was designed to keep them guessing until the last moment. Sixty divisions began their *Aufmarsch*, or deployment march, on the evening of 16 March. Around one million men marched forward night after night, resting under cover during the day, until everyone was in position.

Battalions of hand-picked *Stossentruppen* (storm troops) led the attack. They were composed of four companies of infantry supported by machine guns, bombers and flamethrowers as well as a battery of field artillery.

Some would penetrate along misty valleys while others captured high ground, ready to enfilade the enemy line. The fastest groups would set the pace and 'make headway wherever resistance was weakening'. Orders emphasised the assault troops were to 'push on, keep inside the divisional areas, do not trouble about what happens right or left'.

Timetables for the creeping barrage were arranged but it was accepted that the infantry advance could change according to circumstances and it 'aimed at a breakthrough, not in the old sense but at a general crumbling'. The tactical concept was to reinforce success not failure, pushing through the gaps and looking to enfilade the British troops to the flanks.

Scouts would point out centres of resistance to avoid, so the assault teams could infiltrate as far as possible while it was still misty. Special parties armed with bombs, trench mortars, flamethrowers and field guns would then close in on the redoubts. The doctrines were explained to the officers with the words, 'division must follow division to strike while the iron was hot.'

Typically the spring weather involved an overnight mist lasting well into the morning and while it soon cleared from the high ground, it persisted along rivers and valleys. Some would later believe it helped the assault teams, because the British machine gun and field gun teams could not see them. Others thought it delayed and disorientated the assault teams.

The *Deutsche Luftstreitkräfte*, or German Air Force, did not move aircraft to the Michael front until just before the attack but the Royal Flying Corps observers had seen new airfields and hangars appearing. It left the German pilots with only a few days to familiarise themselves with their area of operations and one of their first tasks was to check that everything was well camouflaged.

Squadrons were devoted to reconnaissance and the photography of targets, both for the artillery and for bombing flights. There were thirty-eight flights of fighters to protect the reconnaissance planes while they did their work. A large number of planes would support the attacks, strafing and bombing targets just ahead of the infantry advance. Another thirty-nine flights would provide air cover, ready to take on the Royal Flying Corps' fighter planes.

The Attack Goes In
By nightfall on 20 March, Seventeenth Army had lined up nineteen divisions against Third Army's six divisions while Eighteenth and Second Armies had assembled forty-three divisions opposite Fifth Army's fourteen divisions. For several days prisoners had been telling their interrogators when they thought the attack would begin. In fact there were so many false

leads that 'one could not help wondering whether these communicative gentry were not being sent over, according to plan, to upset our nerves or render us careless by constant cries of wolf.'

Lookouts watched as gaps were made in the wire but no man's land became quiet as the mist thickened into a fog late on 20 March. A few raids were made and the prisoners were anxious to leave the trenches before the bombardment started. Everyone was convinced that the time had come and some divisions even issued instructions to man battle stations.

Lieutenant Colonel Prior of the 9th Norfolks patrolled no man's land: 'In the Boche lines there was a stillness which, at the same time, was not a complete silence. Just as if a large number of men were already in position, waiting in intense excitement and speaking to each other in whispers.' The shelling began moments after he returned to his headquarters.

Each German corps had divided its artillery into three types. The *Artilleriebekämpsfungs-Artillerie* (*Aka*) or Counter Artillery Groups would hit the British batteries with field guns, which could rapidly fire gas shells. The heavy guns of the *Fernkämpsfungs-Artillerie* (*Feka*) or Deep Battle Artillery Groups would hit the lines of communication. The *Infantriebekämpsfungs-Artillerie* (*Ika*) or Infantry Artillery Groups were split into four sub-groups: (a) was armed with howitzers, (b) with howitzers and super howitzers, (c) had half the field guns and (d) had the rest of the field guns. They would destroy the infantry defences and then provide the creeping barrage.

Some British corps gave instructions to shell the German assembly areas around 3.30 am but the guns soon fell silent. Gas was released by 61st Division to disrupt any troops gathering around St Quentin. Then at 4.40 am the German guns opened fire across seventy miles of front, hitting part of First Army, most of Third Army and all of Fifth Army. The first phase of the bombardment had begun. The British artillery were hit by a mixture of 4½:1 gas to high explosive shells, with lots of tear gas to encourage the gunners to take off their masks to deal with the irritants in their eyes; they then fell foul of the mustard gas. The trenches were simultaneously hit by mortars firing a 1:1 mixture of gas to high explosive shells.

All along the British line, officers like Lieutenant Colonel Prior issued orders to man the battle stations: 'The men were turning out and getting into their gas masks as they ran to their posts. Having seen that everything was readiness, I went out to the right where I could see more of our front. It was getting much lighter and the bombardment over the whole front was

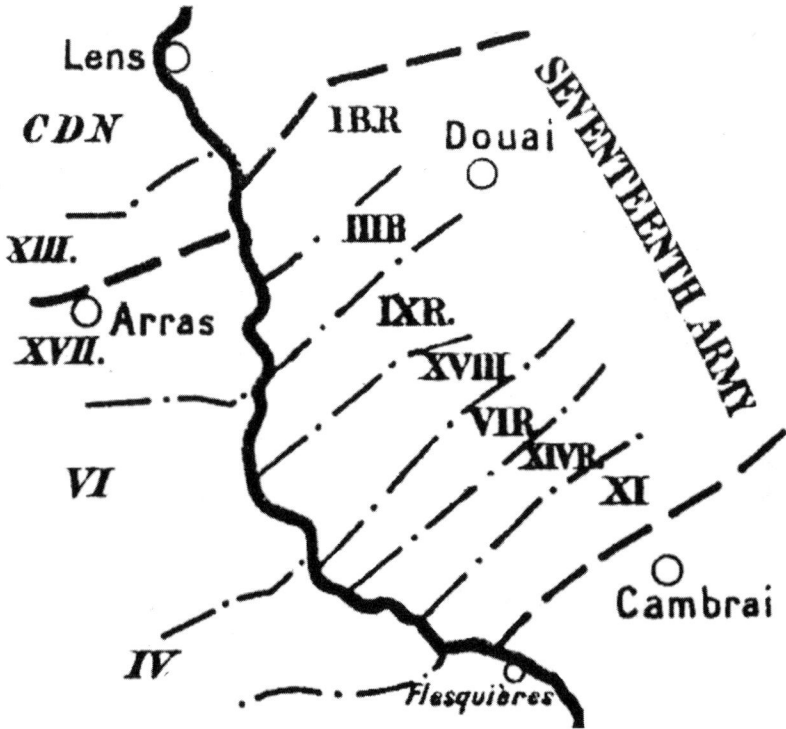

Seventeenth Army faced Third Army.

terrific. Shells were bursting everywhere and the noise was frightful. The gas shelling had stopped and it had been replaced by heavy shells.'

The trench mortars stopped after twenty minutes but the artillery continued to hit the batteries, communication centres, trench mortars and billets for another one hundred minutes. Another burst of intense shelling at 5.30 am hit the first position with high explosive and the second position with gas shells for ten minutes. The gunners engaged on counter-battery fire and then rested for ten minutes before starting again.

At 6.40 am the guns detailed to fire the creeping barrage checked their ranges in three groups of ten minutes each. The Counter Artillery and Deep Battle Groups continued to hit their usual targets but the Infantry Artillery Groups fired short bombardments against the infantry defences, starting at 7.10 am. Half the howitzers hit targets behind the first position for fifteen minutes while the rest of the howitzers and all the super howitzers hit strongpoints for ten minutes. The field guns also fired tear gas and high explosive shells at targets in front of the second position for ten minutes.

Second Army faced the Flesquières salient and Fifth Army's left.

The Infantry Artillery Groups repeated these short bombardments at 8.20 am.

A final crescendo of fire by all guns at 7.35 am warned the storm troops to start deploying into no man's land. The barrage had five belts of fire starting at the front line: howitzers, trench mortars, field guns, super heavy howitzers, deep battle batteries and heavy trench mortars. The remaining guns were used to hit the second line of trenches. Zero hour was only minutes away and many British soldiers were relieved that 'they are coming at last, good business. They will get it in the neck.'

After five minutes, the barrage started to creep forward. This was the *Kaiserschlacht*, or Emperor's Battle, but it was to be an 'assault without hurrahs', to leave the British guessing what was happening in the mist. The infantry had been told to 'keep close behind the barrage regardless of shell splinters. A single enemy machine gun which survives the bombardment does more harm than any number of our own shell splinters.'

The creeping barrage would jump 300 yards and then wait three minutes. The field artillery, 5.9-inch howitzers and light mortars, then moved 200 yards forward every four minutes while the heavy artillery jumped 400 yards every eight minutes. The infantry would fire green flares every time they advanced 200 metres if they had been delayed. Flamethrower teams would also fire squirts of burning fuel at regular intervals, so aerial observers could track their progress.

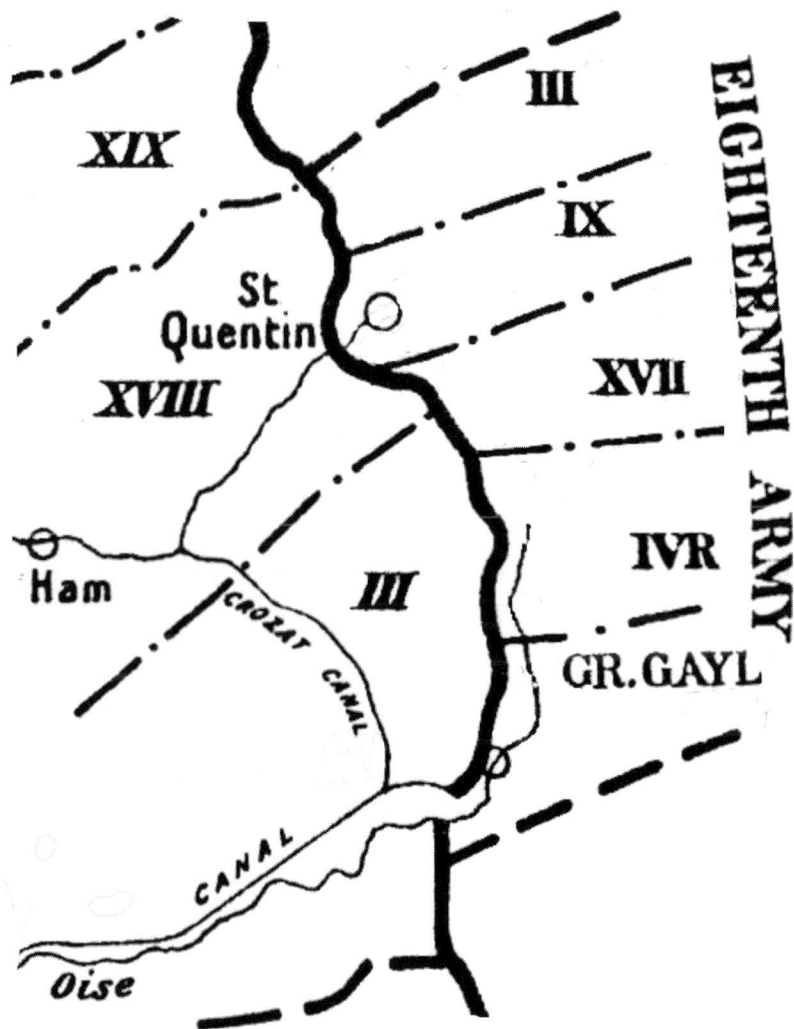

Eighteenth Army faced Fifth Army's right.

There was devastation along Forward Zone; trenches were levelled, strongpoints were demolished and machine gun posts were knocked out. The garrisons in the redoubts and fortified villages had not been hit so hard but the first they knew of the attack was when the Germans emerged from the mist.

The Royal Artillery's gunners had to work in a thick haze of fog and gas. There was no news from the front because the underground and overhead cables had been cut. All battery commanders could do was tell their men to fire at pre-set targets on 'night-counter-preparation lines', unaware that many of the German batteries had relocated during the night.

Battery commanders knew the attack was underway because of the change in sound and tempo in the enemy barrage but they could not see the SOS flares through the mist. The first they knew what was happening was when stragglers moved through their positions or they came under fire. Many battery commanders had moved their horse teams, lorries or tractors close to their positions so they could withdraw at short notice. But the warning came too late for some and the gunners had to disable their guns and escape.

The only way to get messages back and forth was by runners, leaving the men in the Forward Zone to fight on their own. Often there were few men standing to counter the first rush and many battalion and brigade headquarters knew nothing until they came under fire because the German storm troops were moving faster than their runners. The men in the Battle Zone were alerted with the code word 'Bustle' but it was no easy feat getting to their posts. A few groups got lost but the rest shuffled forward in their gas masks, holding onto each other in the mist.

The sun had risen at 6 am but the fog lay thick in the valleys, particularly along Fifth Army's right. It started to thin on the higher ground around 10 or 11 am but it lasted until 1 pm in the Oise valley. Dust and smoke from shell bursts then replaced the mist, so neither aerial nor ground observers could see anything. Even pigeons and runners found it difficult to find their way through the toxic mix of smoke, mist and fog. It was sometime after 11 am by the time Generals Byng and Gough knew the extent of the attack but the news was still sketchy. Haig was told soon afterwards and he, like his generals, was relieved it had fallen when and where it had been predicted.

The Royal Flying Corps was the eyes for the artillery during a battle, tracking the advancing infantry and spotting enemy batteries. Observers were to report targets through zone calls which identified targets with predetermined codes rather than using complicated trench map references. But the plan initially failed due to the poor visibility and because a lot of signalling equipment had been damaged. Problems continued because it was difficult to maintain communications along a fast-moving front line. The battery commanders tended to act on messages delivered by the infantry's mounted messengers rather than the few zone calls which came through. It meant that many lucrative targets were missed.

The RFC's contact patrols watched for friendly troops, close reconnaissance patrols looked out for the enemy but they found it hard to differentiate between the British and German infantry. It was then sometimes difficult to locate the ever-moving corps headquarters. Spare squadrons went looking for targets behind the lines and pilots would fly low, strafing and bombing. It was soon found that columns of troops and supplies strung out along the roads were the easiest to find and hit.

Chapter 4

The Struggle was of a Ding-Dong Nature

Third Army, 21 March

There were bombardments and raids astride the River Scarpe but the Arras–Cambrai road was the northern limit of Seventeenth Army's attack. It was aimed at VI Corps and IV Corps, and the aim was to drive past the north side of the Flesquières salient and cut off V Corps.

At 9.20 am the German assault teams began creeping forward in the mist while the bombardment hit the British trenches. They charged twenty minutes later and most of the outposts were overrun before they knew the attack had begun. Virtually everyone in the front trenches had been killed or captured in thirty minutes.

VI Corps

3rd Division, North of the Sensée Stream

Major General Cyril Deverell's front line was where the battle of Arras had ended in May 1917 and it was overlooked across a narrow no man's land. The bombardment hit the Battle Zone, while raids hit the men in the Forward Zone. The only successful one took trenches from the 1st Northumberland Fusiliers and 4th Royal Fusiliers, south-west of Chérisy. Brigadier General Potter was pleased to hear that Captains Carrick and Chipper had reclaimed the Northumberland line.

The Germans wanted Hénin Hill because of its commanding position, so another bombardment was followed by an afternoon attack. Tank and Dodo trenches were taken from the Northumberland Fusiliers and the Royal Fusiliers but the Germans 'were shaken and scattered by the mad-minute practice' of Lieutenant Colonel Hannay's 2nd Royal Scots. The support line held but the Royal Fusiliers had to pull back their right flank because 34th Division had retired to Hill Switch Trench.

34th Division, North-East of Croisilles

Seventeenth Army's plan was to smash through 59th Division and wheel north behind 34th Division's flank. Major General Lothian Nicholson deployed the reserves of the 22nd and 25th Northumberland Fusiliers when his right flank was under threat and they fired at the columns of infantry advancing towards Écoust as the mist cleared. Then there was a feint attack from Fontaine against 101 Brigade, to draw reserves from the left flank.

Later attacks all along the front drove the 23rd and 22nd Northumberland Fusiliers back to Gollywog Trench. Captain McLauchlan's company of the 25th Northumberland Fusiliers encountered 'masses of the enemy, several battalions strong and had to retire rapidly' from the Hog's Back. Lieutenant Colonel Charlton's two batteries of 160 Brigade RFA stopped three attempts to get behind 102 Brigade before they were overrun because 'the struggle was of a ding-dong nature'.

Lieutenant Colonel Guard was surprised to hear the enemy were behind his flank but the 15th Royal Scots fought a fierce bombing contest to stop the breach widening. Meanwhile, Major Warr prevented them from crossing the Sensée stream at Croisilles. A fresh bombardment was followed by 'wave after wave of Huns' advancing across 101 Brigade's front towards Hénin Hill. The 15th Royal Scots and 11th Suffolks poured enfilade fire into them, reducing the impact of the attack on 3rd Division's right flank.

The main problem was on 102 Brigade's front where the headquarters of the 22nd, 23rd and 25th Northumberland Fusiliers were trapped in a railway cutting called Bunhill Row. Captain McKellen, Captain Kirkup and RSM Peterkin organised the stragglers and their staff into an all-round defence. Sergeant Collins even found an escape route but Lieutenant Colonel Acklam was killed trying to lead his men out. During a lull 'the Boche shouted a message intimating that we had three minutes in which to surrender' or they would use their heavy trench mortars. With so little ammunition and so many wounded, there was no option but to give themselves up. A few able men made a run for it and they fought on in Factory Avenue under Captain McLachlan.

Major General Nicholson ordered Brigadier General Chaplin to move 103 Brigade to his right flank after hearing the Germans had reached Écoust in 59th Division's sector. Lieutenant Colonel Stephenson's 16th Royal Scots held Croisilles while some of Lieutenant Colonel Earle's 1st East Lancashires covered the exposed flank.

The German penetration between 34th and 59th Divisions had been contained but they were close to St Léger at the back of the Battle Zone. 'The day of fighting followed by a night of marching imposed a horrible strain on the men. Hollow-eyed and gaunt, all showed traces of the ordeal but their discipline stood the test and in grim silence they did what was required of them.' The only good news was that the 12th Suffolks had contacted 103 Brigade at dusk; it meant that 40th Division was approaching.

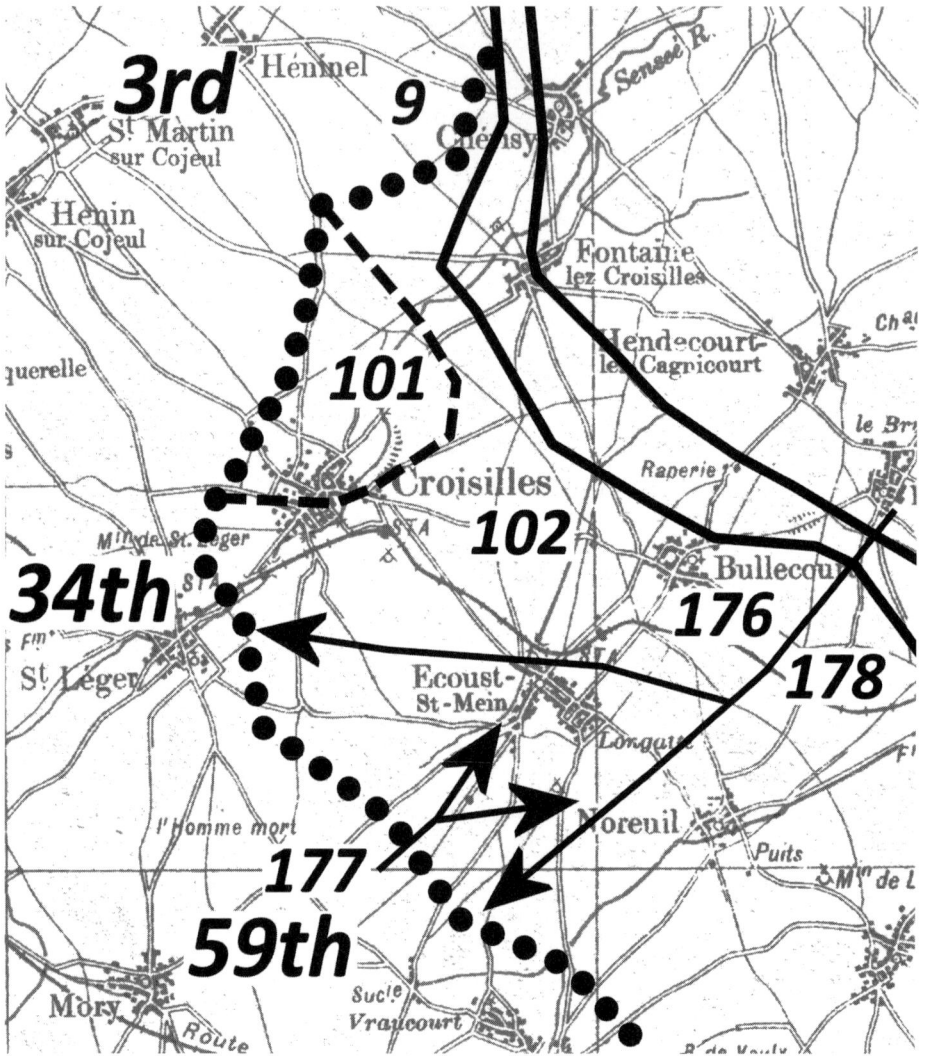

21 March VI Corps: 59th Division was overrun next to the Hirondelle stream, forcing 34th Division to fall back astride the Sensée stream.

59th (2nd North Midland) Division, Bullecourt and Noreuil
Major General Cecil Romer's men faced the first attack at 9.40 am and it was the heaviest. Brigadier General Stansfeld's trenches had been flattened by the bombardment and the assault troops moved rapidly through 178 Brigade's line north of the Hirondelle stream. The 7th Sherwoods were

overwhelmed and while some storm troops followed the Hirondelle stream towards Noreuil, others headed north, forcing the 2/6th Sherwoods back. They then turned on the 2/6th South Staffords, east of Bullecourt. There was a fierce hand-to-hand fight but the Sherwoods had been overrun by midday.

The fog was clearing when the Germans reached Noreuil and the 2/5th Sherwoods held on until they were outflanked. A few dozen men fought on south-west of the village, with 295 Brigade RFA, but the gunners had no idea where the front line was. Lieutenant Colonel Gadd was told to withdraw to Vraucourt and join the 2/5th Lincolns at the back of the Battle Zone but hardly any of his men made it. The same applied to the 2/6th South Staffords and the 2/6th Sherwoods because 178 Brigade had all but disappeared.

The Germans finally forced the 2/5th North Staffords out of Bullecourt, clearing all of 176 Brigade's Forward Zone. Lieutenant Colonel Thorne was organising a counter-attack to retake Longatte when large numbers of Germans approached the 2/6th North Staffords. Thorne asked Brigadier General Cope for help but it never came and only thirteen men escaped Écoust. Some of the Germans wheeled north-west behind 34th Division's flank while the rest attacked the 2/4th Leicesters at the back of the Battle Zone.

The German plan to capture the high ground and then enfilade the British line to the left and right was working. After midday, Major General Romer sent Brigadier General James's 177 Brigade forward, unaware that the Écoust ridge was already in enemy hands. The Lincolns and Leicesters had no artillery support and they were strafed by enemy planes as they advanced into the unknown.

The 2/4th Leicesters came under fire from Écoust, so they covered a battery until the gunners had disabled their guns and then retired to the back of the Battle Zone. The 2/5th Lincolns also encountered the Germans at Noreuil but they were unable to withdraw and 'what happened to these companies is not known as they were never seen again'. The 4th Lincolns deployed at the back of the Battle Zone, east of Vraucourt, finding a line of cut turf and they had to hunt for entrenching tools before they could dig in.

All along across the Battle Zone gunners were firing their last rounds, disabling their guns and making a run for it. Often there was too much machine-gun fire to bring the limbers forward and only fifteen teams managed to get their guns away.

A disaster had befallen 59th Division but help came from 34th Division when Lieutenant Colonels Vignoles and Earle made the 9th Northumberland Fusiliers and 1st East Lancashires run to the trench south-east of St Léger.

They just beat the Germans to it and were then engaged in a fierce battle as 'odds and ends of troops were hurried up to stem the rush'. They had to fight off 'wave after wave of grey figures advancing over the Hog's Back, undismayed by the heavy losses inflicted on them...'

The quick intervention saved the line at St Léger and a weak 177 Brigade was joined by every spare man as they extended the line south-east towards the Hirondelle stream. Major Hart was wounded as the 6/7th Scots Fusiliers (Pioneers) stopped the Germans reaching Vraucourt and Vaulx on the right.

VI Corps' Reinforcements

Lieutenant General Aylmer Haldane had told Major General John Ponsonby to move 40th Division forward at midday but it took the mounted staff officers time to deliver the messages to all the brigades and battalions. Brigadier General Campbell was told to move 121 Brigade south-east of St Léger, behind 34th Division's right. But 'little was known about the general situation, all that was reported was that the enemy was through the line though it was not known to what depth the Germans had actually penetrated.'

They soon found out because both the 12th Suffolks and 13th Green Howards had to drive the enemy out of the trench they were supposed to hold. Second Lieutenant Ernest Beal's group silenced four machine-gun teams so the 13th Green Howards could occupy their trench. Beal would rescue a wounded man under fire later in the day, only to be killed the following morning; he would be awarded a posthumous Victoria Cross.

Lieutenant Colonel Forbes moved 120 Brigade to Vraucourt, behind 59th Division's right and again the Germans had to be driven out of the Battle Zone trench. The 10/11th HLI contacted 121 Brigade on the left but the 14th Argylls could not contact 6th Division in the Hirondelle valley.

Brigadier General Crozier's 119 Brigade reached Hénin Hill, behind 34th Division's centre, around dusk. Major General Geoffrey Feilding moved the 2 Guards Brigade to Mercatel, ready to counter-attack if Hénin Hill was lost. Haldane had, however, allowed 34th Division to abandon Croisilles in the Sensée valley because it was a shell trap. While VI Corps' line was secure for now, the Germans had almost broken through the Battle Zone and the incomplete Green Line was only a short distance behind.

IV Corps

Lieutenant General George Harper's line was between the Hirondelle valley and the Canal du Nord but both the Forward and Battle Zones were on forward slopes in front of the Hindenburg Line. One battalion commander said the defences were 'the most disgusting he had ever met, with little cover to fall back upon once the Forward Zone had been lost, except for a few strongpoints and the old corps system'. Another said there were 'hardly any support trenches and no dugouts'.

6th Division, Lagnicourt

Major General Thomas Marden had all three brigades in line and the Germans moved along three valleys in the mist, heading for Noreuil, Lagnicourt and Morchies. They reached the Battle Zone either side of Lagnicourt within the hour.

Most of the 1st Shropshires and 2nd York and Lancasters were overrun while the survivors fell back towards the 1st Buffs after hearing that Noreuil and Lagnicourt had fallen behind their flanks. Lieutenant Colonel Smith's men made a last stand with some of the Shropshires next to the Hirondelle while Lieutenant Moody was killed trying to fight his way out with his company of the Buffs. The 'remnants of the Shropshires endeavoured to break out through the open with the bayonet' but only a few reached Captain Morgan's company of the Buffs near Vaulx Wood.

Brigadier General Walker welcomed two companies of the 8th Border Regiment because it meant 25th Division was close. Captain Hamilton told them that 16 Brigade had plenty of men but few officers and little ammunition. The Borders deployed while Second Lieutenant Rogers used the men of the Divisional Bombing School to help the Shropshires recapture the back of the Battle Zone. The main attack hit the rest of the 8th Border Regiment and the 11th Leicesters around Vaulx Wood. The guns of 24 Brigade RFA fired as long as they dared before limbering up and cantered to safety; only one battery had to abandon its guns.

The 2nd Sherwoods and the 9th Norfolks were quickly driven out of 71 Brigade's Forward Zone and the Germans took the front of the Battle Zone and Lagnicourt before midday. Lieutenant Colonel Prior sent Captain Hancock's company of the 9th Norfolk to help the Sherwoods and he watched as it advanced 'over the shell swept ground with very mixed feelings; pride at the gallant, unfaltering advance and dread at the cost that would have to be paid'. But the Germans kept coming and Prior burnt all his papers before gathering all the men he could find to counter-attack. Meanwhile, Lieutenant Watson and Captain Harbottle of the 1st Leicesters helped Captain Shelton form a new line south of Lagnicourt.

Brigadier General Brown was under attack from three sides but his men held on until Captain Spencer's 11th Leicesters (Pioneers) arrived. The arrival of the 2nd South Lancashires meant 25th Division was on its way. Brown's men 'fought until their rifles were too hot to hold and their Lewis guns had to be cooled down before they would fire another round. Finally, when ordered to withdraw they had come out carrying all their casualties.' They escaped to the back of the Battle Zone, north-west of Morchies, under cover of darkness.

The Norfolks alone had suffered over 360 casualties and they had been at just over half strength before the battle. Prior lamented that 'there were less than eighty men left of the splendid battalion I had commanded thirty hours previously... It is not too much to say that the enemy must have suffered at least six casualties for every one inflicted on the battalion.'

To begin with, all was well along 18 Brigade's line east of Lagnicourt. The 2nd Durhams even captured four machine guns and turned them on the Germans when the mist cleared. But the Germans had penetrated 51st Division on the right and they outflanked the 1st West Yorkshires. The

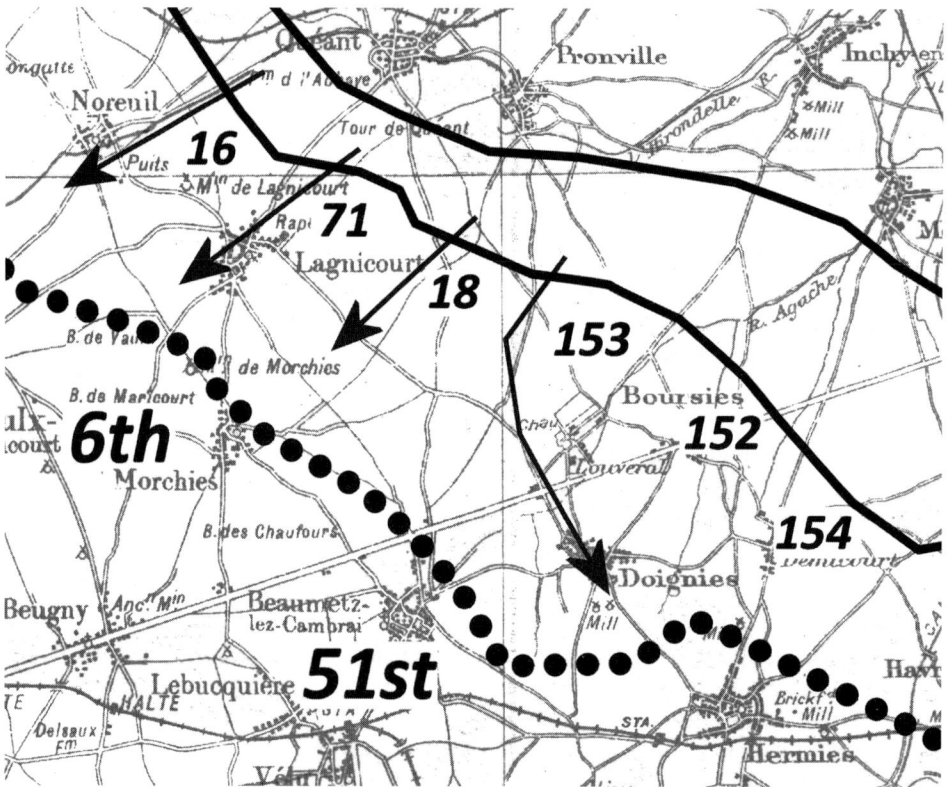

21 March IV Corps: 6th Division face the full brunt of the attack north of the Bapaume road while 51st Division was hit on both flanks.

1/7th Gordons were unable to retake Louverval but some of the 11th Essex helped them hold the open flank.

Brigadier General Craufurd was told a counter-attack was being organised but his men ran out of ammunition before it started and the West Yorkshire and Durhams had to leave their wounded behind because the machine-gun fire was so heavy. Lieutenant Colonel Boyall reported the West Yorkshires were cut off and could not hold on much longer but he stood by his promise to fight to the last. Less than 400 men made it back to the rest of the Essex at the back of the Battle Zone, east of Morchies.

51st (Highland) Division, along the Bapaume Road
The German plan was to break through 6th Division and 17th Division and then turn against Major General George Carter-Campbell's position astride the Bapaume–Cambrai road. Nothing was heard from the outpost line until Second Lieutenants Crowder and Stuart reported enemy infantry around their observation post two hours into the attack; then the line went dead.

The Germans moved east along 153 Brigade's line, using flamethrowers to knock out the posts of the 1/6th and 1/7th Black Watch. A counter-attack by the 11th Essex from 6th Division's Battle Zone failed to stop them and storm troops soon reached Louverval chateau on the Cambrai road. Lieutenant Colonel McClintock and Major Campbell and the two Black Watch battalion headquarters made a stand for another two hours while field guns engaged targets over open sights. Observers relayed targets to the heavy artillery when the mist cleared but the Germans kept coming. Then Brigadier General Beckwith heard that the 1/7th Gordons were under attack at the back of the Battle Zone.

The attack continued behind 152 Brigade's line, forcing the 1/5th Seaforths to regroup in Sturgeon Avenue before stopping the Germans leaving Boursies. But the 1/6th Gordons refused to leave their trench astride the main road and they were overrun.

Second Lieutenant John Buchan had been injured twice by the time he gathered his group of the 1/7th Argylls in Aldgate Trench. Shouting 'to hell with surrender' he shot enough Germans so they could escape but he did not get the order to withdraw with the rest of the Argylls. Buchan was last seen fighting off overwhelming numbers and would be posthumously awarded the Victoria Cross. His last stand gave the 1/4th Gordons time to prepare a defensive flank on 154 Brigade's right.

After taking Louverval, the Germans raked the 1/5th Seaforths position, killing Captain M'Kenzie as he formed a defensive flank. Lieutenant Menzies 'refused to leave his gun, even though wounded six times'. Instead he rallied the survivors in front of Beaumetz, alongside the 1/6th Gordons.

By mid-afternoon 51st Division's reserves were at the back of the Battle Zone where they had 'the best field firing practice of their lives' against the Germans leaving Doignies.

The Scots had held onto the Battle Zone but at tremendous loss of life, as well as forty machine guns and many field guns. During the early hours Harper told Carter-Campbell to withdraw to the back of the Battle Zone, to break contact and prepare for the morning's onslaught.

IV Corps' Reinforcements

General Harper had two divisions to reinforce IV Corps' line. Major General Guy Bainbridge's 25th Division was deployed north-west of Bapaume and Brigadier General Bethell was told to deploy 74 Brigade and 112 Brigade RFA astride the Cambrai road to stop the Germans penetrating at Louverval. Both the 11th Lancashire Fusiliers and 9th Loyals deployed between Morchies and Beaumetz, at the back of the Battle Zone.

Meanwhile, Major General George Jeffreys, of 19th Division, had told Brigadier General Ballard to move 57 Brigade and 29 Brigade RFA towards 51st Division's right flank. Twelve tanks of 8th Battalion headed for Doignies but they were driven back by the time the 10th Worcesters and the 8th Gloucesters were ready. Captain Manley James, of 57 Brigade's staff, persisted in making an attack but they came under such heavy fire that the company commanders agreed to retire to the back of the Battle Zone instead. James was credited with stopping the Germans breaking through and he would be awarded the Victoria Cross.

V Corps

Lieutenant General Edward Fanshawe was responsible for the Flesquières Salient, a 7-mile-wide and 4-mile-deep bulge in the line. It was where Third Army had withdrawn to after the German counter-attack at the end of the battle of Cambrai. Parts of the trenches were made out of converted sections of the Hindenburg Line but the Germans had no intention of attacking the area head on.

The salient was subjected to the same bombardment as the rest of the front, so as not to raise any suspicions and then raids made the British troops 'stand to' and deploy their reserves. Attacks followed against the 17th, 63rd and 47th Division, but there was no intention to go further than the front trenches. Instead the salient was hit with mustard gas shells which resulted in clouds 'the density of a London fog'. Hundreds of men were evacuated and the 4th Bedfords alone suffered over 250 casualties. Mustard gas always hung around in trenches, a clear sign that the Germans had no intention of capturing the salient for some time.

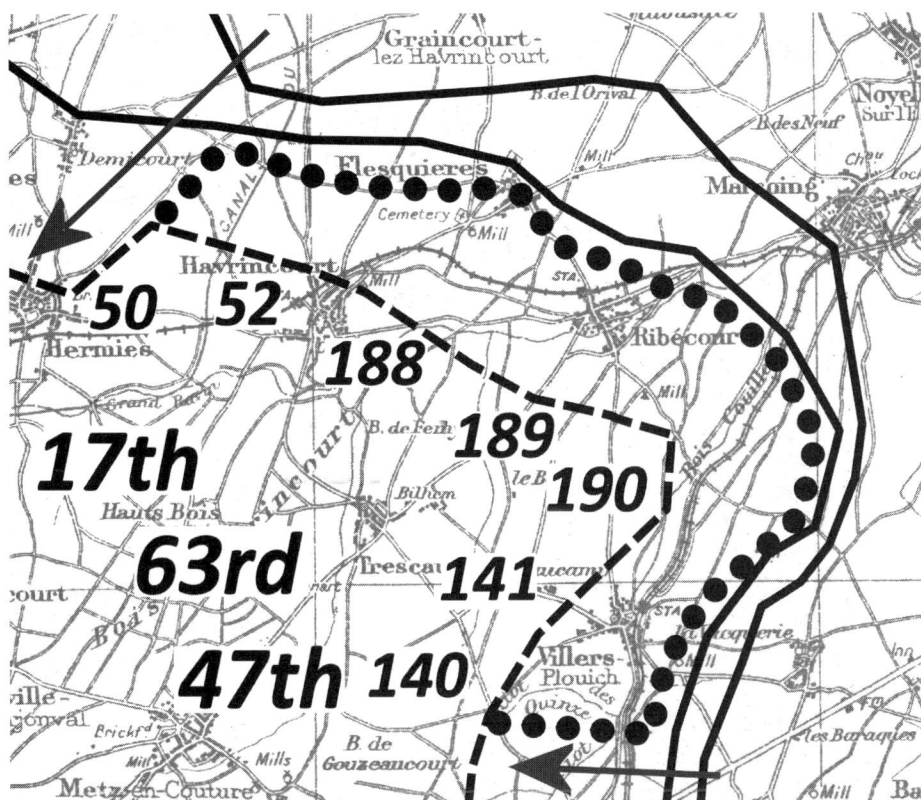

21 March V Corps: There were few attacks against the Flesquières salient but V Corps had to withdraw at night.

Instead Seventeenth and Second Armies would push past the flanks, to trap V Corps in a pincer movement.

17th (Northern) Division, Astride the Canal du Nord

The 6th Dorsets and 10th West Yorkshires lost Hughes Trench astride the Canal du Nord but the West Yorkshires retook their section of 50 Brigade's line. The outpost line of 52 Brigade was overrun but the 10th Lancashire Fusiliers and the 12th Manchesters stopped six waves of men from reaching Owen Trench. The battle was going so well that Lieutenant Colonel Torrens had to be told not to counter-attack because 'it was not the policy to lose men in fighting to retain the forward trenches.'

But Major General Philip Robertson became concerned after hearing that 51st Division had been driven out of Doignies, so he moved the 10th

Sherwoods to Hermies on his left flank. Further attacks against the front line after the fog had cleared also failed and 'the impression that evening was that things were going well.'

<u>V Corps Summary</u>

By dusk it was clear that the Germans were making a pincer move against V Corps so Byng obtained Haig's approval to withdraw everyone from the Salient. But it was dawn before the men at the front heard the news and they then had to withdraw across ground saturated with mustard gas. The Germans would wait until nightfall on 22 March before they dared to occupy the poisoned trenches.

Third Army's Summary

By nightfall General Byng was worried. He knew that both VI and IV Corps had been forced to the back of the Battle Zone and that all four of the front line divisions had suffered heavy casualties. He had also committed three of his five reserve divisions to the battle. The 59th Division had been hit particularly hard, suffering well over 5,000 casualties and 178 Brigade had been reduced from around two thousand men to less than sixty in just a few hours. Only V Corps was safe for the time being and General Gough's optimistic report led Byng to believe that all was well south of the Flesquières salient.

Chapter 5

Here We Fight and Here We Die!

Fifth Army, 21 March

General Gough was responsible for forty-two miles of front but it was doubted that there would be a major attack on the right flank, where the River Oise and canal ran along no man's land. The Forward Zone was well developed, with outposts and strongpoints but the Battle Zone was only half built and virtually nothing had been done to the Rear Zone.

VII Corps

Lieutenant General Sir Walter Congreve had three divisions between the Flesquières salient and the Cologne stream. Most of the Forward Zone had been established where the German counter-attack had ended at the end of the battle of Cambrai while the Battle Zone crossed the Lempire and Épehy ridges close behind. The plan was for the outposts to withdraw when the attack started, leaving defended localities to break up the attack.

<u>9th (Scottish) Division, Gauche Wood and Chapel Hill</u>

Brigadier General Henry Tudor was in command of the division while Major General Cyril Blacklock was on leave; Winston Churchill had described him as 'an iron peg hammered into the ground; immoveable'. The Germans did not attack Brigadier General Kennedy's 26 Brigade, in front of Gouzeaucourt, because it was considered part of the Flesquières salient. The same applied to the 1st South African Regiment but the Germans attacked Lieutenant Colonel Christian's 2nd South African Regiment in Gauche Wood. Lieutenants Bancroft and Beviss held on for over four hours in the mist before they were overpowered. Captain Green then sent the rest of his men to the west side of the wood while Brigadier General Dawson 'directed all the artillery at his disposal to bombard' it.

Quentin Redoubt stopped the Germans going any further when the mist lifted but Dawson was concerned the Germans were pushing through 21st Division on his south flank, especially when he learnt they had been driven

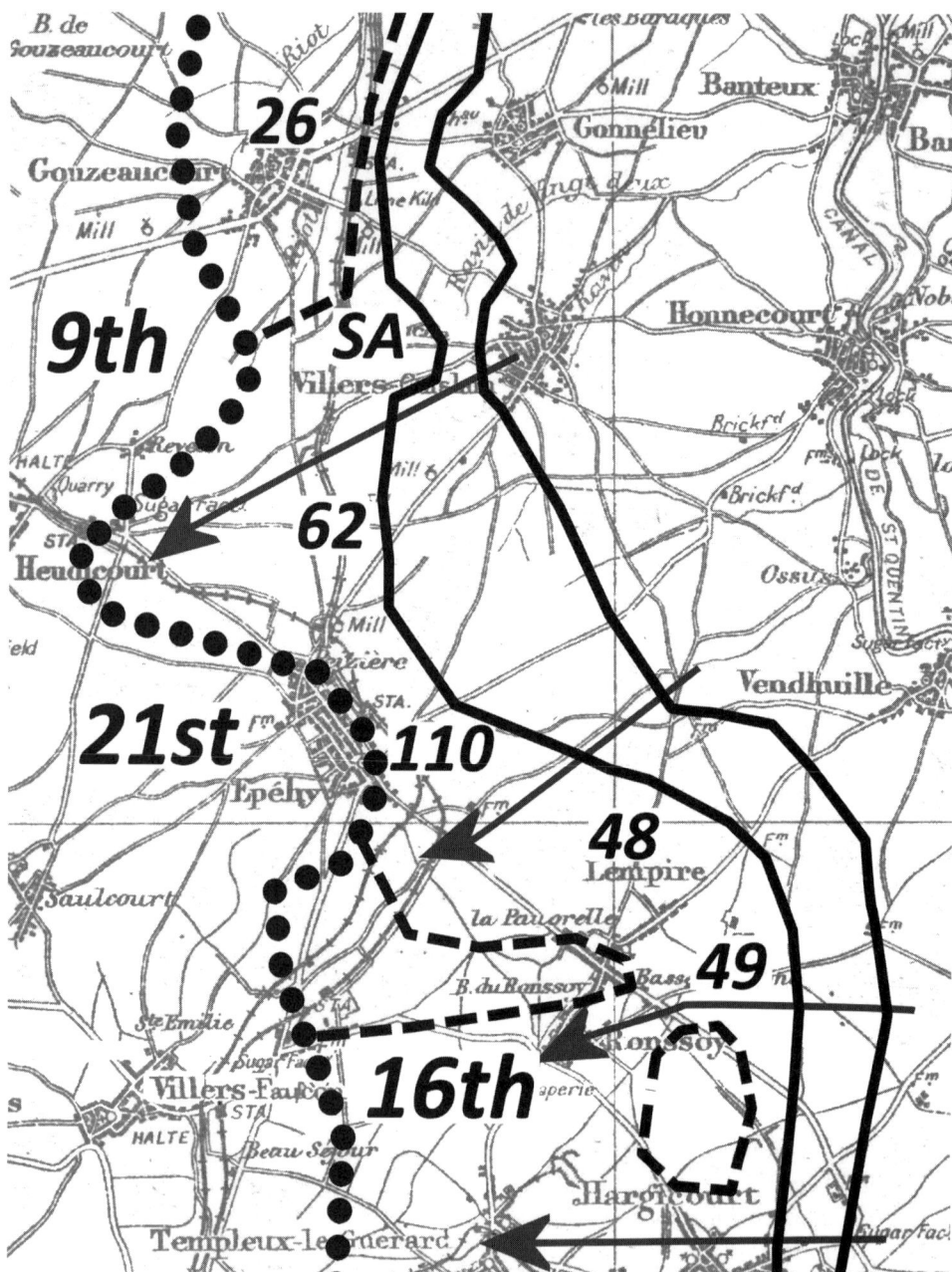

21 March VII Corps: Both 21st Division and 16th Division suffered reverses, so VII Corps had to fall back during the night.

from Chapel Hill. Lieutenant Colonel MacLeod moved a company of the 4th South African Regiment towards the hill, only to find the 1st Lincolns were still there having 'done magnificently'.

Lieutenant General Congreve knew 9th Division was planning to recapture Gauche Wood but 21st Division was struggling to hold the Battle Zone while 16th Division was being forced out of it. Congreve also heard that V Corps was planning to start withdrawing from the Flesquières salient, leaving him no option but to pull back his left to keep in contact; 'it came as a huge surprise to General Tudor when he was ordered to withdraw his men during the night to the Battle Zone.'

21st Division, Peizière and Épehy
The location of no man's land had again been decided by the battle of Cambrai and there was a valley in Major General David Campbell's rear area. It meant the Forward Zone and the Battle Zone were almost touching on the ridge between Chapel Hill and the twin villages of Peizière and Épehy.

The 1st Lincolns and 12/13th Northumberland Fusiliers fought in the mist for 62 Brigade's Forward Zone until midday. The British machine gunners wasted most of their bullets firing along fixed lines in the mist but German stretcher bearers carried ammunition forward for their German counterparts before heading back with casualties. There was a bitter afternoon battle for the front of the Battle Zone because the Germans wanted Vaucelette Farm, so they could see across the division's rear area.

A lookout made sure Lieutenant Colonel Fisher and the 1st Lincolns headquarters had time to escape onto Chapel Hill. But the Germans captured the 12/13th Northumberland Fusiliers' headquarters north of Peizière. Brigadier General Gator had deployed field guns and machine guns around Heudicourt valley and they fired into the advancing mass of infantry and artillery limbers when the mist lifted. Lieutenant Colonel Festing was killed as the 15th Durhams counter-attacked but the line was restored close to Vaucelette Farm.

The first attack at 7 am failed to drive 110 Brigade's outposts back but a second advanced along Linnet and Thrush valleys, pushing the 8th Leicesters back into Épehy. The storm troops then turned north against Lieutenant Colonel Sawyer's 7th Leicesters in Peizière and there was bitter fighting all around the fortified twin villages. Brigadier General Cumming sent the 6th Leicesters forward and Lieutenant Colonel Stewart's counter-attack resulted in a German communiqué which stated, 'the Leicester Brigade at Épehy gave us the most trouble.'

16th (Irish) Division, West of Vendhuille

Major General Sir Amyatt Hull's Forward Zone followed a salient opposite Vendhuile while the Battle Zone was based around Malassise Farm and Lempire one mile to the rear. The mist was particularly dense around the St Quentin Canal and most of the Forward Zone was overrun in the first rush, leaving insufficient men to hold the Battle Zone.

Assault teams pushed past the 1st Dublin Fusiliers to reach Malassise Farm in the centre of 48 Brigade before midday. But it was some time before Brigadier General Ramsey heard that the 2nd Munsters and the 2nd Dublin Fusiliers were still holding on north of Lempire. The survivors would fight their way back by nightfall.

Other storm troops bypassed the 2nd Irish Regiment east of Lempire and the 7th Irish Regiment east of Ronssoy so none of 49 Brigade's outposts escaped. But the main threat came from the Germans moving down the Cologne valley to Templeux-le-Guérard. They then turned behind the 7/8th Inniskilling Fusiliers and captured Ronssoy and its wood. They headed towards the back of the Battle Zone, leaving the support waves to deal with Lieutenant Colonel Walkley's posts.

The rapid advance drove Lieutenant Colonel Crockett's 11th Hampshires (Pioneers) out of St Emilie for a time and two huge railway guns had to be abandoned because the track had been cut. The news prompted Major General Hull to tell Brigadier General Gregorie to counter-attack with 47 Brigade only to countermand the order when it was clear the Germans were pushing past his flanks.

Lieutenant Colonel Weldon of the 2nd Leinsters got the cancellation order in time, as did the 1st Munsters, but an injured Lieutenant Colonel Raynsford did not, so the 6th Connaught Rangers advanced alone. They had no artillery support and their two supporting tanks were knocked out so they were unable to retake Ronssoy. Captains Crofton and Norman were both hit as the Connaughts were 'practically annihilated'. The Munsters and Leinsters were deepening the trench at the back of the Battle Zone when a few dozen Connaughts fell back, to find the 'shelling devilish; dead and wounded everywhere'.

VII Corps Reserves

Brigadier General Hornby was in temporary command while Major General Edward Feetham was on leave. General Gough gave 39th Division to VII Corps shortly after midday and it was directed towards 16th Division. Major General Hull was told to hold the back of the Battle Zone until it arrived and 116 Brigade covered the gap which had developed south of Épehy during the evening.

XIX Corps

Lieutenant General Herbert Watts' line covered nearly six miles of front between the Omignon and Cologne streams. He was relying on the line of redoubts located between the fortified villages of Templeux-le-Guérard, Jeancourt, Le Verguier and Vadencourt, to stop the Germans. As usual, the fog hid the storm troops moving through the Forward Zone but most of it had cleared by the time they reached the Battle Zone. However, there were problems on the flanks where the mist hung around in the Cologne and Omignon valleys.

66th (2nd East Lancashire) Division, Hargicourt and Grand Priel Wood

Major General Neill Malcolm was so sure the attack would begin on 21 March that he issued a warning and cancelled all working parties. Patrols returned during the early hours to report 'abnormally large numbers of the enemy in the trenches'. No man's land was narrow and the mist was thick along the Cologne valley in 197 Brigade's sector. The 2/8th Lancashire Fusiliers were overrun north-east of Hargicourt and the battalion headquarters was captured before Lieutenant Colonel Stokes-Roberts knew the attack had begun; only Second Lieutenant Sayer and a handful of men escaped.

Templeux quarry was kept under fire while the Germans moved along the Cologne valley into the village. A few escaped but the rest only surrendered when their ammunition ran out during the afternoon. Fortunately for Brigadier General Borrett's men, the mist was clearing, and 'lines of Germans on the high ground above the quarries presented a favourable target of which full advantage was taken by the artillery.'

One company of the 2/6th Lancashire Fusiliers stopped the enemy entering Templeux, giving Major Wike time to organise a counter-attack. But the Germans persisted until Lieutenant Colonel Gell's 2/7th Lancashire Fusiliers and some of the 1/5th Border Regiment (Pioneers) were surrounded. Only Captain Smirke's group escaped to join the stragglers collecting under Major Biddolph.

The 2/4th East Lancashires were overrun on 198 Brigade's front. The 2/5th East Lancashires were surrounded in Hargicourt but Lieutenant Colonel Evan Lloyd made sure the 9th Manchesters held on in a sunken road west of the village. Brigadier General Hunter was also pleased to hear the 9th Sussex were holding Trinity and Trinket redoubts, stopping the Germans reaching Hesbécourt.

The first rush overran the 2/5th Manchesters holding 199 Brigade's front line. Enfilading fire stopped the storm troops moving across the high ground south of Villeret while the rest of the Manchesters held onto

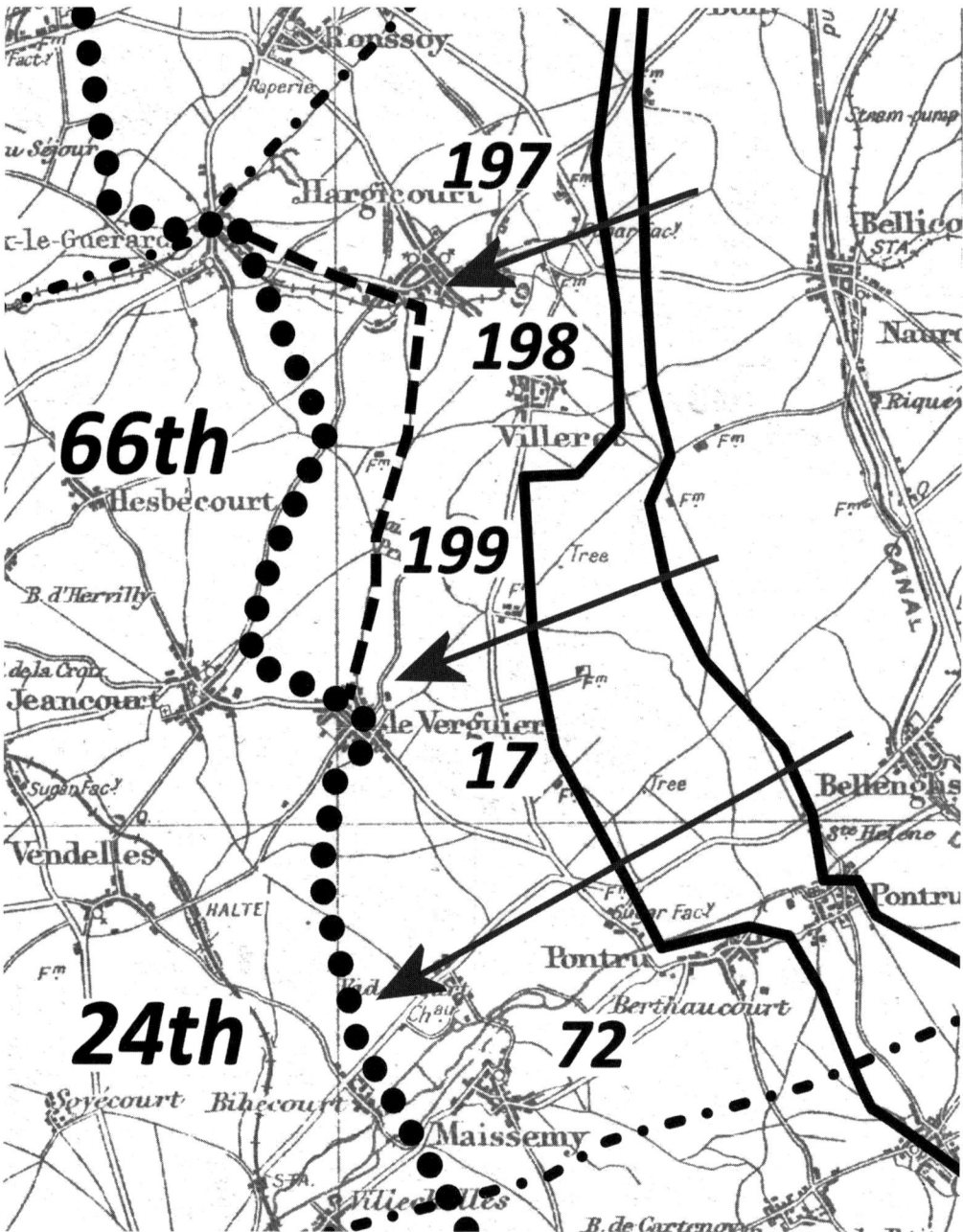

21 March XIX Corps: Both 66th Division and 24th Division were forced back between the Cologne and Omignon streams.

Higson's Quarries. Flamethrowers drove the 2/6th Manchesters from Fervaque Farm and Grand Priel Wood but Lieutenant Colonel Hurlbatt's men held onto Carpeza Copse while the 2/7th Manchesters in Brosse Wood stopped the Germans pushing past the right flank.

24th Division, Le Verguier, Berthaucourt and Maissemy

Brigadier General Stone's 17 Brigade covered Le Verguier, and the front companies of the 8th Queen's and 3rd Rifle Brigade were soon overrun. Lance Corporal John Sayer held one post with a small group of the Queen's, allowing Lieutenant Colonel Peirs time to organise the 8th Queen's in Le Verguier. Sayer died in captivity and he would be posthumously awarded the Victoria Cross.

Lieutenant Colonel Kewley's 3rd Rifle Brigade held on around Cookers Quarry, north-east of Vadencourt, but the German assault teams continued to push east. Eventually, Major General Arthur Daly gave the order to retire while Peirs pulled the Queen's back a short distance; the 3rd Rifle Brigade never got the message and were surrounded.

The 8th Queen's Own were overrun astride the Omignon stream and the storm troops bypassed Pontru. Lieutenant Colonel Wenyon instructed the 8th Queen's Own to evacuate Vadencourt and fall back between Le Verguier and Bihécourt.

Many of the 1st North Staffords were killed or captured around Berthaucourt but the storm troops bypassed Essling Redoubt and followed the Omignon. They came under enfilade fire from the 8th Queen's Own across the stream when the mist cleared but Lieutenant Colonel Pope's 1st North Staffords in front of Maissemy were overrun. Some of Lieutenant Colonel Lawrence's 9th East Surreys fought on for several hours south of Maissemy and only twenty men were left to surrender when they ran out of ammunition. An artillery major made sure the rest of the 9th East Surreys and some of the 12th Sherwood Foresters (Pioneers) stopped the Germans reaching Vermand.

Major General Daly reported the disaster along the Omignon to Lieutenant General Watts when he realised Vermand was being threatened. He also instructed Brigadier General Dugan to deploy his 73 Brigade along the back of the Battle Zone.

XIX Corps' Reserves

Major General Richard Mullens was instructed to move the 1st Cavalry Division forward following Gough's visit to Watts. Brigadier General Beale-Browne was told to put 2nd Cavalry Brigade behind 66th Division while the 2nd Cavalry Brigade Pioneer Battalion garrisoned Roisel in the

Cologne valley. Brigadier General Makins moved 1st Cavalry Brigade to 24th Division's right, where the Queen's Bays and the 5th Dragoon Guards deployed south of Vadencourt. The 11th Hussars garrisoned Villecholles, covering Omignon valley.

XVIII Corps

Lieutenant General Sir Ivor Maxse was holding a 5½-mile sector facing St Quentin. His plan was for the troops in the front line to withdraw to the redoubts, where field batteries would cover the gaps with fire. But the plan soon fell apart because the German assault troops were on top of the redoubts and gun batteries before the fog had lifted.

<u>61st (2nd South Midland) Division, Gricourt and Fayet back to Holnon Wood</u>
Major General Colin MacKenzie's men were ordered to 'man battle stations' north-west of St Quentin when the bombardment started.

The 1/5th Gordons held Fresnoy-le-Petit, in 183 Brigade's sector, until after midday but only thirty men escaped; Lieutenant Colonel McTaggart and Major Robertson were just two of the many prisoners. The 2/4th Ox and Bucks held Enghien Redoubt, north-east of Fayet, in 184 Brigade's zone. Lieutenant Colonel Weatherall was wounded and Captain Moberly never received the order to withdraw. Second Lieutenant John Cunningham's last message to Brigadier General White was 'we are surrounded now sir, what are we to do?' He was told to escape but only a few men made it. The 2/8th Worcesters held Ellis Redoubt, south-east of Fayet, in 182 Brigade's zone and while the headquarters was overrun, some men held until late in the afternoon; none escaped.

Lieutenant Allan Ker, 61st Battalion, Machine Gun Corps, fought on with his pistol and a captured rifle after his Vickers machine gun was damaged, only surrendering when their ammunition ran out. Ker would be awarded the Victoria Cross for stopping around 500 of the enemy for three hours.

Major General MacKenzie threw back his left flank as the Germans moved along the Omignon. Lieutenant Colonel Macalpine-Downie was killed as the 1/8th Argylls fought north of Holnon wood and Lieutenant Colonel Dimmer VC was killed leading the 2/4th Berkshires forwards on horseback. His men could not retake Maissemy but they had stalled the German advance. Dimmer had been awarded the Victoria Cross for deeds while serving as a Lieutenant with the 2nd KRRC in November 1914.

Barely fifty men escaped from the Forward Zone but they had delayed the German advance. They had captured Holnon but Lieutenant Colonel Lawson's 2/5th Gloucesters stopped them entering the wood while the 2/6th Warwicks refused to budge to the south.

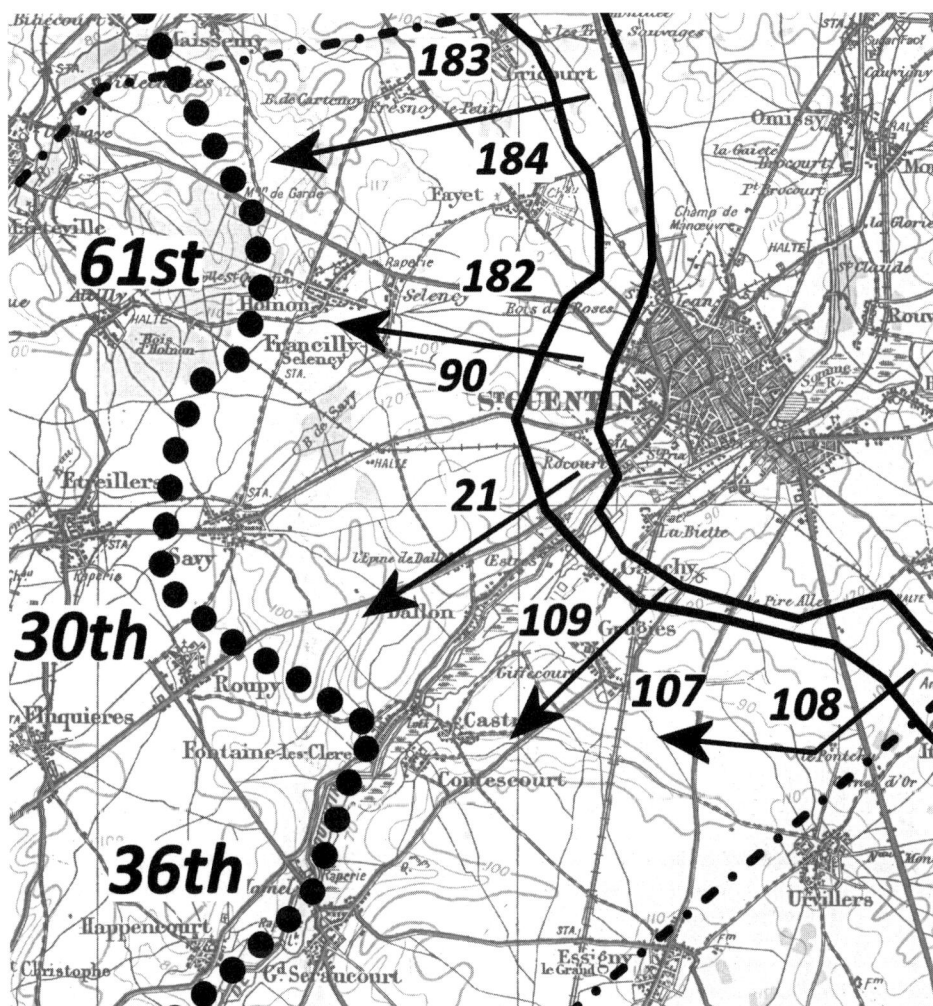

21 March XVIII Corps: 61st Division and 30th Division were pushed back to Holnon Wood and Savy at the back of the Battle Zone while 36th Division had to withdraw behind the Somme Canal.

30th Division, West of St Quentin to Savy and Roupy

Major General Weir Williams' men held the area north of the River Somme and the St Quentin Canal. Lieutenant Colonel Wilfrith Elstob called 90 Brigade's acting brigadier, Lieutenant Colonel Poyntz, to tell him that the 16th Manchesters would 'defend Manchester Hill to the last'. He then checked the redoubts' defences, telling everyone 'you are doing magnificently'. He personally stopped a bombing attack and was wounded twice carrying ammunition to his men. After seven hours, the Manchesters realised their commander's prophecy: 'here we fight, and here we die!' Elstob would posthumously be awarded the Victoria Cross.

In 21 Brigade's sector, the attack penetrated the 2nd Wiltshires' flanks in the mist and then took the front companies in the rear; only Lieutenant Capp and half a dozen men escaped. The first sign of trouble for Lieutenant Colonel Martin was when the fog briefly lifted and he saw 'a party coming like a mob, from the direction of Roupy'. L'Épine de Dallon strongpoint was then strafed by planes, swept with machine-gun fire and hit by artillery. Two pigeons carried messages to Brigadier General Goodman saying, 'the 2nd Wiltshires are still holding.' No more was heard but Martin's men had delayed the Germans for several hours.

As the mist cleared the men in the Battle Zone shot at the columns of infantry moving across the valley. The 2nd Bedfords stopped them reaching Étreillers while Lieutenant Colonel Edwards' 2nd Green Howards held Roupy where 'the many Germans who clustered into the quarry had terrible experiences.' Lieutenant Colonel Peck was killed leading a counter-attack by the 19th King's and they helped the 17th Manchesters hold on between Étreillers and Roupy.

36th (Ulster) Division, South of St Quentin

The 2nd Inniskillings' war diary noted that a 'terrific bombardment opened at 4.30 am' but nothing more was written because they were overrun. Major General Oliver Nugent's artillery could only fire at predetermined targets as the men in the redoubts fought on in the mist. The initial rush of troops came from east to west, along the Grugies valley behind the front line.

After dealing with the 2nd Inniskillings, holding 109 Brigade's line around Gauchy, the assault troops bypassed Boadicea Redoubt, next to the Somme. Lieutenant Colonel Farnham's men were then 'surrounded on all sides by overwhelming forces, smothered with trench mortar shells, subjected to constant bombing and *Flammenwerfer* attacks'. Lieutenant Colonel Crawford's 1st Inniskillings were waiting in Ricardo Redoubt, south-west of Fontaine-les-Clercs, but the Germans again bypassed the position, heading south-west along the River Somme.

Lieutenant Colonel Cole-Hamilton's 15th Irish Rifles held Racecourse Redoubt until the evening, astride the railway south of Grugies. Captain Stewart used grenades to stop the flamethrower teams while a wounded Second Lieutenant Edmund De Wind twice drove the

Germans back. Reinforcements eventually reached De Wind after seven hours but he would be mortally wounded soon afterwards; his 'cold courage' had saved 107 Brigade and he was posthumously awarded the Victoria Cross.

The assault troops followed the St Quentin canal and entered Contescourt because a large shell had hit Captain Brown's company of the 1st Irish Rifles which had been detailed to man its defences. Two pigeons carried Farnham's final message to Brigadier General Hessey at dusk; nothing more was heard of the Inniskillings. Meanwhile, Brigadier General Withycombe was pleased to hear that Major Rose's 2nd Irish Rifles in Quarry Redoubt had stopped the Germans leaving Contescourt until late in the evening.

The 12th Irish Rifles covering the Essigny–St Quentin road were overwhelmed but Captain Johnston fought a running battle on 108 Brigade's front. Once the mist cleared his men spotted reinforcements for the attack against Jeanne d'Arc redoubt to his rear. 'Lewis gun fire opened upon this body in a few seconds killed or wounded every man and horse in it, leaving the whole column in a welter of confusion.' The redoubt surrendered during the afternoon and so did Johnston's weary men when a tank approached, the first time the German A7V tank had been in action (five were deployed but three had broken down). 'As the prisoners were marched back towards St Quentin they had the grim satisfaction of seeing the column of transport they had annihilated still strewn in indescribable confusion about the road.' Part of 1st Irish Fusiliers held out in Station Redoubt, giving Brigadier General Griffiths the time to deploy the 9th Irish Fusiliers and 9th Inniskilling Fusiliers as a defensive flank along the railway cutting west of Essigny.

XVIII Corps Summary

As Maxse reported later, the front battalions had 'simply fought it out on the spot and their heroism will live for ever in the annals of their regiments'. However, the loss of Essigny in III Corps' area meant the Germans could see across Maxse's XVIII Corps' Zone. Gough had already agreed III Corps would withdraw to the Crozat Canal line, so 36th Division had to conform.

The Ulstermen abandoned Quarry and Station Redoubts during the night, wheeling to a line between Fontaine-les-Clercs and Happencourt along the St Quentin Canal. Brigadier General 61 Brigade (20th Division) filled the gap to 14th Division on the Crozat Canal. Everyone got across the canal before the bridges were blown, the engineers sometimes working under fire to complete their work.

III Corps
Lieutenant General Sir Richard Butler was covering over twenty miles, from the south-east side of St Quentin, along the west side of the Canal de l'Oise and across the marshes surrounding the River Oise.

14th (Light) Division, Urvillers, Cerizy and Essigny
Sixty-year-old Major General Sir Victor Couper was not having a good time. He had just received a letter saying he was going to be relieved to make way for a younger man after serving with the division since its training days. He was due to be relieved the following morning but he first had to fight his last battle.

The first attack from Itancourt overran the 8th KRRC on 41 Brigade's left with the help of two A7V tanks. Major Bowden described them as 'larger and faster' that the British Mark IVs and his men surrendered as they crushed the wire. The assault parties bypassed Urvillers and then captured Manufacture Farm and Essigny. Brigadier General Skinner heard that Major Thornton's 7th Rifle Brigade was holding on at the back of the Battle Zone but 41 Brigade's rapid retreat had caused a problem for XVIII Corps.

The Germans now turned south behind the 9th KRRC, holding 42 Brigade's sector, while Lieutenant Colonel Howard-Bury's men held onto Urvillers. The 5th Ox and Bucks and the 11th King's (Pioneers) also held on between Benay and Essigny and 'according to the casualty list at the close of the first day, they must have been engaged heavily with the enemy'.

The 6th Somersets and part of the 7th KRRC were overrun around Benay and Cerizy. Some of the 9th Scottish Rifles helped the rest of Lieutenant Colonel Birch's KRRC hold on as the Germans pushed past. Brigadier Tempest eventually lost touch with 18th Division because the Germans had penetrated Gibercourt Wood on his right.

Most of the Essigny plateau was in enemy hands by mid-afternoon and while Lieutenant General Butler had few facts to go on, it sounded bad. He moved all his reserves forward but they could not stem the tide of troops moving through the Battle Zone, meaning III Corps would have to withdraw behind the Crozat Canal.

Major General Couper stayed with 14th Division headquarters throughout the fighting but Major General Bob Greenly took command because 2nd Cavalry Division's brigades were mixed in with 14th Division – which must have been awkward. Greenly left on 27 March when 14th Division was finally pulled out of the line but Couper stayed on until Major General Cyriac Skinner took command on 31 March.

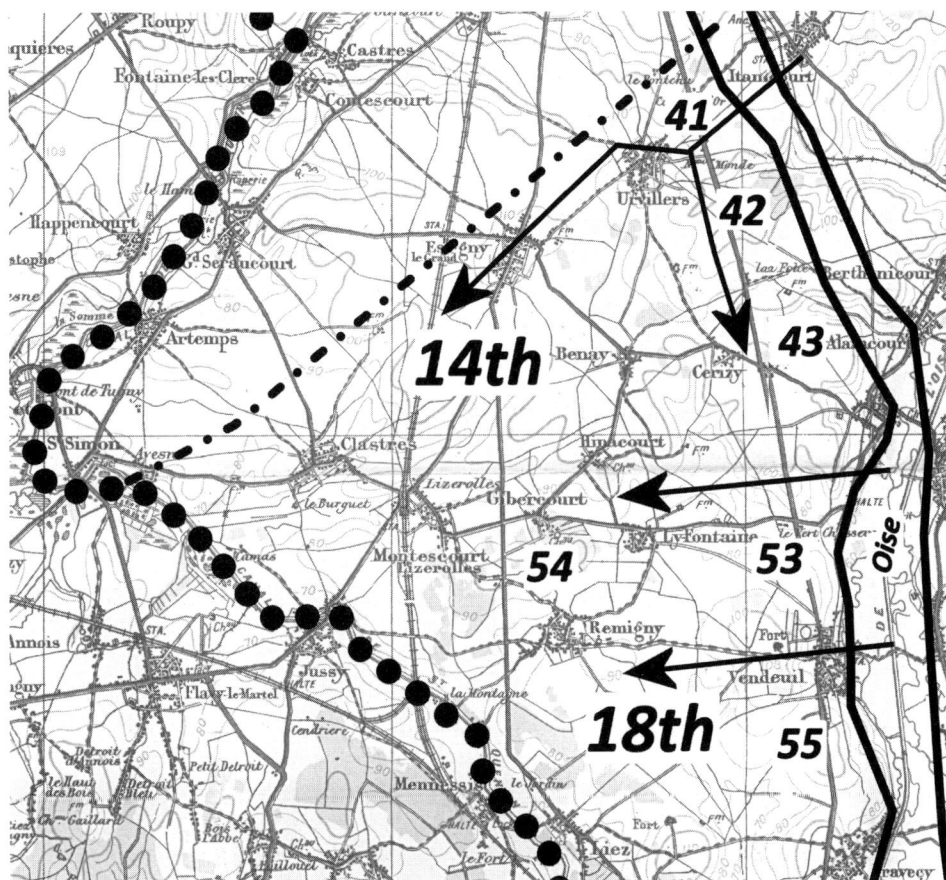

21 March III Corps' North Flank: The loss of the Essigny plateau by 14th Division resulted in an overnight withdrawal to the Crozat Canal.

18th (Eastern) Division, Alaincourt to Vendeuil

It seems Major General Richard Lee was unaware that the Oise River and Canal were low enough to wade across. Raiding parties were sent into the fog, forty minutes before zero hour, to keep the British troops under cover while the storm troops crossed the river.

Both the 8th Berkshires and 7th Queen's Own had been overrun by the time the lingering fog had lifted. Only an injured Lieutenant Colonel Crosthwaite and the Queen's Own headquarters held one strongpoint west of Moy well into the afternoon. But the advance on 53 Brigade's front came to a sudden stop when the assault teams breasted a ridge right in front of the 10th Essex's machine guns. The Essex's left flank was turned when 14th Division abandoned Benay but Lieutenant Colonel Dewing held onto a quarry north of Ly-Fontaine until dusk.

The breakthrough was causing concerns so General Lee sent the 8th East Surreys to Gibercourt to support Brigadier General Higginson. Lieutenant General Butler also moved 54 Brigade from corps reserve to reinforce the same area.

The Germans crossed the canal near Vendeuil and only a few of the 7th Buffs held out along 55 Brigade's front. One group even held out in an old French fort west of Vendeuil until the evening of 22 March, only surrendering when their ammunition ran out. The 8th Sussex fought off all attacks throughout the afternoon but the Buffs defence meant that the Germans did not reach the 7th Queen's. A patrol eventually led the surviving Buffs back to Lieutenant Colonel Ransome.

The 82 and 83 Brigades RFA would lose most of their guns because the Germans could get close in the fog. Gunner Charles Stone stuck by his throughout the day while his battery was hammered with gas and high explosive shells. He ran back with a message and then returned to grab a rifle to help hold the enemy back before capturing a machine-gun team. Stone would be awarded the Victoria Cross.

58th (2/1st London) Division, Astride the Canal de l'Oise
Major General Albemarle Cator's 8-mile-long front straddled the Oise valley, a two-mile wide strip of lakes, reed beds and woods. The canal and river ran parallel to each other and Eighteenth Army only planned to strike Brigadier General Worgan's line, while using the river to protect its left flank.

The storm troops crossed the Oise Canal just after 6 am and overran the 2/2nd London Regiment holding 173 Brigade's line. Captain Houghton's men held on for a time but Travecy was captured after midday. A few of Lieutenant Colonel Read's outposts held out until the fog cleared but one group fought until the evening of 22 March. They only gave up after expending all their ammunition; all 18,000 rounds and 400 grenades.

Meanwhile, Captain Lees' men had escaped to the Crozat Canal at the back of the Battle Zone. The 2/4th London Regiment were driven out of Quessy and across the Crozat Canal but the 3rd London Regiment helped them fight for Fargniers and Condren. Brigadier General Worgan ordered 173 Brigade withdrawal behind the Crozat Canal during night, having learnt that prisoners from over seventy different battalions had been taken.

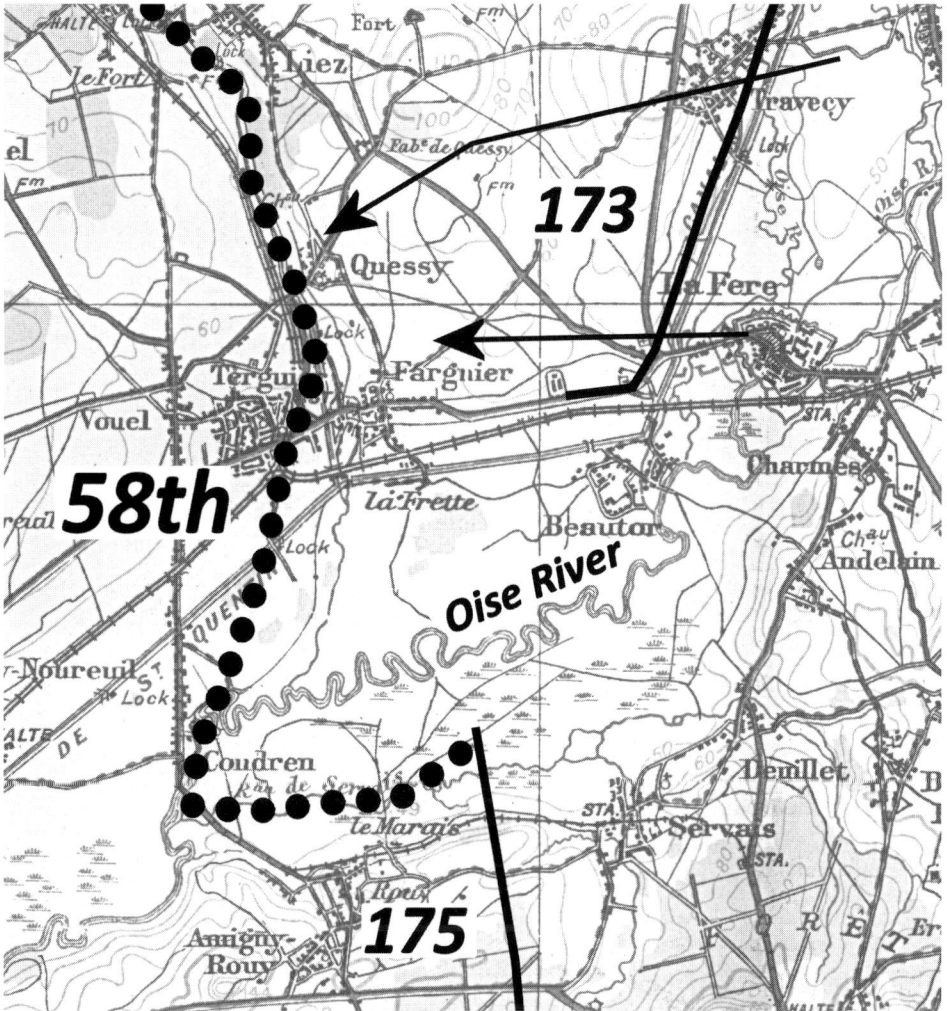

21 March III Corps' South Flank: 58th Division had to withdraw behind the Crozat Canal.

III Corps Summary

The loss of the Essigny plateau had compromised III Corps' Battle Zone. Butler and Maxse agreed that they had insufficient reserves to recapture the plateau and it made sense to fight along the canal until the French reinforced their position. Butler had warned his divisional commanders to be ready for an overnight withdrawal and they had sent as many men back as they dared to prepare a defensive line along the Crozat Canal. The Royal

Garrison Artillery had also withdrawn all their heavy guns and howitzers across the bridges.

All three divisions withdrew across the canal during the hours of darkness without any interference. In many cases the infantry helped the gunners manhandle guns to the limbers so as not to alert the enemy. The engineers had fixed explosives to the canal bridges, detonating them as soon as the last man was across. In many cases it was still possible to clamber across the rubble while the railway bridge east of Jussy was still standing.

Fifth Army's Summary

General Gough had expected to lose the Forward Zone in the initial attack and, so far, that was all that had been lost. Early reports indicated that the troops in the Battle Zone were keeping the Germans at bay, so he called his corps commanders to give them words of encouragement.

General Humbert visited Gough during the early afternoon to tell him the cryptic words 'I only have one flag' referring to the pennant on his car; in other words the French Third Army had no reserves to spare. Pétain was also reluctant to help because he was convinced the bombardment of the Reims front might be the start of something big on the French front.

Gough then embarked on a sixty-mile round trip around his four corps headquarters. Reports from the Forward Zone were sketchy but there had also been heavy casualties in the Battle Zone. Many batteries had been overrun in the mist but the infantry had been able to stop the Germans at most points as soon as it cleared. Stragglers were joining the first officer they could find while the gunners, engineers and pioneers were grabbing a rifle and fighting alongside the infantry.

Gough learnt that Congreve had ordered 39th Division forward to deal with the breakthrough along the Cologne valley on VII Corps' right. Watts had a problem in the same area but XIX Corps' right flank was also being pushed back along the Omignon valley. Maxse was confident about XVIII Corps' situation west of St Quentin but he was concerned about III Corps' loss of the Essigny plateau.

Gough had committed all his reserves and it would be some time before he had any more. The loss of the Essigny plateau meant that XVIII and III Corps had to withdraw behind the Crozat Canal. Gough headed back to his headquarters, concerned how tired his men were but believing they could hold on until reinforcements arrived.

Gough arrived back in Nesle to find more bad news waiting for him. The RFC had started flying as soon as the mist cleared and observers reported columns of infantry, artillery and supply wagons stretching back for over ten miles all along Fifth Army's front. Gough knew his battered divisions could not hold back such large numbers for long enough. Gough called GHQ and Lieutenant General Herbert Lawrence, Chief of the General Staff, reassured him that Haig would support his decision to withdraw from the Battle Zone.

There were mixed reports on the German side because reports were still coming in. The official communiqué was pragmatic: 'After a heavy bombardment of artillery and trench mortars our infantry assaulted on a wide front and everywhere captured the enemy's first lines.' A delighted Kaiser prematurely announced 'a complete victory'. Others were more pessimistic because they had not overrun the Battle Zone or the heavy artillery positions, as hoped for. Crown Prince Rupprecht's Chief of Staff General Hermann von Kuhl said, 'the hoped for objectives were not reached.'

By the end of the first day of the battle, OHL was already reconsidering their strategy based on the results so far. Reserve divisions would now be sent to Eighteenth Army, to keep pushing Fifth Army back. The hope was they could drive a wedge between the British and the French.

Chapter 6

Contest Every Foot of Ground

Third Army, 22 March
General Byng's left was safe but Seventeenth Army had pushed VI Corps and IV Corps to rear of the Battle Zone in his centre. The 59th Division had been so badly mauled that it was being replaced by 40th Division. Byng had another five divisions in reserve but others had a long way to travel. So far Second Army had not pressured V Corps but it was making a pincer movement with its left against the south side of the Flesquières salient. Byng's problem was how to withdraw V Corps while keeping in contact with Gough's Fifth Army.

XVII Corps

15th (Scottish) Division, Monchy-le-Preux
Lieutenant General Charles Fergusson was worried the Germans could push north from 3rd Division's sector during an afternoon attack north of the Cambrai road. The temporary divisional commander, Brigadier General Allgood, was told to protect Monchy-le-Preux and man a communication trench facing Hénin Hill but neither he nor Fergusson had any spare troops.

VI Corps
Lieutenant General Haldane's sector posed several problems. On the left, 3rd Division could only hold the line south of the Arras road as long as 34th Division held Hénin Hill. Meanwhile, a battered 34th Division had been pushed back astride the Sensée stream to the back of the Battle Zone. On the right, 40th Division had relieved a badly mauled 59th Division.

3rd Division, Cojeul Valley
Only the 1st Northumberland Fusiliers were engaged on the division's right flank. Lieutenant Colonel Moulton-Barrett's men caused enormous casualties as massed columns crossed the Sensée valley heading for 34th

Division. The artillery observers could only watch as lucrative targets passed by because the field artillery were out of range and the heavy artillery could not be contacted.

Brigadier General Potter was forced to deploy the 13th King's and then the 20th KRRC (Pioneers) as the troops on his flank fell back. But the loss of Hénin Hill during the evening meant 9 Brigade was in danger, a fact emphasised after Captain Allgood reported a transport column had come under fire when it came forward to supply the Northumberland Fusiliers.

Major General Deverell issued orders for a withdrawal across the Cojeul stream to the high ground between Wancourt and Hénin during the right. But it was no easy task getting the message to the front because no one dared to mention the word 'retirement' over the telephone in case the Germans intercepted the message. The brigade majors hunted for the battalions in the dark but Moulton-Barrett did not get the order. He eventually called brigade headquarters to ask for his orders in Hindustani and the answer came back, 'Go behind immediately and hurry up!'

Sections were left behind to make 'war noises' to keep the enemy patrols away until dawn. But Deverell's men were annoyed to find they had abandoned perfectly good trenches to move back to shallow, unconnected ditches.

34th Division, The Fight for Hénin Hill

Major General Nicholson was holding the west bank of the Sensée stream with three weak brigades but the Germans were intent on taking Hénin Hill. They passed through an abandoned Croisilles in the fog, heading for the 15th Royal Scots. Captain Brown was killed holding the onslaught back while 'friendly' artillery fire forced both the 15th and 16th Royal Scots to withdraw up the slopes of Hénin Hill. They were then spotted by an enemy spotter plane and the bombardment that followed forced both battalions to run for their lives towards Hénin. 'Only by dint of numerous appeals and threats were Lieutenant Colonel Guard and Major Warr able to arrest the rout' at the back of the Battle Zone.

The Germans now turned on the rest of 34th Division but one hundred men of the 22nd Northumberland Fusiliers helped the 11th Suffolks hold on north of the breakthrough. The 23rd and 25th Northumberland Fusiliers formed a defensive flank south of the gap while the 10th Lincolns and 9th Northumberland Fusiliers stopped the Germans entering St Léger. Captain Simpkin was killed steadying the 13th Green Howards but Captain Quetteville secured the line even though

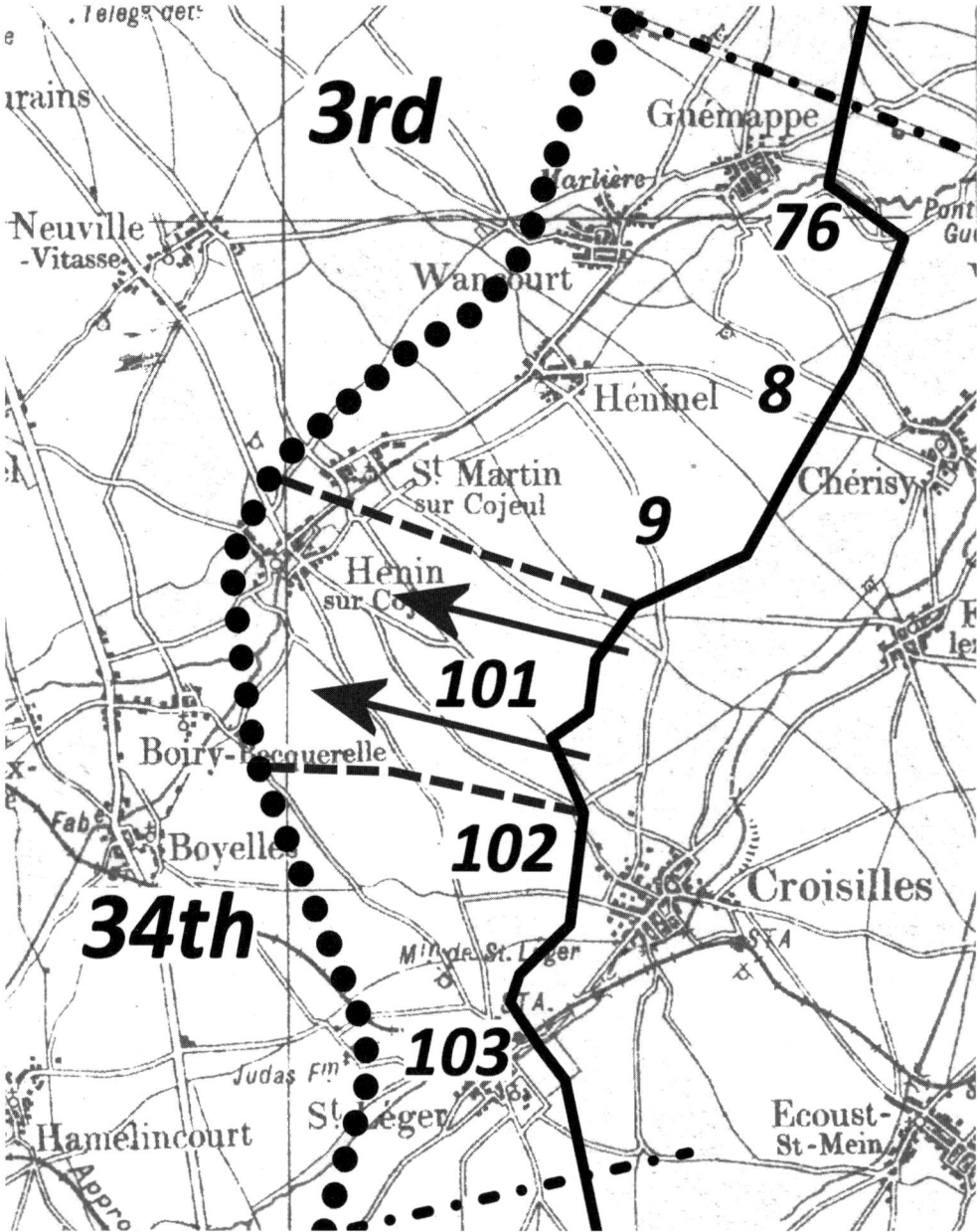

22 March VI Corps: There was a withdrawal behind the Cojeul stream, near the back of the Battle Zone.

two Lewis guns burst from overheating. Brigadier General Chaplin sent the 1st East Lancashires forward in time to stop the Germans breaking through 103 Brigade.

Major General Nicholson sent both the 18th Welsh and the 13th East Surreys forward but Chaplin decided it was time to withdraw to the back of the Battle Zone before it was too late. Lieutenant Colonel Blockley received the message to withdraw the Lincolns and Captain Quetteville covered the 13th Green Howards' retirement. However, the 9th Northumberland Fusiliers and some of the East Lancashires in St Léger did not get the message until it was dark, so Lieutenant Colonel Vignoles waited until the Germans were quiet and then a Lewis gun team fired rapidly as his men escaped.

40th Division, Mory

During the afternoon, the Germans came under heavy fire as they advanced along the Hirondelle stream towards Vraucourt and Vaulx. German planes soon located the British positions and artillery fire forced the 10/11th HLI and the 14th Argylls to fall back, exposing 177 Brigade's flank. Brigadier General James had to tell his battalions to withdraw. 'Though the men were becoming very tired they fought every inch of the way and obeyed all the orders of their officers and ncos in a most exemplary and cheerful manner.' They were less happy when they discovered that the Green Line was just a shallow ditch.

A heavy barrage north of Mory forced 121 Brigade to withdraw to the Green Line at dusk. Most of the 12th Suffolks were cut off but the rest helped part of the 20th Middlesex shore up the line around Mory. At the same time, the 2/4th Leicesters were fighting for the village, in a battle that lasted well into the night. Meanwhile, the Germans pushed around the flanks of the 2/5th Lincolns and 4th Lincolns until they had to retire 'in splendid order with the greatest steadiness until they arrived at a position where they dug in'.

Brigadier General Heathcote-Drummond-Willoughby wanted the 10/11th HLI and the 14th Argylls to counter-attack but his orders did not get through. Instead he had to report Mory had been lost, the only part of the Green Line lost on Third Army's front.

IV Corps

Lieutenant General Harper's line was at the back of the Battle Zone, astride the main road to Bapaume. He had elements of all four of his battered divisions in the line and he badly needed 41st Division to reinforce them.

6th Division, North of the Bapaume Road

The Germans kept up the pressure and Major General Marden received many reports about 'the losses everywhere and asking for reinforcements sufficient to enable the perished lines to maintain such a position they had to take up'. An early afternoon attack against 16 Brigade drove the 8th Border Regiment back near Vaulx Wood, outflanking the 1st Buffs. Captain Hamilton made sure his men followed the order to 'contest every foot of ground, conform as far as possible with the movement of other troops and only retire fighting.'

Men from the divisional reinforcement camp joined the Buffs and the 14th HLI but they were too few to save Vraucourt. The 'other troops had all gone and it became obvious to those on the spot that to remain longer merely meant to be surrounded by sheer numbers, so a general retirement was ordered.' The 2nd York and Lancashires and the 1st Shropshires held Vaulx until their ammunition ran out and they then fell back to find their ammunition wagons waiting at the Green Line, east of Beugnâtre.

On 71 Brigade's front, the Germans concentrated on driving the 2nd South Lancashires and the 11th and 1st Leicesters back around Vaulx wood and Morchies. Lieutenant Colonel Latham, Captain Giles and Lieutenant Bassingthwaite escaped with only 160 men and they ran back to a shallow trench west of Morchies held by Lieutenant Colonel Smeathman's 9th Welsh Fusiliers and Lieutenant Colonel King's 9th Welsh. Meanwhile, the 3rd Worcesters (of 74 Brigade) fought alongside 150 of Brigadier General Brown's men around Morchies. They were eventually overrun and less than 300 of 71 Brigade's men were sent into reserve that night; over 1,500 had been killed or captured in just thirty-six hours.

Brigadier General Craufurd's left flank was exposed when 71 Brigade fell back past Morchies. The few dozen survivors of the 2nd Durhams and the 1st West Yorkshire were ordered to withdraw to 58 Brigade's line, south-west of Morchies, while the 11th Essex formed a defensive flank next to the 51st Division. A wounded Captain Reginald Hayward refused to leave his men and instead moved amongst the 1st Wiltshires until he collapsed. He was awarded the Victoria Cross for making sure the Green Line was held north of Beugy.

A company of 9th Welsh was fighting to fill the gap when twenty-five tanks of Lieutenant Colonel Bryce's 2nd Tank Battalion arrived, ready to counter-attack. Lieutenant Colonel King decided the 9th Welsh could not abandon Beugny because 'information was scant, orders were many and contradictory, rumour was wild and they knew nothing of what was taking

22 March IV Corps: There was a huge battle astride the Bapaume road as the Germans tried to advance towards the town.

place on their left.' So the tanks went forward alone late in the afternoon, hidden by smoke from grass fires.

The German infantry fell back in disorder as Major Prior joined the tanks with two companies of the 11th Cheshires. They crawled around, firing at anyone in sight until sixteen had been knocked out by artillery fire; the survivors returned having 'done their duty'. The tanks had stalled the German attack but there was still a large gap between 7 Brigade in the Green Line and 71 Brigade near Morchies. Brigadier General Craufurd only had 120 men left, most of them staff and details, to cover it.

51st (Highland) Division, Astride the Cambrai Road

Attempts to 'dribble up were dealt with by machine guns, rifles and rifle grenades', whereas the artillery dispersed larger troop concentrations. 'The Jocks were at the top of their form, were inflicting great losses on the enemy and were complete masters of the situation.' Around 200 men ran towards 153 Brigade to escape a German barrage falling short and Major Will's gunners then shot up an artillery battery as the teams cantered forward. Typically each Scottish gun team was firing one thousand rounds a day and the shells armed with instantaneous fuses caused fearful casualties; the 'machine gunners also reaped a fine harvest.'

Both Lieutenant Colonel Gemmill's 1/8th Royal Scots (Pioneers) and the 1/7th Gordons held on east of Morchies until 6th Division's right flank gave way at dusk. 'The first sign of serious trouble appeared when transport wagons came back at full speed' so the 1/7th Gordons and 1/6th Black Watch then fell back south of the Bapaume–Cambrai road. Lieutenant Colonel McClintock made the 1/7th Black Watch use abandoned battery positions as strongpoints as they retired through Beaumetz. They found Major Johnson and the 1/6th Seaforths waiting for them in a new defensive position.

Both the 10th Worcesters and the 8th Gloucesters of 57 Brigade held on east of Beaumetz as did the 1/4th Seaforths. However, the 1/4th Gordons fell back as it went dark because they were running out of ammunition. Brigadier General Buchanan then had to withdraw the rest of 154 Brigade, losing contact with 17th Division around Hermies.

V Corps

Lieutenant General Fanshawe had withdrawn his troops over a mile but the salient was still 4 miles wide and 3 miles deep. A further retirement would reduce it further, release spare troops and maintain the boundary with Fifth

Army. Haig had told Byng to be ready to withdraw but Byng waited until the afternoon before giving the order.

17th (Northern) Division, Hermies and Havrincourt

The first attack against the 9th Duke's in Jermyn Street, east of the Canal du Nord, failed to take Havrincourt but it had distracted Major General Robertson from the real threat, west of the canal. The mist cleared early, revealing around 4,000 men advancing en masse towards 50 Brigade. Every gun in range opened fire and the infantry carried shells to a battery of LXXIX Brigade RFA until the attack was stopped. The 7th Lincolns 'caught them with enfilade and mowed them down. Three successive waves were dealt with and hundreds of Germans were lying in heaps, killed and wounded. The slaughter was prodigious.' Brigadier General Yatman's men had stopped the Germans entering Hermies but 51st Division was retiring, so the 7th Border Regiment extended the 10th Sherwoods' defensive flank around the village.

Bombing parties and flamethrower teams attacked the 7th East Yorkshires in Gong Trench and the 12th Manchesters in Havrincourt all afternoon. Sergeant Harold Jackson reconnoitred the enemy in front of the East Yorkshires and then drove the enemy out of his trench before crawling forward to knock out a machine-gun team. He withdrew his company to a safe position after all his officers had been hit and also rescued several wounded men under fire. Jackson was awarded the Victoria Cross only to be killed in action on 24 August. Major General Robertson reported a 'very satisfactory' situation but he had to withdraw from Havrincourt to keep in line with the rest of V Corps.

63rd (Royal Naval) Division, Withdrawing from the Trescault Salient

The order for a night-time withdrawal back into Havrincourt Wood arrived during the afternoon. The 1st Marines escaped along Grand Ravine but Commander Beak did not realise it was time to leave until he 'came across a demolition party preparing with the upmost zeal to blow up his Drake Battalion'. Beak kept the Germans at bay with a Lewis gun but it was dawn by the time his men caught up with the rest, by which time another order told them to keep going to the Green Line. Lieutenant Colonel John Stanhope Collings-Wells did not get the order to leave the tip of the salient until it was nearly too late either. He led the 4th Bedfords' rearguard until they ran out of ammunition before escaping.

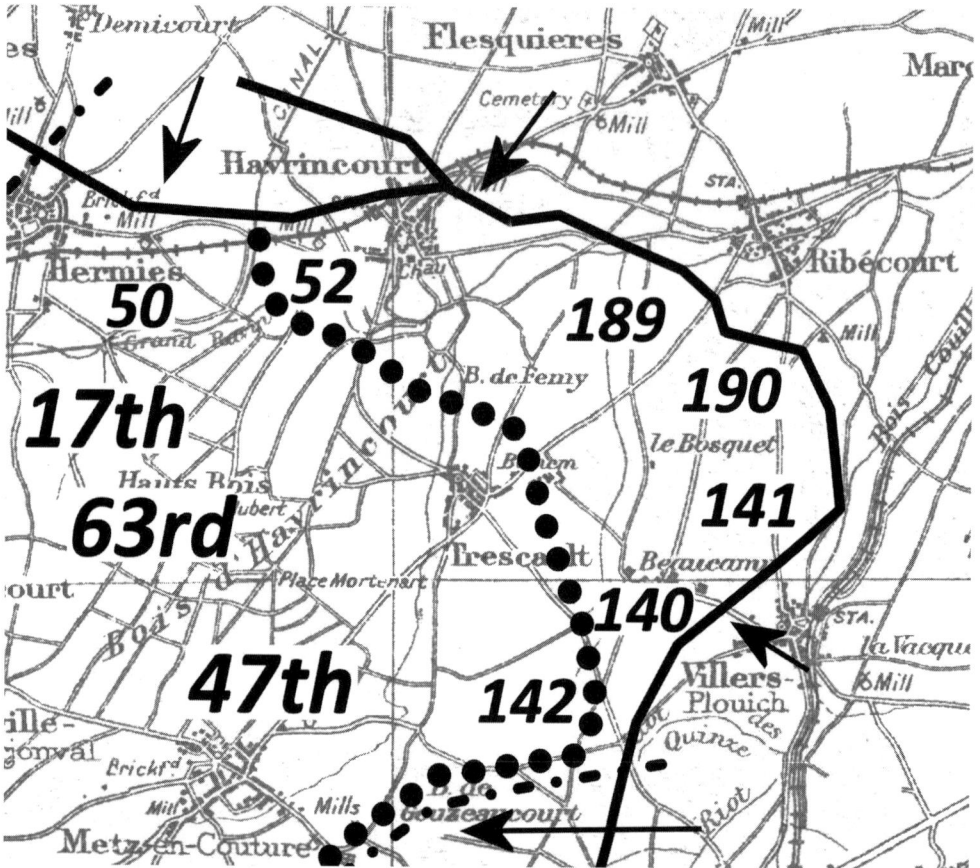

22 March V Corps: There was a struggle to evacuate what was left of the Flesquières salient.

<u>47th (2nd London) Division, South Side of the Trescault Salient</u>
For the second day running, the Germans did not pressurise the Londoners. The 1/18th London Regiment stopped a late attack from Villers Plouich but Brigadier General Mildren was becoming concerned by the Germans pushing through Gouzeaucourt Wood, past 142 Brigade. The 22nd and 23rd London Regiments formed a defensive flank but the gap to 9th Division was increasing. Lieutenant General Fanshawe had been given 99th (2nd Division) to extend the flank past Metz but the Scots kept falling back. Brigadier General Barker only had 1,000 rifles to cover the three miles to Équancourt and that was not enough.

<u>V Corps Summary</u>

Byng did not issue the withdrawal order until the early afternoon and Fanshawe then had to wait until nightfall before executing it. The late withdrawal into Havrincourt wood had got rid of the original salient but 9th Division's rapid withdrawal in Fifth Army's area to the south had exposed the corps' south flank. The key was to hold Hermies on the left and Metz on the right or the men would be trapped in the salient.

Third Army's Summary

Lieutenant General Haldane reported to Byng that 3rd Division had been forced to withdraw across the Cojeul valley, to the back of the Battle Zone, after Hénin had been lost. He had no reserves to work on the Green Line and neither had Third Army. All Byng could do was to tell Lieutenant General Fergusson to pull back his flank and tell 15th Division to evacuate Monchy-le-Preux, even though it had excellent views over the German rear.

Byng explained his dilemma to Haig's chief of staff, Lieutenant General Lawrence and they agreed that Generals Haldane and Harper had to build a new defensive line, called the Red Line, a couple of miles behind the Green Line. In VI Corps' sector, 31st Division took over the part of 34th Division's line facing St Léger. General Harper also welcomed the Guards Division behind his left flank. In IV Corps' sector, 41st Division took over from 6th Division, north of the Cambrai road.

There were concerns over the boundary, which ran from Metz-en-Couture in a south-west direction to Manancourt. Fifth Army's left was withdrawing faster than Third Army's right, opening a gap which was growing by the hour.

Gough visited Byng and they agreed V Corps had to withdraw faster. Brigadier General Barker was also told to move his 99 Brigade to Équancourt to cover the gap. But the plan was upset when there was a warning that German troops were likely to reach the village first. It later turned out that it was only a few men but it had highlighted the vulnerability of the army's boundary.

Byng decided that V Corps had to withdraw all the way to the Green Line. The guns left when it was dark and General Fanshawe was given the go-ahead to move the infantry at 1.30 am. But 63rd and 47th Divisions were not given the orders until dawn. It meant they would have to withdraw over three miles in daylight to a line which had had very little work done on it.

So Third Army was withdrawing rapidly but a German account illustrates the frustration and anxiety felt when their assaults failed:

> *The losses mount up. The German appetite for the attack dwindles. Thoughts of Verdun came back to recollection; can it be that the attack has run itself to a standstill on the second day? Watches show that it is past 2 pm. Not a move relieves the horrible stagnation. Then, unexpectedly, the British front began to waver, for ammunition was running short in some units, and the weight of numbers gradually told.*

Chapter 7

That Night the Devil had Business on his Hands

Fifth Army, 22 March

The mist lasted until mid-morning on high ground but longer along the rivers, resulting in attacks being made at different times along the front. Gough believed Fifth Army could be destroyed if it tried to stand and fight so he wanted to hold the Green Line while a defensive line was organised along the Somme and Crozat Canals. He summarised: 'most important that the corps should keep close touch with each other and carry out retirement in complete cooperation with each other and corps belonging to Armies on the flanks.' He planned to make a stand on the Somme, to give the French time to deploy.

VII Corps

A lot had happened by the time Congreve received Gough's message at midday. He queried the instruction and while he was told to avoid a decisive battle he was not to withdraw behind the Green Line.

9th (Scottish) Division, Withdrawal to Nurlu

The Germans knew Chapel Hill was the key to VII Corps' line and they cut off Captain Green's company of the 4th South African Regiment before capturing Heudicourt station from the 2nd South African Regiment. Two of 150 Brigade's batteries fired until the last moment and were then abandoned. Meanwhile, Major Campbell's 11th Royal Scots held onto Revelon Farm, east of Heudicourt, and 'when last seen the survivors were fighting heroically against a ring of foes under Lieutenant Cowans.'

The Germans entered Heudicourt when 21st Division retired towards the Green Line at dusk, threatening to cut off the South Africans' line of retreat. So Captain Beverley rode along the line telling them to fall back through Fins while Lieutenant Colonel Smyth's 6th KOSBs and the brigade staff covered them. It had been close and 'only the tenacity and courage of the men and the extreme coolness and daring of the junior officers had prevented a wholesale disaster.'

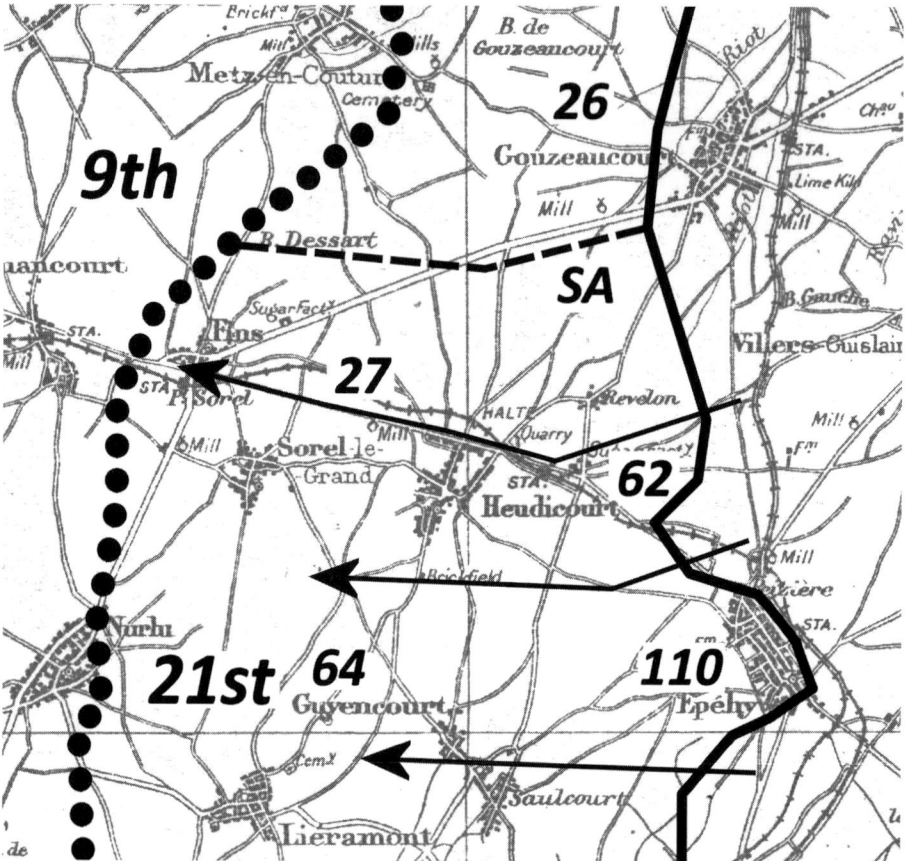

22 March VII Corps' North Flank: 9th Division was in danger because of its open flank and 21st Division had to follow.

The Germans had reached Fins by the time Brigadier General Kennedy instructed the 5th Camerons and 7th Seaforths to withdraw from Gouzeaucourt wood. Fortunately the Germans following 26 Brigade detonated mortar shells as they crossed an anti-tank minefield and Lieutenant Colonel Inglis and Major Anderson's men took advantage of the panic to make a charge through Fins. They reached the 8th Black Watch and Major Hunter with the brigade details in the Green Line, south of Équancourt. They had seen 'streams of wounded, guns, and details were hurrying through the streets' to the rear as shadowy groups of men dug in. 'The inky blackness of the night was ripped by flashes of brilliant flame as innumerable rockets and flares soared skyway.'

Tudor was reorganising his line when he heard that Major General George Gorringe was refusing to cover the two-mile gap to 47th Division, creating 'a most awkward contretemps'. Gough visited Third Army headquarters at Albert to ask for help and while Byng made 99 Brigade from 2nd Division available, Brigadier General Barker had too few men to cover the gap from Metz-en-Couture to Équancourt.

21st Division, Peizière and Épehy

The Germans got around the flanks of 62 Brigade so Brigadier General Gator instructed the 15th Durhams and 2nd Lincolns to withdraw but few made it because they were 'getting it hot'. Some did not get the retirement order and either made a run for it when they ran out of ammunition or were captured. Major Lloyd was proud of his Lincolns: 'although been driven back by vastly superior numbers, with flanks and rear threatened, and with no prospect of immediate help, there was no semblance of panic. The men withdrawing in good order, fighting stubbornly and taking every opportunity of inflicting casualties on the advancing enemy.' Only eighty men reported for duty at the end of the day.

The Germans concentrated on driving the 8th and 6th Leicesters out of Épehy and many, including Lieutenant Colonel Stewart, were killed as they escaped down the communication trenches. The mist had cleared by the time Brigadier General Cumming told the 7th Leicesters to leave. Two of 4th Battalion's tanks stopped the Germans long enough for some to escape from Peizière but the rest were overrun after the tanks were knocked out. The 1st East Yorkshires covered the Battle Zone around Saulcourt while 110 Brigade regrouped.

Although 21st Division had made it to the back of the Battle Zone, General Congreve was worried about VII Corps' right flank. He wanted Major General Campbell to continue withdrawing to the Green Line between Nurlu and Templeux-la-Fosse but the enemy intervened in his plans. The 9th KOYLIs and 1st East Yorkshires were forced out of Guyencourt and Saulcourt before Brigadier General Headlam received the order and Brigadier General Gator's men escaped at nightfall. As 21st Division dug in along the Green Line around Aizecourt-le-Bas they saw a scene from Dante's *Inferno*: 'The flames of burning huts fired by sappers with the dark silhouettes of retiring troops formed an awesome and romantic spectacle. That night the devil had business on his hands.'

16th (Irish) and 39th Divisions, Ste Emilie

Although 39th Division had reinforced the Irishmen between Ste Emilie and the Cologne stream, Major General Hull was finding it difficult to

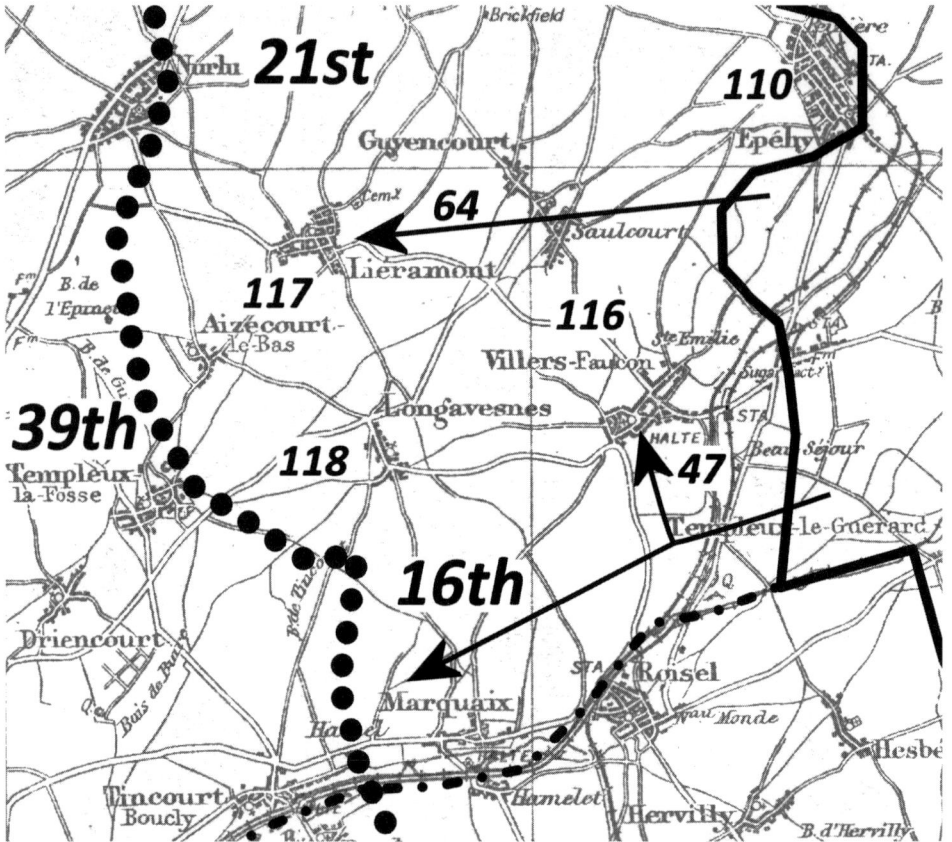

22 March VII Corps' South Flank: Both 16th and 39th Divisions were driven all the way back to the non-existent Green Line.

hold the back of the Battle Zone. Major Freeman's 2nd Leinsters were forced back along the river bank, allowing the Germans to outflank the 11th Sussex. They then headed north towards Ste Emilie where they were stopped by Major Thyne's 11th Hampshires.

The Hampshires had to retire towards Villers-Faucon but Major General Hull's order to withdraw to the Green Line was too late. The 6th Connaughts and the 1st Munsters were fighting for their lives and the 'signallers, police, sappers and all who could be collected' could do little to stop the threat on their flank. Many of the 1/1st Hertfords were hit as they waited for the Irishmen to fall back; they never came because they had all been killed or captured. The last few 'resolved to abandon their trench in spite of murderous fire and to take their chance over the open…

but they had hardly got over the parapet when they were all down. At that moment a hail of bombs landed in the trench, forcing their comrades onto the parapet, where they were quickly surrounded.'

The few survivors eventually reached the Green Line, another shallow trench around the Bois de Tincourt. As 16th Division disintegrated, 39th Division manned the Green Line covering Templeux-la-Fosse and Bois de Tincourt. The Irishmen passed through their position during the night.

<u>VII Corps Summary</u>

By nightfall, Congreve had no reserves left and the gap on his left flank was expanding. There was also a dangerous gap developing on his right flank, where XIX Corps was falling back along the Cologne stream. All along the line, the gunners fired for as long as they dared and the limbers sometimes did not hook up and canter off until the infantry started pulling out. But sometimes they stayed too long and had to disable and abandon their guns, as happened to sixteen guns of 184 Brigade. It brought the total number of guns lost in VII Corps over two days to a massive 120.

XIX Corps

Gough's instruction to withdraw reached XIX Corps headquarters before midday and Lieutenant General Watts told his divisional commanders to prepare for an afternoon move behind the Green Line.

<u>66th (2nd Lancashire) Division, Templeux-le-Guérard to Jeancourt</u>

Major General Malcolm's men were supposed to retire through 50th Division's Green Line position but the Germans attacked early through the mist. Many of the battalions were already being pushed back by the time their commanding officers heard the news, so 'orders were given for every officer to take command of any of his own battalion he could find and make his way towards Roisel.'

On the left, 197 Brigade was attacked from the front while under enfilade fire from across the Cologne stream, where 16th Division was falling back. Many of Brigadier General Borrett's men were overwhelmed in a sunken road south of Templeux-le-Guérard and the 2/6th Lancashire Fusiliers were overrun at the back of the Battle Zone. Captains Barker and Dingley only escaped with a few men after Lieutenant Colonel Biddolph was captured. Some of the 15th Hussars fell back alongside the Fusiliers but the rest defended Roisel until the 1/5th Durhams arrived.

The 2/6th Manchester and the 9th Manchesters escaped from Carpeza Copse while some of the 9th Sussex fought on in Trinket, Trinity and Triple

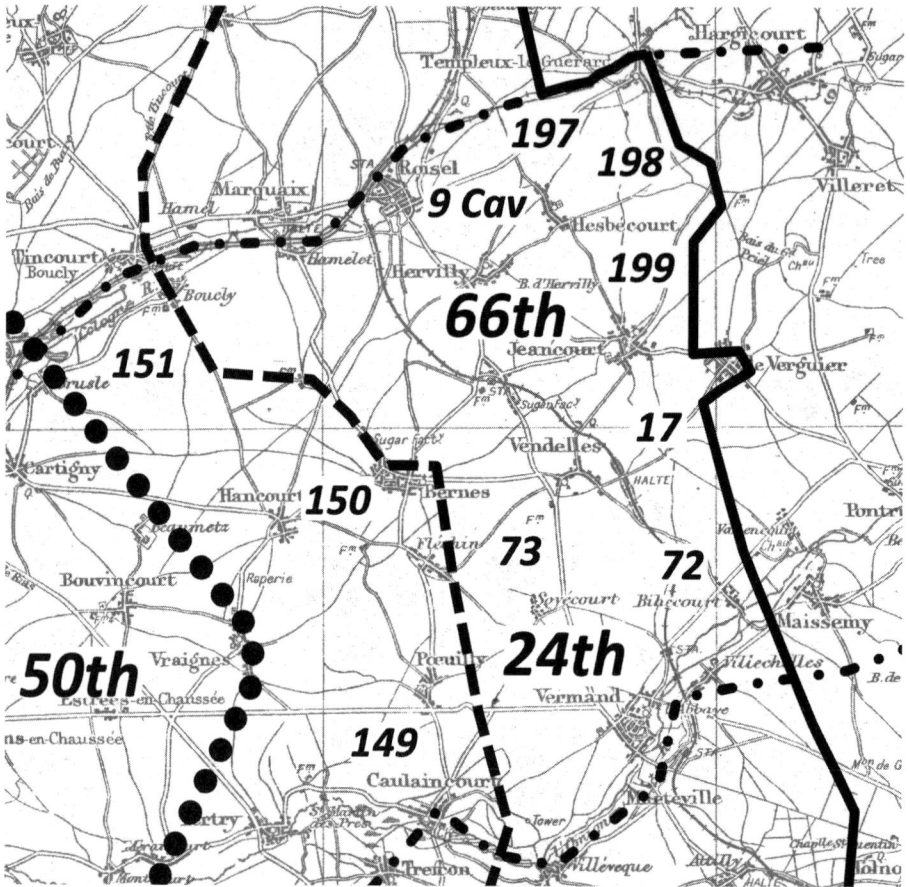

22 March XIX Corps: There were running battles en route to the Green Line while 50th Division established a support line.

Redoubts. The rest of the Sussex held on in Hesbécourt until the Germans pushed through Hervilly wood and they then made a run for it. Only 120 men of the two brigades made it back to the Green Line.

Major General Malcolm wanted to counterattack but the runners could not find the 15th Entrenching Battalion at Nobescourt Farm. Instead the 19th Hussars and 8th Hussars joined the 9th Dismounted Brigade in an attack on the Green Line. Six tanks of the 5th Battalion were knocked out as the troopers cleared Hesbécourt and Hervilly wood and while they had restored 66th Division's front, the Green Line was a poor position to hold.

24th Division, Le Verguier to Bihécourt

The Germans attacked the 8th Queen's in Le Verguier before dawn and Lieutenant Colonel Peirs' men came under accurate artillery fire as soon as the mist cleared. Some men fell back to Fort Lees and Fort Greathead while Peirs gathered the rest in a sunken road south-east of the village. He eventually withdrew to the back of the Battle Zone after Fort Lees was overrun.

Both the 3rd Rifle Brigade and 1st Royal Fusiliers held Le Verguier Switch, south of the village, finding that rifles and mortars were far more effective than machine guns and artillery in the misty conditions. Brigadier General Stone reported 17 Brigade was holding on but the loss of Le Verguier meant the Germans were around his flank. The same applied to 72 Brigade because both the 8th Queen's Own and the 9th East Surreys were holding on astride the Omignon stream.

XIX Corps Withdrawal

Around 11 am, Brigadier Generals Stone and Morgan heard that the enemy were pushing past their flanks and they had to retire beyond the Green Line. The men at the front were surprised when they got the message to pull out because they thought they had a good position. It took two hours to get everyone away and while the 7th Northants and 13th Middlesex covered the retreat, the Germans inflicted heavy casualties on those making a run for it. The 61st Division had withdrawn faster south of the Omignon and the engineers were told to blow up the bridges around Vermand.

50th (Northumbrian) Division, XIX Corps Reserve

Brigadier General Stockley's men had been on the move since the battle started and 'the march was a weary business for already everyone was tired. Thick mist, darkness, heavy traffic on the main road, delayed progress. The men were carrying their packs and, on reaching their bivouacs soon after dawn, were in an exhausted condition.' The division had deployed across a six-mile front between the Cologne and Omignon streams. The Green Line was 'only in a spit-locked condition but a good belt of wire protected the position'. Breakfast was about to be served when the shout went up, 'man the defences immediately'. It was early afternoon before they spotted men from the 66th and 24th Divisions heading for their line and the Germans were close behind.

Brigadier General Martin had sent the 1/5th Durhams forward to reinforce Roisel and while they had a good field of fire, they could also see 16th and 66th Divisions withdrawing either side of the Cologne stream. The Germans did not threaten the 1/6th and 1/8th Durhams around Bouchy but the 1/5th Durhams were forced to withdraw. That left the Germans free to enfilade 151 Brigade's vulnerable position and Martin ordered the Durhams to retire when the divisional artillery started firing short.

The Germans were only interested in capturing Nobescourt Farm from the 1/4th Green Howards on 150 Brigade's left and Lieutenant Colonel Charlton and Captain Bainbridge were killed leading a counter-attack. But the biggest attack hit 149 Brigade north of the Omignon stream when waves of infantry drove the 1/4th Northumberland Fusiliers out of Caulaincourt as the 1/5th Northumberland Fusiliers fought on. Lieutenant Colonel Robb was wounded as 1/6th Northumberland Fusiliers formed a defensive flank around Poeuilly and Brigadier General Riddell sent his brigade details to cover the bridges across the Omignon.

Brigadier General Stockley heard the Green Line was in danger during the evening even though only his right flank was in difficulties. So Watts asked Gough for permission to retire and he agreed because Maxse was withdrawing XVIII Corps to the Somme. It was, after all, better to fight during the day and withdraw during the night, to keep the Germans guessing about the British line. The decision might have made tactical sense but the men disagreed after a long day's fighting. The last thing they wanted to do was to follow their officers on a compass bearing though the misty darkness. It also left many men short of ammunition and not knowing where fresh supplies were. South of the Omignon, some battalions knew where there were abandoned ammunition dumps opposite 24th Division's front. Enterprising officers led battalion wagons through the enemy lines at the canter, loaded up and then returned as fast before the Germans realised what they were doing.

8th Division, XIX Corps Reserve
Although Watts had a fresh division behind his front, he had a four-mile gap to XVIII Corps on his south flank on the Somme Canal. Gough had detailed XVIII Corps to cover Croix-Moligneaux but Lieutenant General Maxse had already fallen back to the Somme. Instead the plan was for 8th Division to fill the gap and Brigadier General Haig led his men across the canal after dusk. They found the Germans waiting for them around Croix-Moligneaux, so 24 Brigade withdrew back across the canal.

Major General William Heneker was instructed to deploy along the Somme but it would take until late morning before the rest of 8th Division was in place. It left Watts with two divisions deployed along the Somme and another three divisions five miles east of the canal; as yet none of them were in touch with other.

<u>XIX Corps Summary</u>
Watts may have chosen a good position to defend but events to his north and south left Fifth Army with a ragged and broken line. His left was one mile west of VII Corps, along the Omignon stream, and his right was four miles north-east of XVIII Corps, along the Somme Canal.

The three corps commanders were trying to achieve different objectives and XIX Corps' headquarters was out of action for a time when it was bombed after dusk. The explosions caused many casualties, including Watts' chief of staff and his GSO2. It was many hours before Lieutenant General Congreve knew XIX Corps was a mile behind his flank. The rapid retirement had also caused problems for the artillery. Over sixty field guns and twenty-eight large calibre guns had been abandoned.

XVIII Corps
The German plan was to clear Holnon wood and while the shelling began at dawn, the fog cleared at 10 am to reveal large attacks developing all along XVIII Corps' front.

<u>61st (2nd South Midland) Division, Holnon Wood to the Somme Canal</u>
Captain Darby's 2/4th Berkshires stopped the attack north of Holnon wood but Brigadier General Spooner had to tell them to retire to the Green Line early in the afternoon. While 183 Brigade's rearguards held the Germans at bay, the rest found that little work had been carried out on the Green Line east of Beauvois.

The Germans had infiltrated behind Lieutenant Colonel Lawson's 2/5th Gloucesters in Holnon wood during the night and they turned on Major Edyvean's 1/5th DCLI (Pioneers) and Captain Beaumont's two companies of the 17th King's at dawn. They all held on until Brigadier General White ordered a retirement to the Green Line but they then faced a withdrawal across the open ground south of Vermand. Captain Barnes's company of the Gloucesters was overrun but Captain Dudbridge's men escaped. Both battalions suffered heavy casualties en route and White was injured when the Germans attacked 184 Brigade's new line.

The Germans did not trouble 182 Brigade, south of Holnon Wood, but Brigadier General Evans also had to tell his men to retire to the Green Line. Both the 2/6th and 2/7th Warwicks suffered many casualties heading back and the officers believed they should have waited until it was dark before they moved. Even more so when they saw that the 'uncomplete trenches at Beauvois were shallow and meagrely wired.' The only good news was they had found a large ammunition dump.

30th Division, Étreillers

In 90 Brigade's sector, the 2nd Bedfords faced a tough fight west of Savy and Major Wynne ordered a withdrawal after making six counter-attacks. Two companies were overrun but the rest made a stand in Stevens Redoubt, north of Étreillers, with help from Captains Lawson and Sheard of the 18th King's. Captain Edwards of the 18th King's helped Lieutenant Colonel Utter-Kelso's 2nd Scots Fusiliers hold Étreillers and they then withdrew in small groups to the Green Line.

In 89 Brigade's sector, the 19th King's stopped an attack near Roupy but Lieutenant Colonel Edwards was wounded when the Germans infiltrated the 2nd Green Howards west of Fontaine-les-Clercs. Aerial observers now knew where Brigadier General Stanley's line was, so the German artillery directed a new bombardment before an afternoon attack overran the 17th Manchesters between Roupy and Savy. The battalion headquarters and a reserve company stopped it at Goodman Redoubt and nearly one hundred men managed to escape to the Green Line before dusk.

Other men fell back on the headquarters of the 2nd Green Howards and the 19th King's in Stanley Redoubt. They too fought their way back to the Green Line around Fluquières only to find that 'as these trenches were only three feet deep they afforded no protection' so they withdrew to the village defences.

36th (Ulster) Division, Withdrawal to the Green Line

III Corps' retirement to the Crozat Canal had compromised 36th Division's position along the Somme Canal. Second Lieutenants Knox and Stapylton-Smith of the 150th Field Company RE spent the morning blowing up twenty-three bridges along on the canal but the Germans got behind the 1st Inniskillings around Fontaine-les-Clercs. They fell back to Ricardo Redoubt only to find 109 Brigade was now threatened from the flank and rear.

Major General Nugent then heard that Lieutenant General Maxse wanted him to withdraw south-west, in line with Fifth Army orders. Lieutenant Colonel Crawford's 1st Inniskillings and Lieutenant Colonel Peacock's 9th Inniskillings covered the withdrawal of 107 and 109 Brigades. Ricardo Redoubt was overrun but the rest fell back to the Green Line between Fluquières and Happencourt, only to find the shallow trench full of men from 20th Division. Strafing from planes and artillery fire caused many casualties before the prone men could scrape some cover.

The 108 Brigade was undisturbed along the canal between St Simon and Happencourt to begin with but the Germans were soon

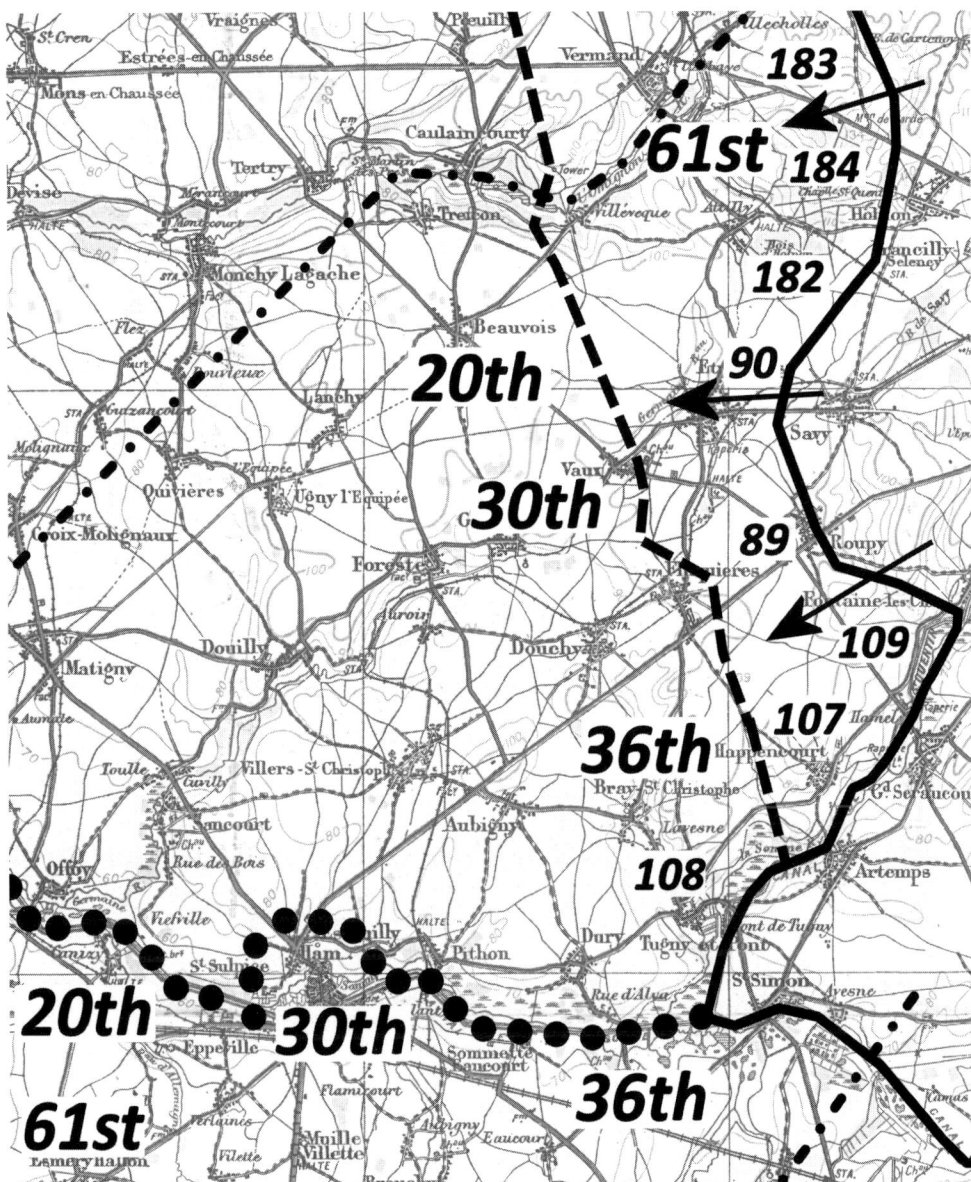

22 March XVIII Corps: There was a hurried and costly withdrawal to the Green Line followed by a confused retreat through the night to the Somme Canal.

attempting to force the 12th King's of 61 Brigade back from Tugny-et-Pont bridge. Second Lieutenant Cecil Knox ran forward when the explosives failed to blow up and the Germans were crossing as he manually lit the fuse. He then ran for safety as the explosion demolished the structure. Knox would be awarded the Victoria Cross. Captain Stapylton-Smith blew up nearby St Simon bridge while the Germans were running across it.

XVIII Corps' Reserve
Major General William Douglas Smith had deployed 20th Division along the Green Line, as a position for 61st, 30th and 36th Divisions to fall back on. However, little work had been done on it and the men had few tools or materials to improve it. Maxse was also concerned that part of the division had already been committed to the battle. Brigadier General Hyslop was preparing to counter-attack with 59 Brigade when he was told to pull back to the Green Line to cover 61st Division's retirement along the Omignon stream.

XVIII Corps; Withdrawal to the Somme
By late afternoon, XVIII Corps had retired to the Green Line, only to find poorly sited and incomplete trenches. Maxse took the decision to withdraw the whole of his corps back to the Somme, involving a march of between 6 and 10 miles. The problem was, the decision would impact on Fifth Army's situation for several days.

61st (2nd South Midland) Division's Withdrawal to the Somme
The plan to use 59 Brigade to cover 61st Division's withdrawal had failed because Brigadier General Hyslop's men had already been committed to a counter-attack. It meant that the South Midland men would have to break contact before they made the long, disorganised march south-west towards the Somme. 'A terrific barrage fell on 61st Division and overwhelming forces of infantry attacked with great determination' during the evening. The men of 182 Brigade were driven out of Vaux only to make a stand at Foreste, two miles to the south-west. Captain Dandy had to pull back the 2/4th Berkshires before an injured Brigadier General White issued 184 Brigade's withdrawal order.

Brigadier General Spooner finally issued orders for 183 Brigade to withdraw from Villévêque when he realised the rest of the division had left. They all then faced a ten-mile march to the Somme, reaching it just before dawn. The 2/6th Warwicks never received the order and only eighty men reached Voyennes.

30th Division's Withdrawal to the Somme

Major General Williams sent out despatch riders to tell his brigades to withdraw to Ham on the Somme during the evening. Many battalions lost heavily as they broke contact and companies then had to march through the dark night. Brigadier General Stanley's 89 Brigade joined 60 Brigade along the Green Line between Fluquières and Happencourt, while the rest of 30th Division headed for the Somme. The three King's battalions of 89 Brigade would man the Ham bridgehead while the rest of the division moved into reserve.

20th (Light) Division Withdrawal to the Somme

In the centre, 60 Brigade was attacked as soon as 36th Division had passed through their line. Brigadier General Duncan withdrew at dusk and the 12th KRRC fought rearguard actions all the way back to Offoy. The Germans were advancing just as fast in a chaotic dash for the Somme. Some even pushed down the river, past the KRRC, engaging the rest of the brigade en route.

Lieutenant Colonel Maclachlan was killed as the 12th Rifle Brigade stampeded a column of German transport. Some of Lieutenant Colonel Welch's 6th Shropshires surprised another column marching past Happencourt 'shouting and singing' before withdrawing. But the rest of the 6th Shropshires and some of the 11th Durhams (Pioneers) were cut off near Tugny. The rest of 60 Brigade escaped across the Somme at Ham without incident, bringing to an end a disastrous withdrawal.

XVIII Corps, Summary

Gough had wanted Maxse to withdraw across the Somme during the night and he had sent the 21st and 23rd Entrenching Battalions back to prepare the defences. But the Germans followed so fast and in such strength that the rearguards could not hold a line connecting XIX Corps' right flank, at Guizancourt, to the Ham bridgehead. However, most of XVIII Corps was across the Somme by dawn, except where the river and canal split around the town of Ham. Unfortunately, the Royal Garrison Artillery had not had enough traction engines to move all their heavy guns and forty-three had been lost over two days.

Bridges were blown along the Somme but Brigadier General Stanley had been told to prepare the Ham bridgehead with 30th Division's engineers, ready for 89 Brigade to man. It meant that the bridges around the town were left intact until the bridgehead had been evacuated. British engineers thought the French railway engineers were going to blow up the Pithon railway bridge, east of Ham, but 'working in haste and with insufficient explosives, [they] did all the damage in their power to it'. It would not take the Germans long to bridge the damaged spans.

The rapid withdrawal behind the Somme worried everyone because it had stretched the corps front to nearly twelve miles while leaving a large gap on the left. It had also scattered some units, in particular 20th Division's. Major General Douglas Smith would learn that 59 and 60 Brigades were holding five miles of the Somme west of Ham. Both brigades had suffered many casualties as had 61st Division in support. Major General Williams was responsible for the Ham bridgehead and while 89 Brigade was north of the river, the rest of the division was south of the canal. The third brigade of 20th Division, the 61 Brigade, was east of the town and in touch with III Corps.

III Corps

Lieutenant General Butler's men had spent the night crossing the Crozat Canal. The Germans spent the morning moving up under cover of the morning mist, ready to push 18th and 58th Divisions back from the canal.

14th (Light) Division, Crozat Canal

Major General Greenly (2nd Cavalry Division) took command of 14th Division during the day. Fortunately the front was quiet for the time being because the Germans were preparing to cross the canal.

18th (Eastern) Division, Jussy on the Crozat Canal

As the fog began to clear, the German infantry crept towards the canal while their trench mortars hit 54 Brigade's positions. The bridges in Jussy had not been destroyed because 'adequate supplies of explosives were not on the spot' but the 5th Lancers and 9th Scottish Rifles stopped them crossing at dusk. The 8th Rifle Brigade sent men to help while Major St Aubyn was killed leading the 7th KRRC's cooks and clerks. The Lancers stopped another attempt during the early hours.

A bend in the canal meant machine-gun fire raked the 11th Royal Fusiliers from end to end so Brigadier General Sadlier-Jackson sent the 6th Northants to drive the Germans back from the towpath. A large number charged across the La Montagne railway bridge, pushing Lieutenant Colonel Percival's 7th Bedfords back until Second Lieutenant Alfred Herring of the 6th Northants helped Captain Browning retake it. Herring would help Lieutenant Colonel Percival's men hold off attacks throughout the night. Herring would be awarded the Victoria Cross and Browning received the Military Cross; Brigadier General Sadlier-Jackson was wounded during the fighting.

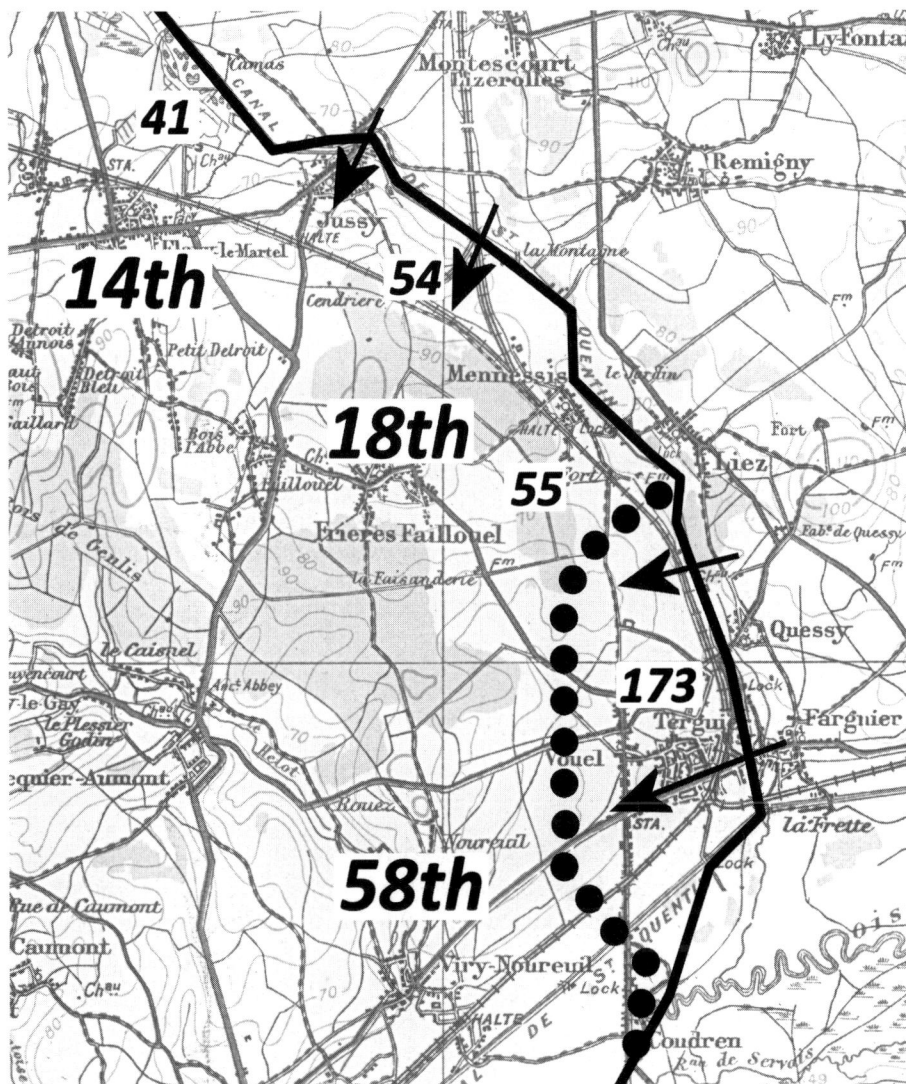

22 March III Corps: The loss of the canal line around Tergnier compromised III Corps line before the French had deployed.

58th (2/1st London) Division, Tergnier on the Crozat Canal

German troops clambered across the ruined canal bridges at Quessy and Tergnier and pushed west. Teams from 58th Machine Gun Battalion helped Lieutenant Colonel Dann and the 8th and 3rd London Regiments hold on but they could not recover the canal line. All that Major General

Cator could do was to deploy Brigadier General Pitman's 4th Dismounted Brigade on the edge of Bois Hallot.

<u>III Corps Summary</u>
Most of III Corps' line was holding on along the Crozat Canal but the Germans had established a bridgehead around Tergnier. The only consolation was that French troops were starting to arrive behind his line.

Fifth Army's Summary
Lieutenant General Watts had been given no time to prepare any defensive line behind the Green Line, so nightfall found half of XIX Corps behind the Somme and the other half five miles to the east. The rapid withdrawal by XVIII Corps to the Somme had left a wide gap in Fifth Army's line and the Germans were pushing through it.

Gough's strategy to dig in during the night was proving to be dangerous. The German infantry were locating the British line during the afternoon so artillery could register it. They then spent the night probing it, looking for weak points. A bombardment and an attack in the morning mist then forced the British to make fighting withdrawals while it was light. It would have been much safer to hold on during daylight and slip away at night. That gave the troops time to dig in and rest while the enemy spent the morning finding the new position.

It would also turn out to be unwise to man a defensive line behind a canal. It was easy to register guns onto a linear feature while the infantry could choose where to attack. The Somme was fordable while woods hid the gathering troops from observers and the canal was easy to cross, especially when it was foggy. Most of the bridges had been destroyed but in many cases it was easy enough to scramble across the rubble.

Chapter 8

Fighting Both to their Front and to their Flanks

Third Army, 23 March

General Byng's left was holding firm and his centre was along the Green Line. So far the penetration at Mory was being contained but there was a gap in the line north of the Bapaume–Cambrai road. The salient on his right had been reduced but V Corps was struggling to keep in contact with Fifth Army.

XVII Corps and VI Corps

Both the 15th and 3rd Divisions had withdrawn to the back of the Battle Zone, to keep in touch following the loss of Hénin hill. Major General Hamilton Reed VC (awarded in the Boer War) had 15th Division abandon Monchy and Major General Deverell had withdrawn 3rd Division across the Cojeul stream. In both cases the exasperated men had to abandon perfectly good trenches and begin preparing a new defensive position. The German artillery shelled the abandoned trenches before their infantry ran into 'strong wired trenches in which the brave defenders, unshaken and not disheartened, were standing firm. There were more heavy losses, and the attack came to a standstill.'

There was little pressure on the Guards Division and 31st Division between the Cojeul and the Sensée streams. The problem was at Mory, where the Germans had broken through VI Corps' Green Line.

40th Division, Mory

German troops assembled north of Mory at dawn but the attack came from the south. Lieutenant Colonel Murdoch's 15th Hampshires reinforced the 20th Middlesex and the 10/11th HLI, opening fire whenever the enemy infantry came over the crest until 'their corpses were piled high in heaps in front of the wire.' The 21st Middlesex and 13th East Surreys recaptured Mory late in the afternoon, only to find the Green Line had been levelled by artillery fire. A counter-attack forced Brigadier General Crozier's men to abandon the village.

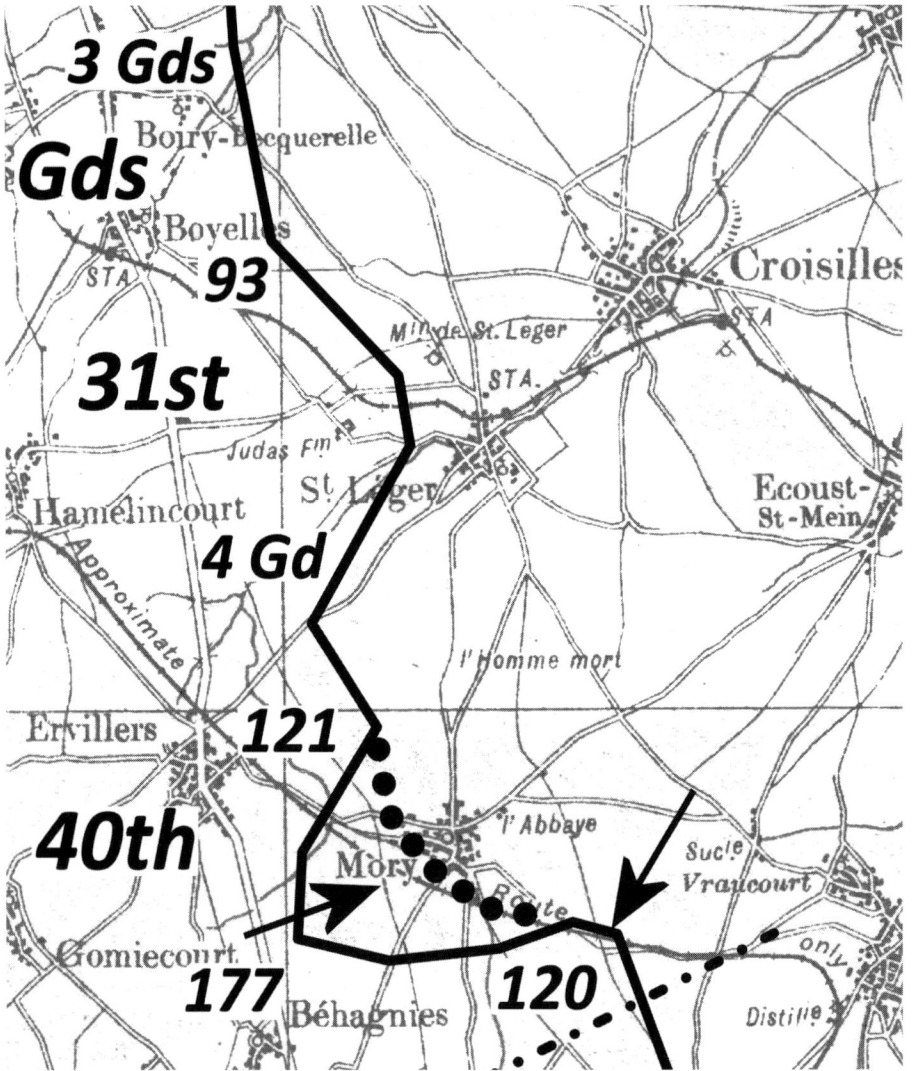

23 March VI Corps: VI Corps held its whole line, even counter-attacking at Mory.

IV Corps

Lieutenant General Harper issued orders to evacuate most of the Battle Zone astride the Cambrai road before dawn, after hearing V Corps was withdrawing on his right. His plan was for 41st and 19th Divisions to hold the Green Line while the exhausted divisions headed for Bapaume.

Harper's main problem was, could 51st Division help 17th Division hold the northern hinge of the salient?

41st and 19th (Western) Divisions, Astride the Cambrai Road

The 10th Queen's held on west of the Hirondelle while the Germans concentrated driving on Lieutenant Colonel Williams' 10th Cheshires and the 1st Wiltshires back astride the Bapaume road. They were 'shelled heavily by the heavy artillery and the machine guns were extraordinarily active but not a single German reached our trenches'.

Two battalions each of 123 and 58 Brigades were holding a vulnerable salient north of the Bapaume road but no one was covering the large gap on their left flank. By midday the 10th Queen's Own and the 11th Queen's were falling back on Beugny but runners could not get through the heavy

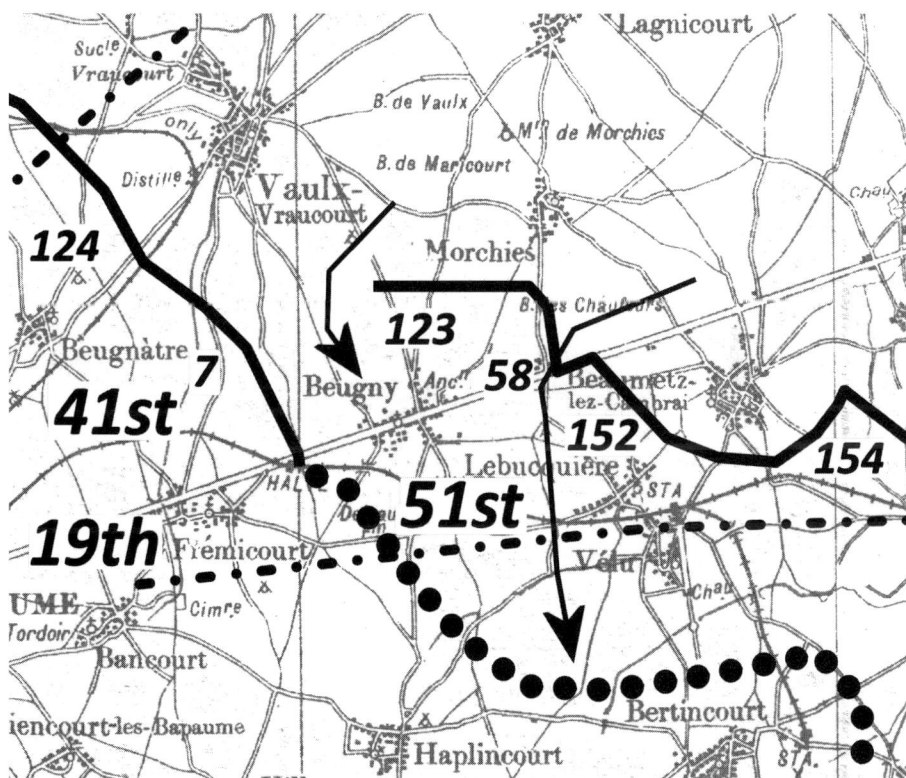

23 March IV Corps: The left of the corps held on but the right faced a difficult withdrawal in line with V Corps.

fire to ask for reinforcements. Captain Davies of the 9th Welsh Fusiliers reported how 'the enemy concentrated a fierce shelling with whiz-bangs on our posts; the machine-gun fire became more and more intense and then the "flying circus" came down on us. A few minutes later, Jerry came at us at the double, bayonets fixed and looking like a cup final crowd. I then gave the order to hop it.'

Most of the 10th Queen's, 11th Queen's Own, 9th Welsh Fusiliers and 6th Wiltshires were overrun. But it could have been worse: 'had it not been for the gallant defence of Beugny by the 9th Welsh, the whole line must have been driven back.' Instead the survivors were able to fall back on the 8th North Staffords and 9th Cheshires south of the Bapaume road.

Immediately north of the road Captains Rufus and Stead of the 11th Lancashire Fusiliers fought the Germans off until the 6th Wiltshires were overwhelmed on their left flank. Lieutenant Colonel Martin and then Major Massey were hit so Captain Potts took command as the Lancashire Fusiliers fell back on Lieutenant Colonel Bowden's 1/4th Shropshires.

51st (Highland) and 19th (Western) Divisions
The 1/5th and 1/6th Seaforths stopped anyone leaving Beaumetz but 19th Division's withdrawal allowed the Germans to reach Lebucquière behind 152 Brigade's flank. Brigadier General Burns gave the order to retire and they fought their way back through Vélu and the adjacent wood to the Green Line. Major Johnson was mortally wounded as the 1/6th Seaforths fell back 'in perfect order, fighting both to their front and to their flanks'.

The 1/4th Seaforths and 1/7th Argylls held on too long west of Hermies and 'it was obvious to all that they were almost cut off'. Ammunition ran low and there was no answer to the last SOS flare so 154 Brigade escaped across the Grand Ravine but some of the Argylls 'hung on in a sunken road with both flanks turned' until they were overrun. 'The fighting of these two battalions certainly constitutes one of the finest performances of the division.'

Major Harcourt had galloped back and forth along the line dropping off water and ammunition for the machine-gun teams until he was badly wounded. The field artillery batteries, like Major Leake's, also stayed in the line as long as possible, only leaving once the infantry reported they had all passed through; only one battery was lost. Meanwhile, steam engines hauled the heavy howitzers back in relays, always leaving them close to the roads so they could be moved quickly.

Brigadier General Ballard told 57 Brigade to retire west of Beaumetz but the 8th Gloucesters and 10th Warwicks never received the order. They soon discovered that the Scots had retired from both their flanks and that the Germans were in Vélu Wood behind them. Twenty-one-year-old Captain Julian Gribble decided to 'hold on to the last' until his group of the 10th Warwicks was overrun. Captain Manley James helped RSM Hopcroft of the 8th Gloucesters hold on until 104 Brigade's field guns escaped. Manley was leading a counter-attack around Beaumetz when he was wounded and taken prisoner. Both Gribble and Manley were captured and they were awarded the Victoria Cross while in captivity but while Manley made it home, Gribble died of pneumonia shortly after the Armistice.

The gallant defence had given the engineers time to prepare the Red Line but Lieutenant General Harper had to change his orders to keep in touch with V Corps. Both 41st and 19th Divisions occupied the Green Line while 2nd Division had to help hold a perimeter around the huge dumps at Bertincourt while they were being emptied. The Germans were impressed by the Highlanders' defence and the message 'Good old 51st. Still sticking it?' was received.

V Corps

Byng received GHQ's order to withdraw across the Canal du Nord to the Green Line before 1 am. Fanshawe was told straight away but it was nearly 5 am before the divisions heard the news and they would not be ready to withdraw until 10 am at the earliest. Eventually it was decided to start abandoning Havrincourt Wood at 1 pm while the men on the flank would follow two hours later. It had taken twelve hours from the initial order being issued to the move being made; and a lot would happen in twelve hours.

17th (Northern) Division, Hermies to Barastre

Major General Robertson's men had to wait until the Green Line defences were organised, the heavy guns had been withdrawn and the dumps had been emptied, before they could leave. They faced a difficult withdrawal, moving at ninety degrees to the fighting line, and the problem increased when the Germans pushed 51st Division back into Vélu Wood behind Robertson's flank.

Despite the danger, the men withdrew 'working by time-table with clockwork precision and with no serious loss. The men were 'quite happy and were not worrying'. Each brigade sent one battalion back at a time while motor machine guns (machine guns mounted on motorbike and sidecar combinations) covered the line. The infantry and the guns took it in turns to withdraw in bounds but the gunners often had to decide when to fire as the infantry fell back to their battery positions.

Brigadier General Eden made sure 52 Brigade escaped from the head of the salient and along the Canal du Nord. 'A considerable amount of fighting took place before the pursuing enemy could be shaken off,' but his men were confident that they had done their bit and that the problems were elsewhere. Brigadier General Yatman's 50 Brigade was next and the 6th Dorsets had to engage a group of Germans dressed in British uniforms and helmets en route. A battery of 76 Brigade continued to fire over open sights until the last moment, allowing the 10th Sherwoods to escape from Hermies. Captains Carr and Wotherspoon were cut off and captured while Lieutenant Colonel Metcalfe was wounded, so it was left to Major Peddie to find a way around the Germans in Vélu wood. Brigadier General Bond brought up the rear, escaping though the Grand Ravin, and joined the rest of 17th Division on the Red Line around Rocquigny.

63rd (Royal Naval) Division, Havrincourt Wood to Bertincourt
Both 188 and 190 Brigades fell back through Havrincourt wood to find 189 Brigade manning the back of the Battle Zone around Ruyaulcourt and Neuville. Both 188 and 189 Brigades continued across the Canal du Nord tunnel and reached the Green Line by mid-afternoon, only to find 'a group of trenches about two feet deep with no field of fire and no dug-outs. There was no cover and no communication. There was no water, no transport and little ammunition.'

Lieutenant Colonel Malone of the 7th Royal Fusiliers was wounded by the deluge of shrapnel and bullets which hit Brigadier General Hutchinson's rearguard. Captain Forster repeatedly blew his hunting horn to rally the men and many stragglers flocked to the calls. By dusk 190 Brigade had reached the Green Line but Major General Charles Lawrie had to give Brigadier General Hutchinson new orders. He had heard that 47th Division had disintegrated during its withdrawal across the Canal du Nord tunnel. It meant 190 Brigade had to deploy facing south towards Ytres, leaving 63rd Division in a tiny salient around the huge dumps at Bertincourt.

47th (2nd London) Division, Metz to Rocquigny
The 24th and 22nd London Regiments were east of Metz while the 21st and 17th London Regiment were south of the village. The infantry were out of touch with the artillery but they caused many casualties with their rifles and machine guns when the Germans advanced en masse. Early attempts tried to push between 142 and 140 Brigades and the field artillery added to the slaughter as soon as they saw their targets over open sights.

Brigadier General Mildren discovered a large gap in the line north of Fins early on. The Germans soon found it and forced their way past

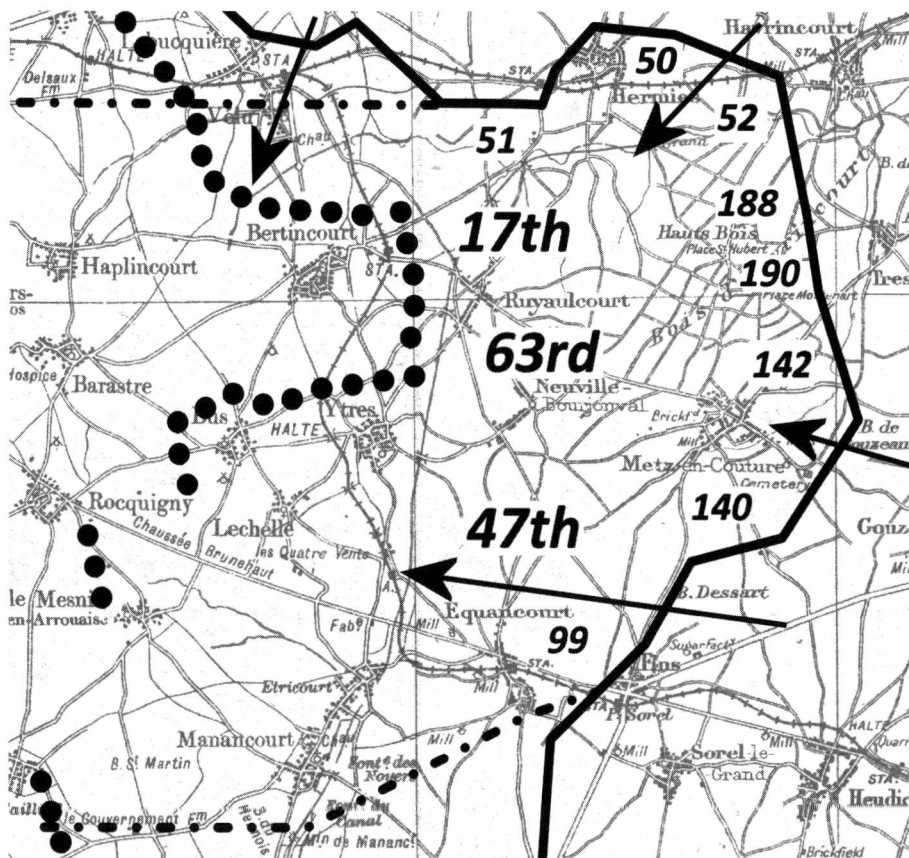

23 March V Corps: V Corps had to hold on while the huge stores at Bertincourt were cleared as the gap on its right flank grew.

the 15th London Regiment, getting behind 140 Brigade and 99 Brigade. Mildren sent the 18th, 19th and 20th London Regiment to stop them while Major General Gorringe warned Brigadier General Bailey and Kennedy to withdraw. Both 142 and 140 Brigades reached the Green Line around Vallulart Wood but the Germans were close behind.

The artillery were often taken by surprise by the rapid withdrawal and one battery officer reported, 'this line my men are holding will be the front line in a few minutes.' They then had to limber up and canter away under fire. All along the line gun teams were finding it increasingly difficult to find ammunition dumps with the right calibre shells or forage stores for their horses.

Brigadier General Bailey made sure 142 Brigade stopped the Germans advancing across the Canal du Nord tunnel while 140 and 99 Brigade fell back to the new line. However, the line 'was disintegrating' because battalion and company commanders had to keep moving back to avoid being outflanked. Gorringe rushed up one hundred details to help what was left of 140 Brigade's rearguard around Lechelle. Fortunately, the Germans were exhausted and the Londoners ended the day south-east of Rocquigny. The retreat had not turned into a rout but the gap between Fifth and Third Armies was now three miles wide.

99 Brigade, The Right Flank Problem

Brigadier General Barker had been given the impossible task of covering the gap between Third Army and Fifth Army. His men found 'huts, camps, wagon parks and even horse lines were abandoned, whilst various bodies of troops moved about in apparently aimless fashion.' The 23rd Royal Fusiliers fell back when the Germans pushed past Fins but Lieutenant Colonel Winters found that the Green Line did not exist, so he withdrew beyond Équancourt looking for a better position.

Barker had ridden out to see what he could do only to find that his men were fighting for their lives as they tried to dig in. They only had their entrenching tools, so men 'just lay down and started to throw up a light cover of earth.' The situation was eased when Private Crabtree drove a group of Germans away from an engineers' dump so they could grab some tools. But Lieutenant Colonel Hunt was killed 'rallying and organising' the 1st Berkshires as they fought off attack after attack while Lieutenant Colonel Stafford's 1st KRRC lost heavily as they dug in.

German planes strafed the shallow trenches time and again but Barker had to stop everyone firing skyward because they were short of ammunition. He even had to cancel a counter-attack after a nearby ammunition dump blew up.

A Further Retirement

It appears that neither Byng nor Fanshawe realised how serious the problem was on the right flank. They made Major General Gorringe responsible for closing the gap with Fifth Army during the evening unaware that 47th Division only had around 1,000 rifles.

Brigadier General Bailey did his best to form a line across the Canal du Nord tunnel but the 1/23rd London Regiment was overrun, allowing the Germans to take the 1/22nd and 1/24th London Regiment in the rear. Lieutenant Colonel Pipon had formed a firing line behind Bus with the 24th Royal Fusiliers, the Hawke Battalion and all the stragglers he could find. Lieutenant Colonel Stafford was explaining how to recapture Bus to Pipon when the Londoners came running past the 1st KRRC, so everyone grabbed their rifle and waited for the attack to begin.

It was sometime before the Germans appeared because they had found a stock of whisky in Ytres. After indulging, 'they rushed down the slope in considerable numbers with a great deal of noise and singing and shouting Hoch, Hoch.' Some foolishly set fire to the British dumps as they advanced, making it easier for Pipon's and Stafford's men to see them.

It was dawn before Lieutenant General Fanshawe knew that 47th Division was at Rocquigny, three miles behind 63rd Division. He told Brigadier General Bond to fill the large gap with what was left of 51 Brigade but it was an impossible task. All across V Corps front, exhausted men wandered around in the darkness looking for their units. In many cases officers gathered them up, made sure they had some food and let them have a nap before it all started again.

Chapter 9

Everybody Seems to be on the Run

Fifth Army, 23 March

By the third morning of the battle, things were looking serious for Fifth Army. General Gough's battered divisions were spread along a forty-mile ragged line and the plan to get everyone back to the Green Line had failed. There was a large gap next to Third Army on the left and another along the Cologne stream, where XIX Corps was falling back faster than VII Corps. There was a third gap on XIX Corps' right because XVIII Corps had withdrawn to the Somme Canal. The fact that the Germans had already crossed the Crozat Canal in III Corps' sector showed that waterways were not the barriers they were thought to be. The only consolation was that French troops were arriving behind Fifth Army's right but they had no artillery and little small arms ammunition.

VII Corps

Brigadier General Tudor was concerned about his north flank, where 99 Brigade was spread across a two-mile gap. Fanshawe was absent when he visited V Corps headquarters but his chief of staff, Brigadier General Boyd, agreed to make arrangements with 47th Division to cover it. Unfortunately, General Gorringe was never told, so Brigadier General Barter was left covering the Équancourt area with just the 23rd Royal Fusiliers and the 1st KRRC. During the day, 9th Division was pushed back west while 99 Brigade was forced north-west, widening the gap. The story of 99 Brigade has been covered in 47th Division's narrative.

So far, the Germans had not realised there was another large gap on VII Corps' right, along the Cologne stream. Congreve argued that his southern flank would be compromised even further if Watts insisted on carrying out his plan to fall back to the Somme, another six miles to the rear. The problem was, XVIII Corps' rapid retreat to the Somme Canal had exposed XIX Corps' southern flank. Gough confirmed Watts' plan to withdraw to the Somme and Congreve had to confirm.

9th (Scottish) Division, Withdrawal to the Canal du Nord around Vaux Wood
Brigadier General Tudor planned to retire behind the Canal du Nord and
make a stand around Vaux wood but the Germans attacked before his orders
reached the front line. Brigadier General Kennedy never received the
retirement order but he decided to withdraw 26 Brigade from Équancourt
when the Germans started pushing past his south flank. The 5th Camerons
and the 8th Black Watch had to fight off an attack before withdrawing
through the 7th Seaforths and across the Canal du Nord into Vaux Wood.
Second Lieutenant McCash held the bridge at Manancourt but it was blown
too early and Second Lieutenant Govan's company of the Black Watch had
to swim across the canal.

A problem developed when 21st Division was driven out of Bois de
l'Epinette on 9th Division's right. The 12th and 11th Royals Scots were
fighting off an attack against Nurlu when they got Brigadier General Croft's
order to withdraw but the South Africans had to counter-attack before
Lieutenant Colonel Smyth's 6th KOSBs could escape. Captain Cockburn's
rearguard, 'fighting every inch of the way, withdrew in a series of bounds
on the principles of fire and movement down the slope, crossed the canal
and passed through Moislains'. All three of 27 Brigade's battalions escaped
but many struggled to find the bridge at Moislains in the mist.

Evening Withdrawal to St Pierre Vaast Wood
Congreve ordered another withdrawal around 4 pm but it would take
Brigadier General Tudor several hours to find his three brigadiers while the
Germans advanced across the canal. The 8th Black Watch held their ground
around Étricourt but the 7th Seaforths were driven out of Manancourt and
back into St Pierre Vaast Wood. Tudor found 26 Brigade holding a thin line
and with both flanks exposed, so he told Kennedy to shift south and fill
the gap around Saillisel. But the Germans were close and 'time after time
the enemy was allowed within 50 yards of our line and then on the word
of command a shower of well-aimed bullets abruptly halted him.' Kennedy
had to wait until dusk before he could withdraw and he then discovered
Saillisel had been abandoned, so he had to move further south.

Croft was holding on along the Canal du Nord between Vaux wood
and Moislains until he realised the Germans were behind both his flanks.
By the time Tudor found 27 Brigade, it had already been driven out
of Vaux Wood, having run low on ammunition, and both the 11th and
12th Royal Scots had fought their way back to St Pierre Vaast Wood.
Lieutenant Colonel Smyth of the KOSBs was wounded when he stumbled
on Germans gathering 'en masse' east of the wood during the evening; it
was his fifth injury of the war. Tudor had told Brigadier General Dawson

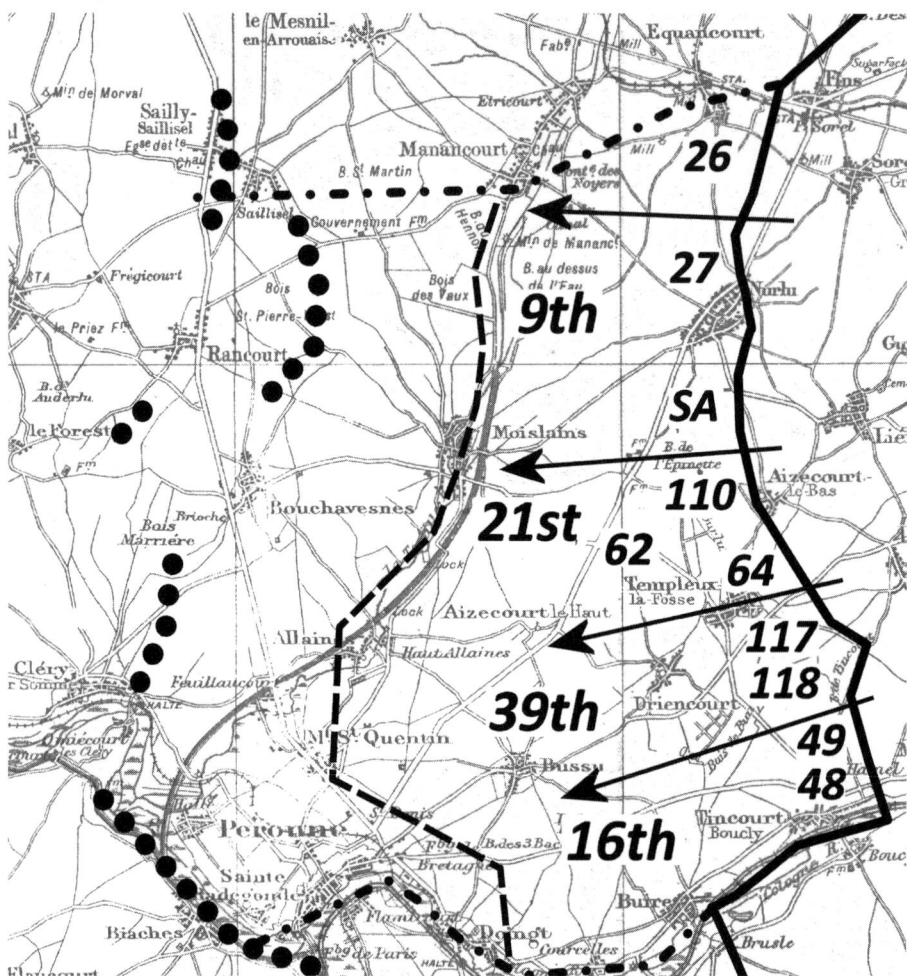

23 March VII Corps: VII Corps experienced a chaotic retreat across the Canal du Nord, resulting in a broken line and open flanks.

that the South African Brigade 'had to hold at all costs', but he had to deploy further west of Bouchavesnes because the chosen position was too exposed.

The withdrawal resulted in a ragged line around St Pierre Vaast Wood and Tudor was most concerned about the gap on his left flank. He found Congreve, who in turn told Gough and he informed Byng he had no reserves to cover it. Fanshawe was told to link up with VII Corps but he also had insufficient troops to rectify the problem.

21st Division, Withdrawal across the Canal du Nord around Allaines
Major General Campbell's order to begin retiring came too late. There were many casualties from the bombardment as the men waited to leave their knee-deep trenches. It hid the fact that German machine gun teams had crept forward through the mist and they soon forced the 7th, 6th and 8th Leicesters to retire through the Bois de l'Epinette. Both Lieutenant Colonels Lloyd and Fisher were hit as the 1st and 2nd Lincolns and the 14th Northumberland Fusiliers withdrew through Bois de Gurlu. The mist cleared before 110 Brigade and 62 Brigade left the cover of the woods and they were raked with machine-gun fire as they made a run for the Canal du Nord.

The rapid retreat by 62 Brigade carried the 15th Durhams and 13th Gloucesters (Pioneers) back towards Moislains on the Canal du Nord. The 9th KOYLIs and the 1st East Yorkshires followed when they discovered the Germans in Templeux-la-Fosse. Only the 15th Durhams halted briefly on the halfway line around Aizecourt-le-Haut but they too joined the retreat to the canal when they realised everyone else was retreating.

Major General Campbell had to order a withdrawal across the canal to try and break contact. A few engineers panicked and blew some of the bridges too early, so the rearguards used fallen trees to get over the Tortille stream. Then Campbell gave a third order to withdraw to Bois de Marrières and Cléry on the north bank of the Somme, after hearing that 39th Division had abandoned Mont St Quentin.

39th Division, Withdrawal North of Péronne and astride the Somme
Both 117 and 118 Brigades were holding on around Bois de Tincourt when they got the order to withdraw while Captain Stewart covered them with some of the 4/5th Black Watch. The 17th KRRC, 1st Cambridgeshire Regiment, 1/6th Cheshires and 4/5th Black Watch reached 116 Brigade but there was no one on their flanks so they all kept marching east.

Major General Edward Feetham rejoined the division as it deployed around Mont St Quentin with orders to cover Péronne as long as possible to allow the crowds of refugees, supply wagons and ambulances to pass through. Men were grabbing what they could before the engineers burnt the stores and blew up the ammunition dumps before continuing on their journey.

But the Germans kept coming, forcing Feetham to tell his brigadiers to make good their escape. They faced the confluence of the Somme and the Tortille and the division had to split due to a lack of bridges. Brigadier General Hornby was seriously wounded, so Lieutenant Colonel Millward took command of 116 Brigade as it crossed the Canal du Nord at Feuillaucourt and Hallé alongside 117 Brigade. They would both deploy at Cléry, on the north bank of the Somme. Major Cruickshank of the Divisional Training School made sure every straggler was rounded up and they joined all the engineers, labourers and pioneers at the front line.

The Germans cut the 13th Sussex off so they joined the 118 Brigade, passed through Péronne and crossed the Somme via Bristol Bridge. Brigadier General Bellingham deployed them between Buscourt and Biaches. The only disaster of the day was when eleven of 282 Brigade's gun teams were caught by machine-gun fire in the act of limbering up; the gunners had to abandon their stricken horses and guns and make a run for it.

16th (Irish) Division, Withdrawal across the Somme

All of Major General Hull's men were heading to the Somme before dawn. They were at the halfway position by midday but the Germans were closing in, so they had to continue their journey. The 1st Dublin Fusiliers and 11th Hampshire (Pioneers) fought a rearguard action as 'great masses of transport were making their way' over the Bristol Bridge. Major Hazard was the last man across before the engineers blew it up.

XIX Corps

Dawn found Lieutenant General Watts' divisions in two lines with gaps in many places. While 50th Division covered a four-mile sector between the Cologne and Omignon, what remained of 24th Division was covering its south flank. There was a two-mile gap on his left which the Germans had not found yet but they had found the three-mile gap on his right. Watts wanted everyone behind the Somme, so the rear guards kept the Germans at bay while field guns continued firing until the infantry had left; they all then faced a race to the river.

66th (2nd East Lancashire) Division, Across the Somme at Péronne

Major General Malcolm deployed all his machine guns along the river bank and told Brigadier General Williams to cover Bristol Bridge with his 199 Brigade until 16th Division had crossed. As we have seen, the bridge was blown up but the nearby railway bridge was left standing after Captain Barker of the 2/6th Lancashire Fusiliers failed to find any engineers.

50th (Northumbrian) Division, Withdrawal Across the Somme South of Péronne

Acting commander Brigadier General Stockley issued orders to withdraw to the Somme at dawn, saying 'the whole movement will be carried out as rapidly as possible consonant with steadiness and control.' A few units got their 'wind up' but there was no panic as they left the Green Line in the mist with the Germans in hot pursuit.

The three Durham battalions of 151 Brigade encountered few Germans as they headed for Éterpigny and the 1/5th Durhams covered the withdrawal across the bridge. Motor machine guns cut off one company of the 1/4th East Yorkshires around Vraignes and only thirty men escaped. The plan was for the 1/4th Green Howards to cover the first stage of 150 Brigade's withdrawal while the 1/4th East Yorkshires covered the second. They both fell back to Brie and then waited while the transport crossed but five tanks had to be abandoned because they were too wide to cross the bridge. Orders often took time to get through and the 1/5th Green Howards were the last to cross the bridge at 3 pm. The bridge was then demolished, leaving some of the 1/4th Green Howards to clamber across the debris.

The Germans were also hard on the heels of 149 Brigade as the Northumberland men headed for St Christ. Lieutenant Balden was last seen fighting off attacks with the 1/6th Northumberland Fusiliers' rearguard, south of the road. Captain Hicks' group of the 1/4th Northumberland Fusiliers was also cut off but they made a break for it when British cavalry drew the Germans' attention. Some of the 1/5th Northumberland Fusiliers held Ennemain until the rest of 149 Brigade had crossed the Somme. The engineers then blew the bridges, leaving the rearguards to swim across. Major General Henry Jackson took command of 50th Division as it lined out along the Somme north of the Amiens road.

24th Division, Withdrawal to Pargny on the Somme

Major General Daly's line south of the Omignon stream was a shambles. The Germans were pushing past Guizancourt on his right flank, so he ordered Brigadier General Stone and Dugan to head for Pargny on the Somme, some 7 miles to the south-west, while Brigadier General Morgan's 72 Brigade formed a rearguard. They fought off attacks before leaving, only to find the enemy were simultaneously advancing through the gap around Croix-Moligneaux. British and German soldiers reached the Somme around the same time so a sergeant demolished the bridge at Pargny without orders, leaving some of 9th East Surreys having to swim for it.

1st Cavalry Division, Around Falvy on the East of the Somme

The Germans pursuing 24th Division to the Somme spotted the 19th Hussars in a quarry east of Falvy and then an aeroplane guided artillery onto the crowded target, stampeding the horses. The 19th Hussars crossed the bridge at Épénancourt just before it was demolished but the 8th Hussars

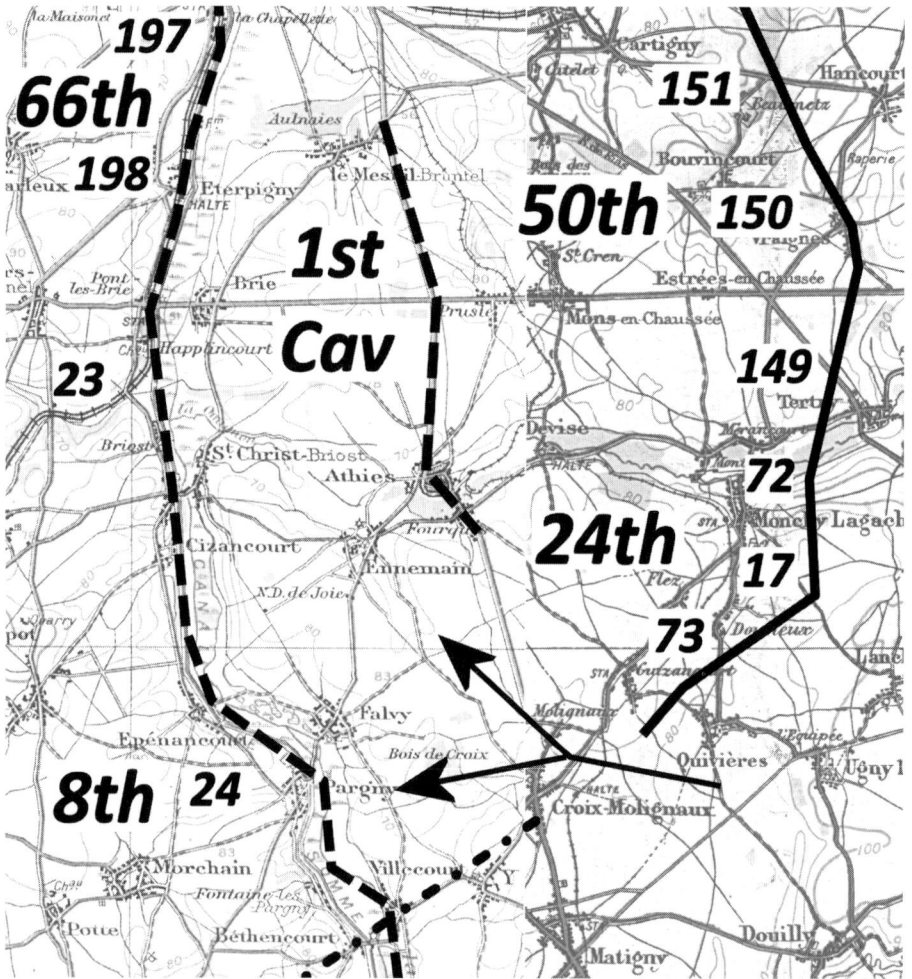

23 March XIX Corps: XIX Corps faced a challenging running battle back to the Somme Canal.

found St Christ bridge was down. Épénancourt and Falvy bridges had also been blown up and the river bank was too marshy for the horses to walk through. There was nothing else to do but to abandon their steeds and scramble across the wrecked bridges under fire.

8th Division, Along the Somme, South of the Amiens Road

The Béthencourt bridges had been destroyed while the five bridges between Falvy and Pargny were being prepared for demolition. Major General

Heneker's men had to cover the remaining bridges until 24th Division had crossed. The message from corps headquarters was 'all bridges may be destroyed at the discretion of divisional commanders, according to circumstances and as soon as all troops have crossed. All such demolitions to be reported to corps.' Lieutenant Colonel Wyatt gave the order to blow as soon as the last troops crossed each bridge.

Lieutenant Colonel Watson was killed as the 1st Sherwoods stopped the Germans scrambling over the ruined bridges south of the Amiens road after sundown. They seized a foothold at Pargny so Lieutenant Colonels Peyton and Roberts organised a counter-attack by the 2nd Rifle Brigade and 1st Worcesters to drive them back across the canal. They 'went hell-for-leather up the street, firing at anything we saw and using the bayonet in many cases. From the beginning every man screamed and cheered as loud as he bloody well could. By the time we reached the church, the village was in an uproar and Boche was legging it hard to the bridge or else chucking his hands up. We only took a very few prisoners as the men had been told to kill, so as to prevent the brutes again coming up in our rear.' Lieutenant Colonel Frank Roberts would be awarded the Victoria Cross for holding the canal line; Peyton was mortally wounded two days later.

XVIII Corps

The rear guards had crossed the Somme bridges just before dawn, leaving them little time to dig in. The river was fordable and there were causeways through the marshes which were hidden by trees. Most of XVIII Corps was behind the canal but 30th Division had to form a bridgehead around Ham because the river went around the north side of the town.

30th Division, The Ham Bridgehead

Brigadier General Stanley's 89 Brigade had spent the night digging trenches around Ham but the three weak battalions had too much ground to cover. The 17th King's stopped an attack from the north while the Germans ignored the 18th King's on the right. However, troops got behind the 19th King's because no one was covering the river bank in the fog. Only a few of the King's escaped with Captains Edwards, Lawless and Redhead while Major General Williams knew nothing of the disaster until it was too late.

The survivors re-formed south-west of Ham while Lieutenant Colonel Poyntz deployed the 2nd Scots Fusiliers and 2nd Bedfords to cover Verlaines on their right flank. But the Germans pushed them back until Brigadier General Goodman sent the 17th Manchesters and the 2nd Green Howards forward to secure the village. A disaster on 30th Division's front was only averted because the Germans chose to turn east against 36th Division, rather than west.

20th (Light) Division, Along the Somme West of Ham

Major General Douglas Smith's cold and hungry men were instructed to 'stand to' along the canal in the thick mist. It was a quiet morning between Béthencourt and Canizy but there were problems on the division's right flank where 30th Division had been driven across the canal at Ham. The roads north of the town were crammed with enemy troops but no one could direct the artillery onto them through the fog. Maxse asked Douglas Smith to help but he could only find 200 men to spare. Lieutenant Colonel Bilton led them to Verlaines but their attack failed because there was no artillery support. There were 'no machine guns to give covering fire, only four low-flying planes strafing the German infantry and to attack a town like Ham with a few men was absurd'.

The Germans tried to push Bilton's small force back but time and again they opened rapid fire as the swirling mist lifted to reveal the 'German hordes' then, just as quickly, it dropped to hide them again. As luck would have it, most of the reinforcements pouring across the Ham bridges were directed east, against 36th Division. Lieutenant Colonel Odo Vivian's 23rd Entrenching Battalion stopped an afternoon attempt to cross at Offoy, otherwise 20th Division's front was quiet until the alarm was sounded at dusk. There was 'a great noise of traffic and shouting was heard on the enemy's side of the river but machine and Lewis-gun fire was not long in restoring quiet.'

36th (Ulster) Division, Along the Somme East of Ham

A despatch rider warned the Ulstermen that the Germans were heading for them. Major General Nugent ordered the 21st Entrenching Battalion to cover Vert Galant on his left flank but it was soon forced back to the railway line. Lieutenant Colonel Peacocke's 9th Inniskillings helped them stop the onslaught but Germans were pouring across the Pithon railway bridge. They soon captured Aubigny but a mounted Captain Bruce, brigade major of the 109 Brigade, led the 9th Inniskillings and Major Montgomery's composite battalion back into it. Nugent sent every man he could to the front line; Captains Smyth and Drummond took forward 300 orderlies, servants, grooms and signallers while Brigadier General Cochrane welcomed 100 engineers. They all carried a rifle and dug in alongside the infantry.

The Germans had also crossed the Somme at Jussy, in 14th Division's sector, and they were squeezing the Ulstermen men into a narrow salient.

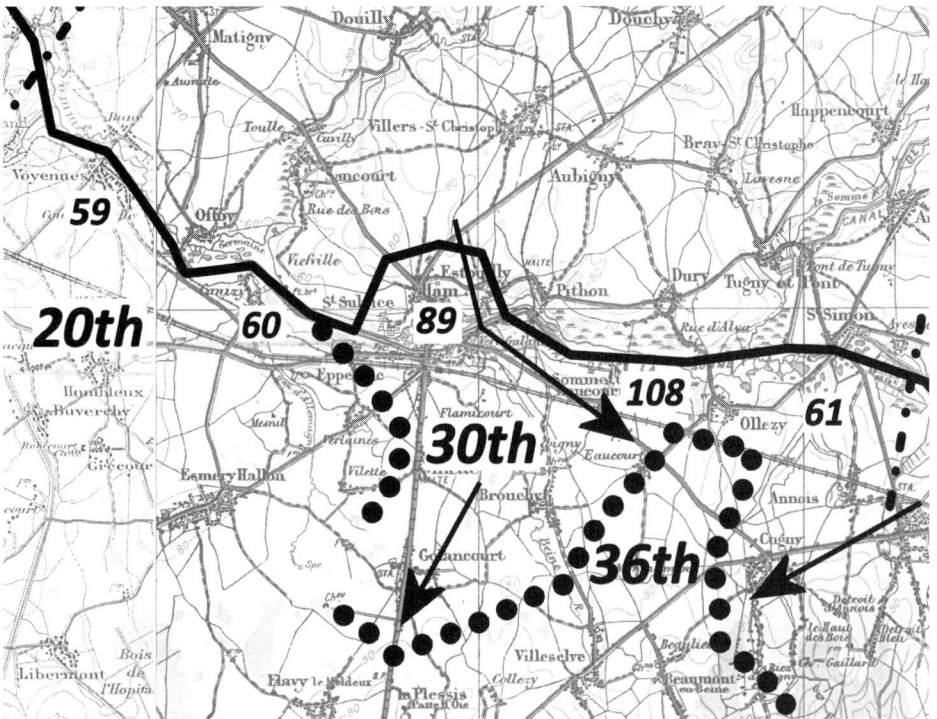

23 March XVIII Corps: The early loss of the Ham bridgehead resulted in a dangerous re-entrant in XVIII Corps' line.

They had reached Annois by the time Brigadier Generals Griffiths and Cochrane heard they had to withdraw 108 and 61 Brigades (attached to 36th Division) from the canal. The 1st and 9th Irish Fusiliers escaped across the railway 'under great pressure' while some of the 7th DCLI joined the 12th King's along the railway. The rest of Lieutenant Colonel Burges Short's men would be pinned down around Ollezy until the following morning. Some of the 7th Somersets stayed with the DCLI and tried to bring down a damaged bridge with grenades but the rest were cut off opposite St Simon and forced to surrender.

As many men as possible had withdrawn from the canal but the Germans continued pushing forward. Those heading south had again forced the 9th Inniskillings out of Aubigny and Brouchy while Captain Thompson's 2nd Irish Rifles had been driven from Cugny. By nightfall, 36th Division had been squeezed into a narrow salient with Lieutenant Colonel McCarthy-O'Leary's 1st Irish Rifles at the head.

III Corps
The morning mist meant Lieutenant General Butler's men could not see the far bank of the Crozat Canal. All three divisions had suffered many casualties during the first two days of battle and the surviving officers had to form ad-hoc units with the survivors. They had heard about the French units deploying behind their line and had been reassured that more were on their way.

<u>14th (Light) Division, Jussy on the Somme Canal</u>
The Germans crossed the canal in the fog and 8th and 9th Rifle Brigade were both driven behind a railway embankment. Some of Brigadier General Skinner's 41 Brigade then scattered west into 36th Division's salient while others retired through the French line and into Bois de Genlis.

The Germans clambered across ruined bridges to drive the 11th Royal Fusiliers and Scots Greys out of Jussy on 43 Brigade's front. The 5th Lancers and 9th Scottish Rifles were then pushed back onto the 7th KRRC and the 5 Dismounted Brigade holding the same railway embankment. Brigadier General Tempest could find no one on his flanks, so he gave the order to withdraw through the French line in Bois de Genlis. Neither Lieutenant Colonels Kirby nor Collins received Brigadier General Pitman's order to withdraw but they soon realised everyone else was retiring and they too fell back through Bois de Genlis.

Brigadier General Forster had gathered 400 divisional details to help 42 Brigade hold the embankment but they came under enfilade fire when the German infantry crossed it at Flavy-le-Martel. Aerial observers guided the German artillery onto the embankment as soon as the mist cleared, forcing Major General Greenly to order a withdrawal soon after midday. 'Everybody seems to be on the run. On almost every road that was visible we could see columns of transport or troops moving. Some of the French peasants appeared to be taking the risk and holding onto farms. On entering Noyon we found many of the inhabitants clearing out.'

<u>18th (Eastern) Division, From the Crozat Canal through Bois de Frières</u>
Major General Lee's men were holding the Crozat Canal around Mennessis but his right flank had been pushed back to Bois Hallot. The problem on 54 Brigade's front began when 14th Division was forced out of Jussy and the 11th Royal Fusiliers came under enfilade fire. Second Lieutenant Smedley stopped the first attack but German reinforcements were crossing the railway bridge east of Jussy. Major Deakin and Captain Pearcy were captured but the colonel escaped with just twenty-five men; Captain Brooking fought on until his ammunition ran out.

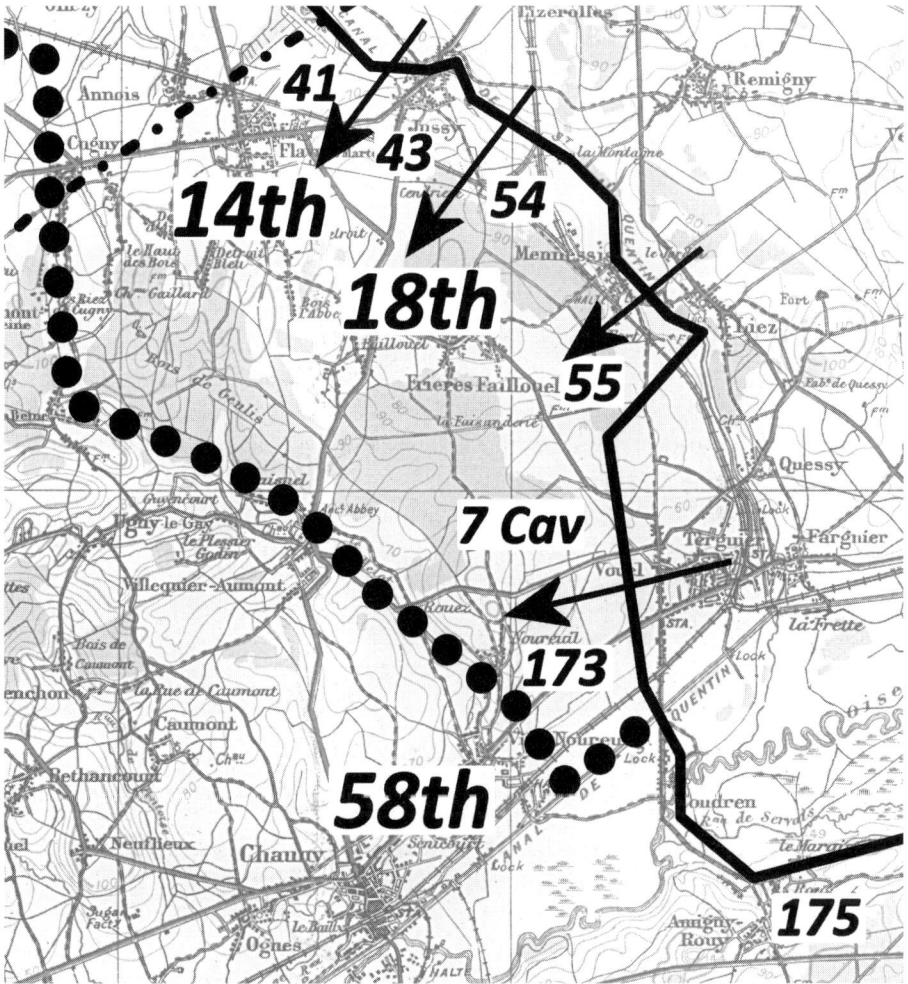

23 March III Corps: The British line collapsed through the French before they were ready to engage the enemy.

Lieutenant Colonel MacDonald's Canadian Dismounted Cavalry Brigade had reinforced 54 Brigade but Brigadier General Sadleir-Jackson deemed it wise to withdraw the 6th Northants and 7th Bedfords through Haute Tombelle wood, while the Royal Canadian Dragoons covered them. The Germans kept following up 14th Division's retreat and both 54 Brigade and the Canadian troopers retired through the French troops deployed in Bois de Frières.

Brigadier General Wood had ordered a relief of 55 Brigade along the Crozat Canal but it took longer than expected. The 8th East Surreys and 7th Queen's were taking over when the Germans clambered out of their boats and rafts and charged through the fog. They moved quickly through Bois Hallot and into Bois de Frières only to be stopped by two companies of the 7th Queen's. Lieutenant Colonel Christopher Bushell was severely wounded but he stayed with his men, cheering them on until he fainted; he would be awarded the awarded the Victoria Cross (unfortunately Bushell was killed in August 1918).

The Queen's were pinned down and the French hesitated to fire towards them when the Germans advanced. They all fell back into Bois de Frières where troopers from the 7 Dismounted Brigade and French armoured cars steadied the line. Major Tween was killed leading a counter-attack in which the 10th Essex were overwhelmed and everyone rallied back after French cavalry failed to clear the wood.

58th (2/1st London) Division, North of the Oise Canal
Brigadier General Worgan's weak London battalions had been reinforced by men from various units but they were not strong enough to drive the Germans back to the Crozat Canal at Tergnier. Two French battalions had been sent forward to try but they did not know the ground nor that they faced a stronger enemy. They soon fell back through the mist, taking 173 Brigade with them, through or south of the Bois de Frières.

III Corps Summary
Lieutenant General Butler was concerned that his right flank had been driven further from the Crozat Canal but he was more worried about the crossing at Ham, in XVIII Corp's sector to his left. That penetration could easily trap his troops against the Oise Canal, so 700 cavalry were attached to a similar number of infantry led by Lieutenant Colonel Theobald. They were placed under Major General Wentworth Harman, 3rd Cavalry Division's commander, and told to watch the vulnerable left flank.

As the third day of the offensive came to a close, one signal officer's account illustrates how the battlefield had changed since the recent days of trench warfare when everything was hidden below ground:

> *In the valley in front of me a field battery was in action, loosing off salvo after salvo at full speed, the flashes lighting up the darkening sky, the crack of the 18-pounders and the drone of the departing shells filling the air. To my right was a great hog's back of a hill, along the crest of this groups of*

horsemen were moving... In front and from either flank came the intermittent crackle of machine guns and occasionally in the woods a pale Very light sailed upwards.

23 March Summary

By 23 March, most of Third Army and all of Fifth Army were falling back fast. Haig told Byng and Gough that they had to prepare a defensive line using the trenches dug prior to 1 July 1916. They crossed the Ancre valley in Third Army's area north of the Somme and then ran five miles west of the river in Fifth Army's sector.

Pétain visited Haig at his Advanced GHQ at Dury to tell him wanted to keep in touch with the British right, north of the Oise Canal. They agreed the French would eventually take over Fifth Army's front, allowing Haig to send his reserve divisions to Third Army. Lieutenant General Thomas Morland and the staff of X Corps would be waiting for them west of Arras. Byng had also been told to organise the Purple Line connecting the defences covering Arras to the 1916 trenches on the Ancre.

Lieutenant General Hamilton-Gordon was also instructed to move IX Corps' staff behind Third Army. He would be given every spare engineering officer and they would mark out the GHQ Line some eight miles to the west of the Purple Line and the Ancre Line. Thousands of men would be sent to Third Army's rear to erect wire entanglements and dig as many shallow ditches as possible, ready to be turned into trenches. They would sketch out 5,000 miles of trenches and erect 23,500 tons of barbed wire in just two weeks.

Haig told Gough that he had two objectives. He had to re-establish touch with Third Army, and 'hold the River Somme at all costs. There will be no withdrawal from this line' until the French arrived. Gough repeated GHQ's message to his corps commanders but it was too late. While XIX Corps had a solid position along the Somme, XVIII Corps had already been pushed back. The French had taken over control of III Corps but it too had been driven back from the Crozat Canal and the British and French troops were very mixed up.

Meanwhile, a delighted Kaiser gave Field Marshal von Hindenburg the Iron Cross with Golden Rays on 23 March. It was the first time it had been awarded for a century. But while the accolades were being handed out, Ludendorff was having to decide what to do about the British retiring in the wrong place. Should OHL reinforce Seventeenth Army's failure south of Arras or reinforce Eighteenth Army's success astride the Somme? Ludendorff decided to change his original plan and follow the second course, hoping Eighteenth Army could force a gap between Fifth Army and the French.

Chapter 10

That Splendid Spirit in which Grit and Enthusiasm Outran Prudence

Third Army, 24 March

It was Palm Sunday but there would be no let-up in the German attacks. On the left, VI Corps was in a strong position in the Battle Zone but IV Corps was struggling to hold the Green Line and it had even lost a section around Mory. On the right, V Corps was in a small salient around Bertincourt but there was still a gap between the two armies.

Initially, Brigadier General Tudor had sent 26 Brigade to locate Third Army north of Sailly Saillisel but he had to recall it before 9th Division withdrew west. So General Byng told Lieutenant General Fanshawe that he was responsible for the line as far south as Sailly Saillisel and 51 Brigade was sent to cover it. Brigadier General Bond did contact 9th Division, but only briefly because the Scottish troops were heading west.

VI Corps

Lieutenant General Haldane's main concern was Mory, where the Green Line had been lost.

<u>3rd Division, Cojeul Stream</u>

The Germans wanted to drive Major General Deverell's men off the ridge north of the Cojeul stream. So they 'dribbled forward to their places of assembly and then advanced in waves; all their movements performed quickly and with precision, flags and discs being used to mark the flanks and to ensure the right direction of the advance.' The 7th Shropshires and 1st Scots Fusiliers stopped them from reaching the crest of the ridge between St Martin and Hénin.

<u>Guards Division, North of the Sensée</u>

The 1st Grenadier Guards and 2nd Scots Guards poured fire into the troops advancing against 3rd Division around Hénin. The machine-gun teams fired 20,000 rounds and some inexperienced men even stood on

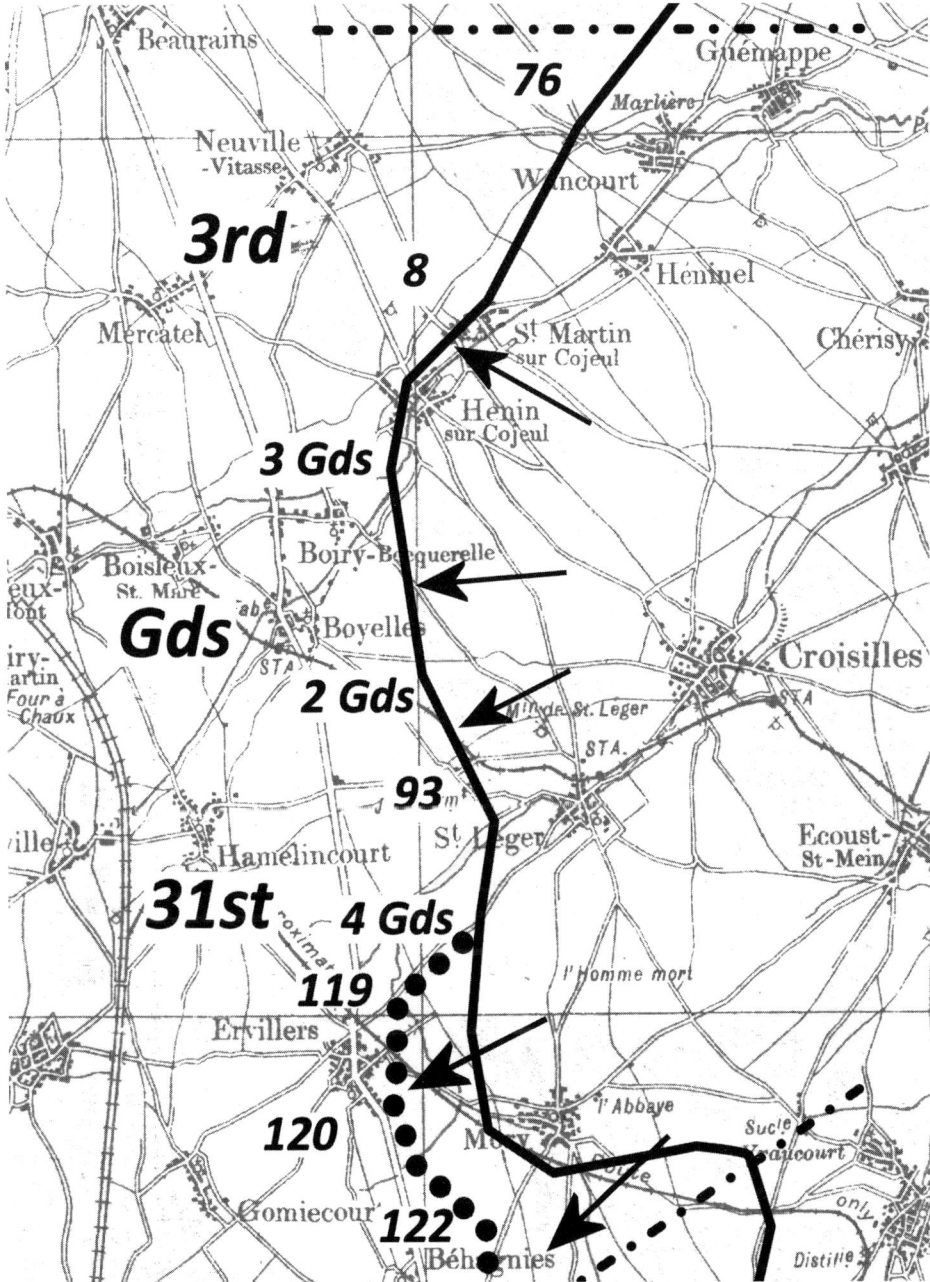

24 March VI Corps: Most of VI Corps held on in the Battle Zone but the right had to fall back in line with IV Corps.

the parapet to get better targets. Lieutenant Colonel Alexander's 2nd Irish Guards and the 3rd Grenadier Guards stopped the morning attacks in the direction of Boyelles.

31st Division, South of the Sensée
On 93 Brigade's front the 13th York and Lancasters and 15th West Yorkshires stopped the Germans advancing north of the Sensée stream. The 4 Guards Brigade were also holding on but Brigadier General Lord Ardee had to deploy the 3rd Coldstream Guards on the division's right flank after 40th Division fell back towards Ervillers. Major General Robert Bridgford also moved up the 11th East Yorkshires to help. They held their fire until the last minute and then stopped the Germans reaching Ervillers. But the main problem for the men at the front was that the British artillery was shelling their trenches and British planes were strafing them.

40th Division, Mory
Major General Ponsonby's men had been engaged all night, leaving them unable to reorganise the line facing Mory. An attack towards the high ground around Ervillers pushed the 21st Middlesex and 13th East Surreys back on 119 Brigade's front. Enfilade fire from 31st Division to the north gave Second Lieutenant Page time to form a flank with the 13th Green Howards but the battle in front of Ervillers continued well into the night.

An early attack out of Mory forced the 2nd South Lancashires of Brigadier Dobbin's 75 Brigade back, south of the village. The 12th East Surreys and 15th Hampshires were then pushed back towards Béhagnies followed by 120 Brigade heading for Sapignies.

The situation along 40th Division's front was chaotic and Major General Ponsonby sent Brigadier General Campbell to find as many stragglers as possible to reinforce his crumbling line. Fortunately for him the Germans were also disorganised and many were found wandering around in the darkness having been told no more than to march through an imaginary gap in the British line.

42nd (East Lancashire) Division, In reserve from Ervillers to Sapignies
Buses had driven Major General Arthur Solly-Flood's men towards VI Corps line, so they could relieve 40th Division around Mory during the night. He planned to establish a support line between Ervillers and Sapignies, so 40th Division could fall back through them. Unfortunately, a staff officer stopped Brigadier Generals Fargus and Seymour, as they marched towards Bucquoy, to tell them that the Germans had broken through. The two brigades halted while patrols went forward but they could

not find the enemy and found few friendly troops either. Fargus then moved 126 Brigade to Ervillers while Seymour took 125 Brigade to Béhagnies.

IV Corps

Lieutenant General Harper's men had a quiet night astride the Hirondelle valley and the main Cambrai road. They were holding the Green Line but casualties were rising faster than reinforcements were arriving. On the left, 41st Division had formed a defensive flank facing Mory but the problem came on the right flank. The plan would be to form another defensive position as V Corps pulled out of its salient after three days.

Unfortunately, V Corps' withdrawal turned into a full-scale retreat across the 1916 battlefield, thanks to the gap on the boundary with Fifth Army. Byng gave instructions to disengage and withdraw behind Bapaume around 4 pm and Harper in turn gathered his divisional commanders at Achiet-le-Petit to tell them. There was no time to make a plan, their men had to destroy everything they could not carry and retire.

Harper warned his subordinates to keep contact on their flanks and he also told Major Generals Bainbridge and Carter-Campbell to get their battered 25th and 51st Divisions out of the line. The divisional commanders returned to their headquarters but it took time to get the message to their brigadiers and battalion commanders, so long in fact that most were retreating before they heard the news.

<u>41st Division, Beugnâtre to Sapignies</u>

The breakthrough south of Mory compromised the flank of Brigadier General Clemson's 124 Brigade.

Lieutenant Colonel Tuite was mortally wounded as the 20th Durhams, 26th Royal Fusiliers and 10th Queen's fell back through Beugnâtre and his men could not carry him back due to the volume of fire.

Major General Sydney Lawford issued orders to break contact at dusk and it would take them all night to establish to a new line north of Bapaume. The 10th Cheshires and the 1st Wiltshires were already falling back along the Hirondelle stream and they both rejoined 25th Division. This left a large gap between 41st and 19th Division around Biefvillers and Lawford only had three field companies to cover it. Fortunately, his engineer chief, Lieutenant Colonel Stockley, found 74 Brigade behind them during the night.

<u>19th (Western) Division, Astride the Cambrai Road</u>

The first attack drove both the 8th Staffords and the 9th Cheshires, holding 56 Brigade's line, back south of the Cambrai road. Captains Milner and

Palmer recaptured their trench around Delsaux Farm, only to find it so full of dead and wounded Germans that they could not use it. The attack then spread to 58 Brigade's sector and both the 6th Wiltshires and 9th Welch were driven back along the Bapaume road to Bancourt.

Major General Jeffreys also wanted to break contact and he instructed his artillery to pull back after hearing 2nd Division was retiring on his right. Both 58 and 56 Brigades withdrew through 57 Brigade's position along the Red Line. The 10th Worcesters and 10th Warwicks left when it was dark after seeing a large group of Germans advancing towards them. They passed through Bapaume but the Germans refused to enter because their guns were shelling it. This lack of coordination allowed 19th Division time to reorganise west of the town.

51st (Highland) Division, In support south-east of Bapaume
Major General Carter-Campbell's Scots were supposed to be resting but they saw men from 19th Division were falling back towards their position

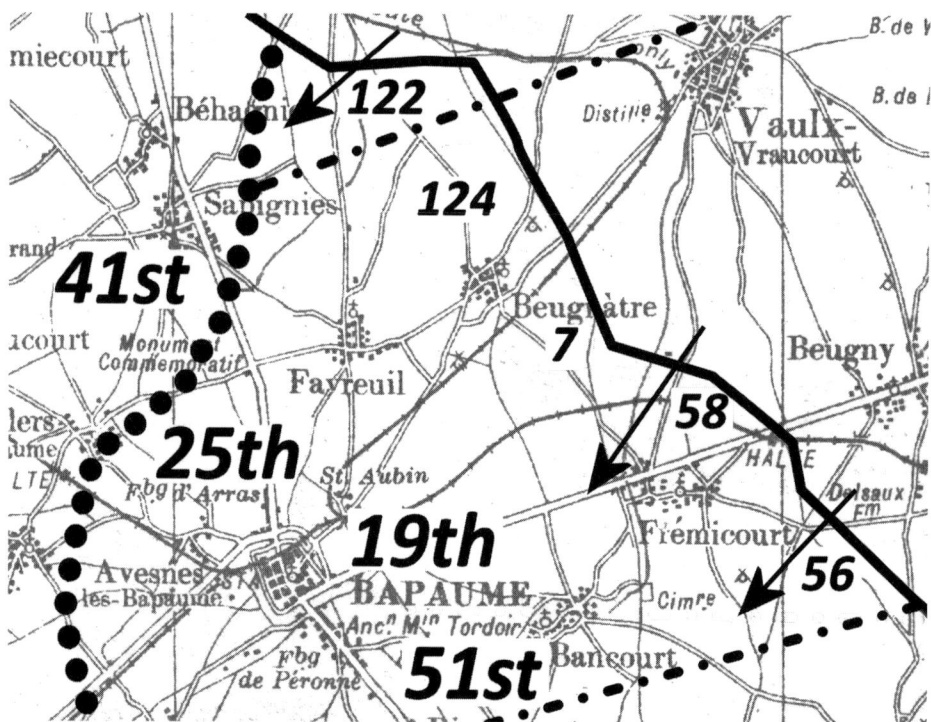

24 March IV Corps: IV Corps had to abandon Bapaume in an attempt to break contact with the Germans.

during the afternoon. Then 152 Brigade came under fire after 17th Division retired from Barastre on their right. Brigadier General Burn's men fell back in a north-west direction, moving 'deliberately and gradually, platoons retiring in succession from the right and was splendidly covered by the fire of the reserve platoon'. They passed through 154 Brigade and stopped for a time on the Cambrai road. Meanwhile, 153 Brigade had been stopping the Germans from leaving Frémicourt for a time.

The three brigades faced a testing withdrawal as they moved through and to the south of Bapaume. 'Shells, steadily arriving from high velocity guns, some bursting in the air, some on the ground, some containing gas; dense masses of guns, transport and troops packing the road.' En route the Scots helped themselves to everything they could carry from an abandoned canteen and then looted Bapaume, before the Germans arrived. They were relieved to find Lieutenant Colonel McDonald with one thousand reinforcements and sixteen machine guns waiting for them on the far side of the town.

IV Corps Summary
IV Corps had escaped but the men were tired and hungry while units were in the wrong place and mixed up. The road network meant that most of the guns had headed for Achiet-le-Grand, causing a traffic jam, and ten batteries were still waiting to pass through the village at dawn. One group of heavy batteries had been delayed by the mass of traffic moving through Bucquoy.

V Corps
Lieutenant General Fanshawe's men were in a tight salient around Bertincourt, the site of a huge dump, where men worked through the night to remove the engineering stores and ammunition under shell fire. Fanshawe wanted to withdraw into reserve at dawn but the Germans attacked first, hoping to overrun the salient. A massive explosion before dawn caused many casualties to the 1/28th London Regiment, but the flames lit up the battlefield as the Germans advanced resulting in heavy casualties.

2nd Division, Withdrawing from the North Side of the Salient
Fanshawe was unable to contact Major General Cecil Pereira by telephone, so he sent Brigadier General Boyd to find 2nd Division's headquarters. He learnt that the men of 19th Division were already withdrawing from his left flank. Around one hundred men of the 10th Worcesters were sent to fill the dangerous gap. They were never seen again, so tanks from 8th Battalion deployed behind a belt of old wire to cover it.

A wounded Lieutenant Sheridan and some men of the 2nd HLI stayed with the tanks until the 2nd Oxford and Bucks, 24th Royal Fusiliers and the rest of the HLI escaped. However, Brigadier General Bullen-Smith's 5 Brigade retired south-west rather than east and the 'absence of landmarks, pressure of time and shell fire all contributed to the mistake.'

Brigadier General Walsh's 6 Brigade drove off an attack and then withdrew but Second Lieutenant Atkinson was killed as the Germans pursued the 2nd South Staffords. Lieutenant Christopher made sure his machine-gun teams 'inflicted terrible casualties and, after terrible slaughter, drove the enemy back towards Vélu Wood,' but a second attack pushed between the 1st King's and the 17th Royal Fusiliers.

Pereira's men had made it to the Red Line but they could see 63rd Division falling back to the south, so many decided to keep going. There were too few officers to stop them and the division fragmented as it retreated across the 1916 battlefield towards Gueudecourt. Lieutenant Lewis and Second Lieutenant Armstrong fought on around Lieutenant Colonel Murray-Lyon's 1st King's headquarters, north-east of Haplincourt. Some of the 2nd South Staffords held on with 'that splendid spirit in which grit and enthusiasm outran prudence,' but Lieutenant Colonel Alban was hit as the rest made a run for it. He was carried to the rear, one of the few to escape the onslaught.

Time and again, the teams from No 2 Battalion, Machine Gun Corps, 'fought with unflagging energy and cool heroism' for every yard of ground, often running forward to rescue wounded men. Second Lieutenant Craig's teams fired over 100,000 rounds in just four hours in front of Barastre. To the south, Lieutenant Robinson's teams of the 2nd Machine Gun Battalion helped a group of stragglers from the Bedfords and the London Regiment hold Rocquigny. Lieutenant Colonel Dunlop's men had enabled V Corps to escape from Bertincourt but they lost twenty-nine machine guns in doing so.

63rd (Royal Naval) Division, Abandoning the Salient and Across the Somme Battlefield

The three brigadiers decided to escape from their narrow salient before they became trapped because Major General Lawrie's order had been delayed. Brigadier General Coleridge instructed 188 Brigade to withdraw from Bertincourt while Brigadier General Hutchinson had 190 Brigade withdraw past Bus. The Hood and Drake Battalions saw them leaving as the mist cleared, so Brigadier General Du Pree told them to escape while the enemy was still firing high.

All three brigades crossed the Red Line before midday and Lieutenant Colonel Malone's 7th Royal Fusiliers made a brave stand in front of

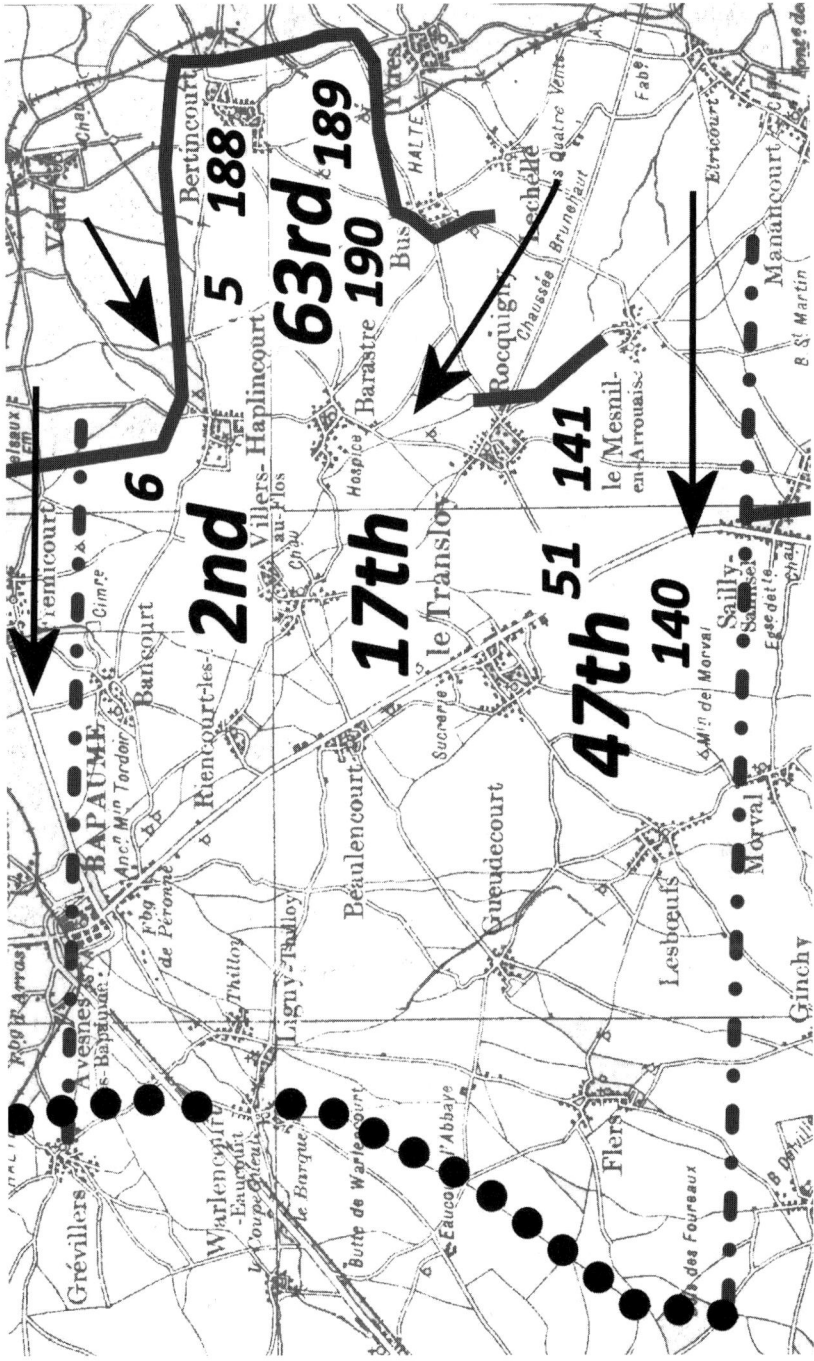

24 March V Corps: After finally escaping the Flesquières salient, V Corps faced a long and confusing march across the 1916 battlefield.

Rocquigny. They continued through Le Transloy and again everyone was already retiring before they received their withdraw orders. Lieutenant Anderson's machine-gun teams delayed the German pursuit at Lesboeufs while the rest of the division negotiated the 1916 crater fields. They finally assembled at what once was High Wood where the outposts were amused to hear the German patrols thrashing about in the undergrowth shouting English bingo calls (such as Kelly's Eye, Legs Eleven and Clickety Click) to keep in touch.

The retreat had been a chaotic affair. Some companies were lost while others were cut off. The rapid march meant that many of the wounded had to be left behind, a gut wrenching decision to make for those leaving and those left behind.

17th (Northern) Division, Covering the South Side of the Salient

Major General Robertson was in support around Barastre, at the west end of V Corps' line. He instructed Brigadier General Bond to move his 51 Brigade to fill the gap between 47th and 9th Divisions around Sailly Saillisel. They found hundreds of stragglers, many of them wounded, heading west while the Germans were in Sailly Saillisel. Major Peddie of the 7th Lincolns held on around Le Mesnil while 63rd Division withdrew. His men were just 'a very thin brown line' but most of the Germans preferred to move past, rather than engage them.

Most of 17th Division was moving by the time Robertson was told to withdraw to Bazentin-le-Grand and Montauban, seven miles to the southwest. He returned to his headquarters to discover that Brigadier General Glasgow had already told 50 Brigade to head for Gueudecourt while 51 Brigade was being driven back towards Le Transloy. It also looked like the Germans had cut their line of withdrawal through Lesboeufs, so new routes had to be planned. To complicate matters, 63rd Division was blocking the route through Le Transloy.

In the confusion of battle, Brigadier General Bond did not get his orders because 51 Brigade was already retiring. Brigadier General Eden misunderstood his orders and 52 Brigade withdrew too far. Only Brigadier General Yatman both received his orders and headed in the right direction. Robertson soon lost contact with all three brigadiers and his command became scattered during the night.

47th (2nd London) Division, The South Side of the Salient

By dawn, the division was spread out between Le Mesnil and Le Transloy while large numbers of Germans passed through the gap to their south. The three infantry brigadiers decided to make a stand around Le Transloy and Major General Gorringe told them to stay in touch with Fifth Army, unaware that the Germans were already in Sailly Saillisel.

South of the gap, 9th Division was soon falling back rapidly towards Combles. Byng told V Corps to restore contact with VII Corps, the first Fanshawe knew the gap was increasing, but he had no troops to close it. All he could do was to tell 47th Division to extend its flank as far south as Combles. Major General Gorringe sent the 1/4th Welsh Fusiliers (Pioneers) and some engineers towards Ginchy and Lesboeufs, unaware the Germans had already entered them; it meant they were two miles behind the Londoners' flank.

It was late when Gorringe received the order to fall back to the Bazentin area. The message reached Brigadier Generals Kennedy and Mildren and 140 and 141 Brigades picked their way across the old battlefield, looking for landmarks they recognised from 1916. The messenger heading for 142 Brigade was captured while the brigade major was killed and a wounded Brigadier General Bailey was captured. Most of the Londoners eventually assembled between Bazentin-le-Petit and Contalmaison 'practically walking in our sleep, yet conscious of a great contentment. The sky behind glared with the blaze of the burning ammunition dumps in Pozières, now abandoned to the enemy.'

Brigadier General Barker had withdrawn 99 Brigade to Gueudecourt only to be killed when a shell hit the tent serving as his headquarters. Lieutenant Colonel Winter of the 23rd Royal Fusiliers took over and he instructed a retirement when he saw the London Brigades falling back. The brigade ended up joining 50 Brigade, east of the Butte du Warlencourt.

Third Army's Summary
The old Somme battlefield was a nightmare maze of decaying trenches, shell holes and entanglements. Some troops kept moving west but others turned and fought when the enemy got too close. 'Spread out like a chessboard on which the pieces moved at random, troops of several British divisions checked and counter-checked the enemy... They marched back through the bright evening sunshine, over the shell holes and long grass of the old battle ground due west.'

Stragglers, walking wounded, ambulances and refugees mixed in with formed bodies of soldiers but 'there was a self-imposed order in the retirement and no panic anywhere.' All night long, there was 'a slow march of columns and smaller detachments of tired, hungry and thirsty men, plodding wearily westwards over rough tracks and broken cratered ground'. All the time, the Germans were in close pursuit, sometimes moving close behind the British and at other times parallel to them, unaware they were so close in the darkness.

It would take the officers until dawn to establish where they were, and where the rest of their command was. The men were shaken by the long retreat and they knew they were in trouble because they had passed so many old trench systems, where they could have fought. They had not seen any fresh troops either and they knew they were still in the front line as dawn approached.

Byng's plan had been for IV and V Corps to break contact, withdraw and then re-establish a new line stretching from the west of Bapaume, in a south-west direction across the 1916 battlefield. While IV Corps had fallen back five miles, parts of V Corps had to march over ten miles. The men were tired, hungry, disorganised and low on ammunition.

The Germans 'skilfully carried out' their advance and their 'front was covered by large patrols, each carrying one or two light machine guns. The use of light signals by these patrols was most remarkable. They signalled each stage by sending up a Very light, with the result of light signals going up as far as the eye could reach.'

The patrols fired a different flare if they found a gap in the British line and those following headed straight for it. It also appeared that the infantry often ditched their rifles so they could carry extra machine gun ammunition. But the German troops moved cautiously across the old battlefield, concerned there could be British troops waiting in the next trench. They were also tired and hungry, wondering if their supply wagons would be able to find them.

Lloyd George used underhand methods to replace General Robertson with General Wilson.

General Julian Byng of Third Army and General Hubert Gough of Fifth Army.

Tens of thousands of German troops assembled for the attack moving by night marches into position.

Storm troops making an assault, in this case training for Operation Michael.

Just a few of the many thousands of British prisoners taken.

One of the dozens of British artillery pieces disabled and captured.

Soldiers had to learn how to fight in the open after three and a half years in the trenches.

The artillery had to rely on written messages or SOS flares from the infantry to find their targets.

The chaos typical of a division in retreat with their enemy in close pursuit.

Time and again the Royal Field Artillery's guns stayed in the line, firing until the last minute.

The Royal Garrison Artillery never had enough traction engines to haul the howitzers to the rear.

Ammunition and supplies were evacuated when possible, otherwise they were blown up or burnt.

The Germans faced the nightmare of supplying their troops across the 1916 Somme battlefield.

Refugees escape with a few possessions ahead of the German advance.

German troops were surprised the British were so well stocked with supplies.

After a week of attacking and marching, the German soldier was as exhausted as his enemy.

Chapter 11

Open Warfare with Vengeance

Fifth Army, 24 March

General Congreve had a gap on his left flank and the 1916 battlefield to his rear. General Watts was holding on along the Somme but General Maxse's right had been driven back from the Ham bridgehead. French troops had taken over from General Butler, north of the Oise, but they were relying on British artillery. Gough's centre might have been a solid line but the flanks faced another day of fighting and marching.

VII Corps

Congreve's men were holding a ragged line west of the Canal du Nord. There was no one around Sailly Saillisel on the north flank, where Third Army should have been. Gough promised 1st Cavalry Division and 35th Division were on their way but Congreve pointed out the next line of defence, in case they had to retire.

9th (Scottish) Division, St Pierre Vaast Wood, Bouchavesnes and Maurepas

Brigadier General Tudor issued the order to hold 'at all costs', but few received it because they were already falling back as they fought a battle of 'open warfare with vengeance. There were targets aplenty; the gaunt wilderness was seething with field grey uniforms.' Brigadier General Kennedy's orders were confusing, so the 5th Camerons, 8th Black Watch and 7th Seaforths fell back two miles.

German troops had got behind the 12th and 11th Royal Scots in St Pierre Vaast Wood during the night. Brigadier General Croft's men made an early attack and Major Anderson and Lieutenant Colonel Ritson escaped with their men while the 6th KOSBs acted as the rearguard. It was an orderly withdrawal towards Combles with 'both infantry and artillery moving back as though at an old fashioned field day, with mounted officers conveying orders'.

Another attack forced Croft's men to abandon the Combles ravine before withdrawing south-west towards Hardecourt and Curlu. They fought rearguard actions every step of the way, grabbing food handed to them by the engineers who were busy burning down canteens.

The only good news was that they had met the 12th HLI on Maurepas ridge marching east and it was stronger than the two Scottish brigades combined. It meant 35th Division had arrived but the HLI did an about turn and joined the Scots and Lieutenant Colonel Hunt's scratch battalion, on the north bank of the Somme.

The South African Brigade was the only one to get Brigadier General Tudor's order to hold on 'at all costs'. The fight started with Dawson's headquarters being shelled by British guns but they stopped when the gunners withdrew. Brigadier General Dawson reported the Germans were behind his flanks at 11.10 am but nothing else was heard from him. His men only had around 200 rounds each and they made every one count, taking what the dead had when they ran out. 'All wounded who could possibly hold a rifle were stopped on their way to the dressing station and sent back to the front line.' Those who could not carry a rifle were searched for ammunition.

Smoke from fires hid the Germans when the mist cleared and Major Cochran was mortally wounded stopping men falling back. Time and again the South Africans drove the Germans back, cheering as limber teams galloped forward under fire only to get 'out of hand and men and horses went down in a struggling mass'.

A badly wounded Major Ormiston eventually reported there was no one to the left because 27 Brigade had withdrawn across the Combles ravine; 21st Division had also fallen back. The survivors were in desperate straits: 'Every machine gun and Lewis gun was out of action, the ammunition was nearly gone, the rifles were choked and the breaking point of human endurance had been reached.' Eventually, Dawson called a cease fire and walked forward with his two surviving battalion commanders to be met with shouts of 'why have you killed so many of us' and 'why did you not surrender sooner?'

The South Africans had delayed the German advance by seven hours. As the one hundred survivors were marched into captivity, they had the satisfaction of passing along roads backed up with guns and transport. The Kaiser allegedly said 'that had all divisions fought as well as the 9th Division, he would have no more troops to carry on his attack with.'

But the action had all but wiped out Dawson's command. The Germans saw the aftermath of the last stand when they passed 'the trenches full of dead from bayonet and hand-grenade wounds, a proof that there had been bitter hand-to-hand fighting. A South African Brigade had defended the hill to the last.'

21st Division, North Bank of the Somme

An early attack against 64 Brigade in the mist forced 9th KOYLIs and 15th Durhams back along the river bank, through Cléry. The 2nd Lincolns and 1st

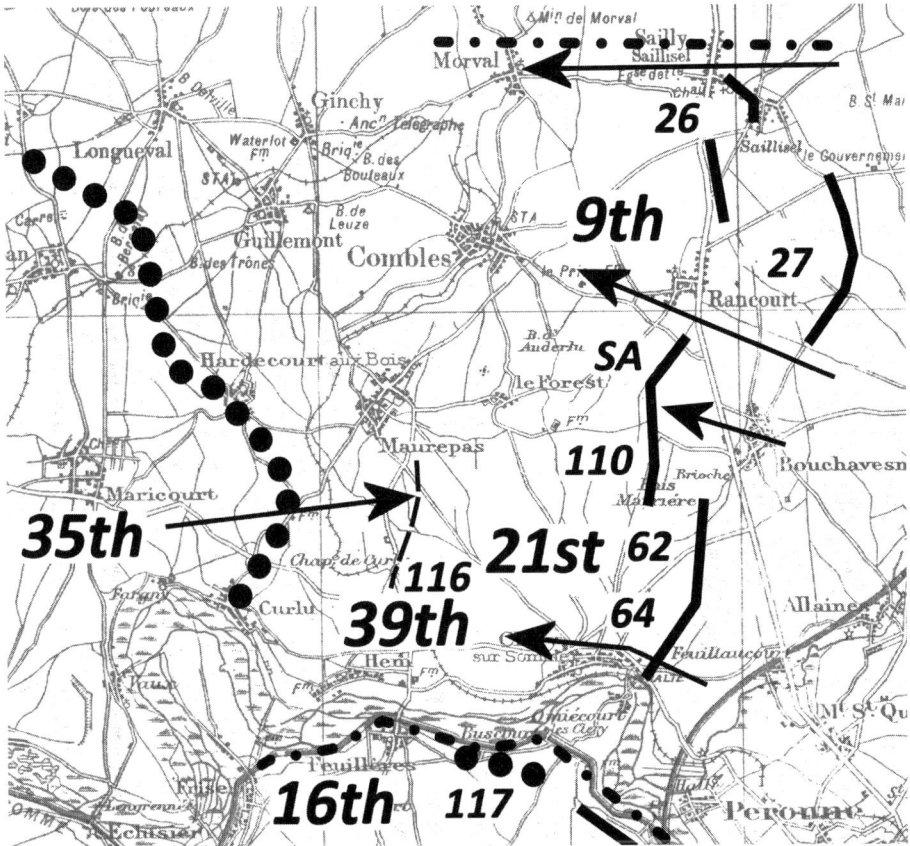

24 March VII Corps: VII Corps disintegrated as it fell back along the north bank of the Somme.

East Yorkshires followed and they all passed through 116 Brigade, en route to Curlu. On the left flank, the Germans had pushed past the flank of the 7th Leicesters and the 14th Northumberland Fusiliers but 110 Brigade fell back north-west, towards Maurepas. Major General Campbell's shattered command eventually assembled around Maricourt and the survivors were withdrawn into reserve. The 2nd Lincolns had started the day with only ninety men and only eighteen had escaped.

39th Division, Astride the Somme
Major General Feetham's problem was on the north bank where Lieutenant Colonel Millward saw 21st Division fall back through 116 Brigade around Hem. Lieutenant Colonel Murray made sure the 4/5th

Black Watch poured enfilade fire into the Germans across the river as they advanced towards Curlu. Brigadier General Armytage deployed 117 Brigade, extended the line as far west as Feuillères to maintain touch across the river.

16th (Irish) Division, Somme around Cappy and Frise

Late in the afternoon Lieutenant General Congreve ordered Major General Hull to guard the crossings of the Somme because of the rapid withdrawal along the north bank. Lieutenant Colonel Crockett saw to it that the 11th Hampshires, the 6th Connaughts and 2nd Irish Regiment took their toll on the Germans across the river.

35th Division, Maurepas Ridge

Major General George Franks' men were exhausted after a seventeen-mile night march onto the battlefield 'which was seriously delayed through the congestion of the roads. They were full of columns of transport moving back, troops moving forward and civilians fleeing for safety with such belongings as they could transport on farm vehicles.' There was no time for breakfast because 'tired troops came streaming back saying that the Hun were on top of them.'

Brigadier Generals Marindin and Pollard moved 105 and 106 Brigades along the north bank of the Somme and they deployed on Maurepas ridge with a Canadian battery of motor machine guns and 4th Tank Battalion's crews, who had abandoned their tanks due to a lack of petrol.

The 12th HLI and 18th HLI were driven back to Hardecourt even though 'every available man, including clerks and cooks of brigade headquarters, were used to stem the tide.' The 15th Sherwoods were overrun while Lieutenant Colonel Cochran, Major Le Mesurier and Captains Barnett and Kidd were killed during the Cheshires' last stand near Hem. Only the 17th Royal Scots held back the German infantry moving along the north bank of the Somme, escaping to Curlu at the last moment.

1st Cavalry Division, North of the Somme

Major General Mullens reached VII Corps' area at midday and Congreve told him to reinforce his crumbling line as it fell back. Brigadier General Legard found that 47th Division was heading for High Wood while VII Corps' left was heading for Bernafay Wood. Legard only had 300 troopers, too few to cover the three-mile gap, so he reinforced 9th Division's left around Montauban instead. Another composite brigade of dismounted troops deployed behind Bois Favières while a third reinforced the Curlu area, next to the Somme.

XIX Corps

Lieutenant General Watts was to continue holding the Somme Canal between Biaches and Béthencourt. He told Major Generals Malcolm, Jackson and Heneker that it was 'to be clearly understood that there is no intention to withdraw, but to fight the battle out on the line now held'.

The Germans tried scrambling across the rubble and girders at the bridge sites in the dawn mist 'but these attempts were by no means confined to the recognised points of passage. Owing to the dry weather the river and marshes did not constitute a very formidable obstacle to infantry, while the trees and undergrowth along the valley afforded good cover to the enemy and limited the field of fire of the defenders.'

66th (2nd East Lancashire) and 50th (Northumbrian) Divisions, Somme Face Péronne

Major General Malcolm's men were under fire from across the river around Péronne. During the evening, the Germans crossed a temporary footbridge south of La Chapelette and occupied an old fort. The 2/8th Lancashire Fusiliers could not drive them back, even with the help of the 1/6th and 1/5th Durhams.

8th Division, Along the Somme, Astride the Amiens Road

Major General Heneker's men were safely behind the Somme but 23 Brigade was attacked at several points. Lieutenant Colonel Lowry's 2nd West Yorkshires stopped them crossing at Éterpigny and Brie while the 6th Northumberland Fusiliers reinforced the Amiens road position. Lieutenant Colonel Cope's 2nd Devons held Haplincourt and Brigadier General Grogan placed Lieutenant Colonel Page's 2nd Middlesex in support after Second Lieutenants Maunder and Huntingford drove back several attempts to cross the ruined bridge.

Brigadier General Haig's 24 Brigade was lined out along the Somme between St Christ and Pargny. On the left, Lieutenant Colonel Watson was killed as the 1st Sherwoods stopped all attempts to cross at St Christ while the 2nd Northants and 1st Worcesters were holding on around Épénancourt. However there were problems on 25 Brigade's front.

German patrols had discovered a path across the river north of Béthencourt during the night and the infantry used rafts, temporary footbridges and fallen trees to cross the canal. They drove Major Hollingsworth's 2nd East Lancashires and two companies of Lieutenant Colonel Stirling's 2nd Berkshires out of the village before turning north. Lieutenant Colonel Paton's 2nd Rifle Brigade fought off attacks at Pargny

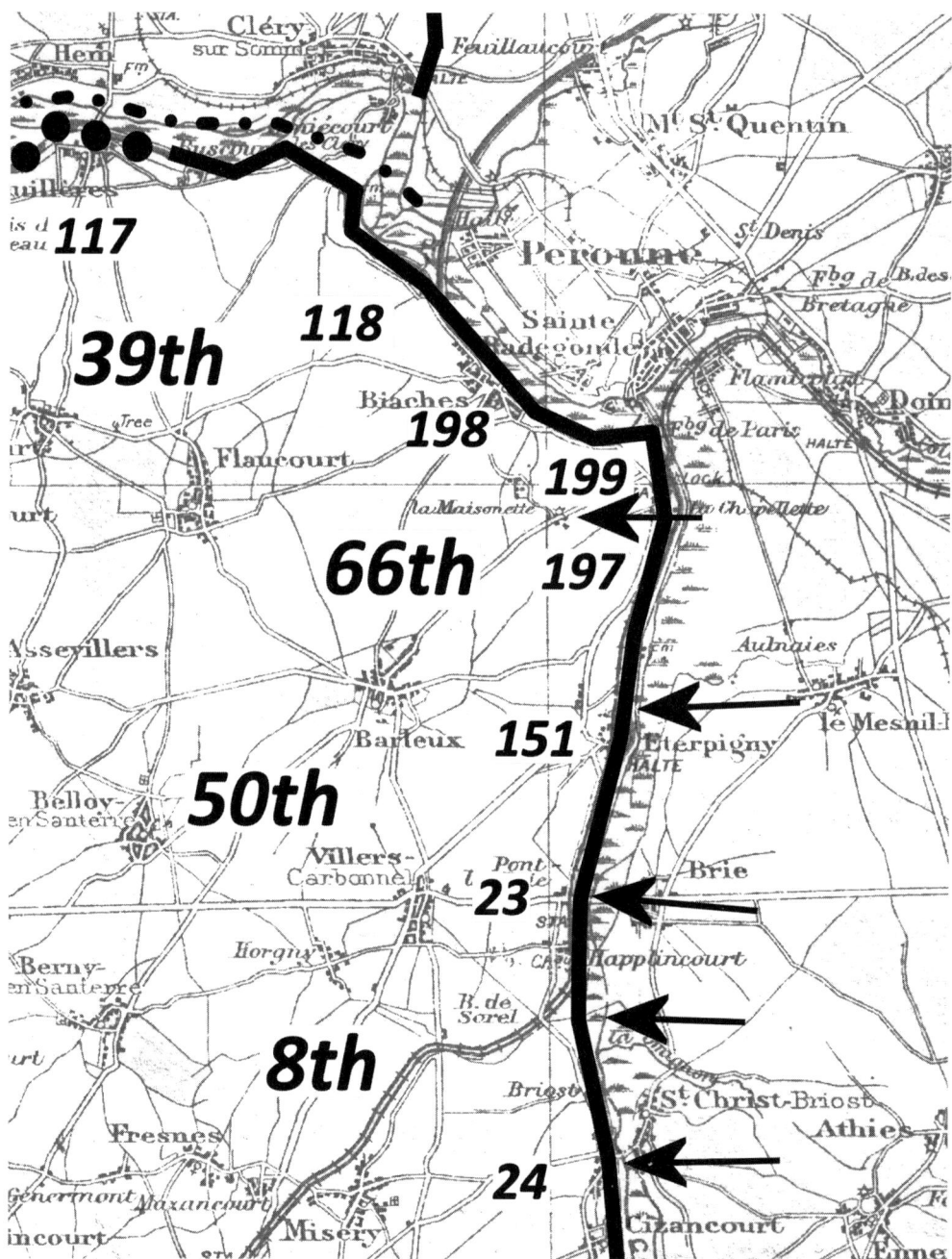

24 March: XIX Corps' north flank held onto along the Somme.

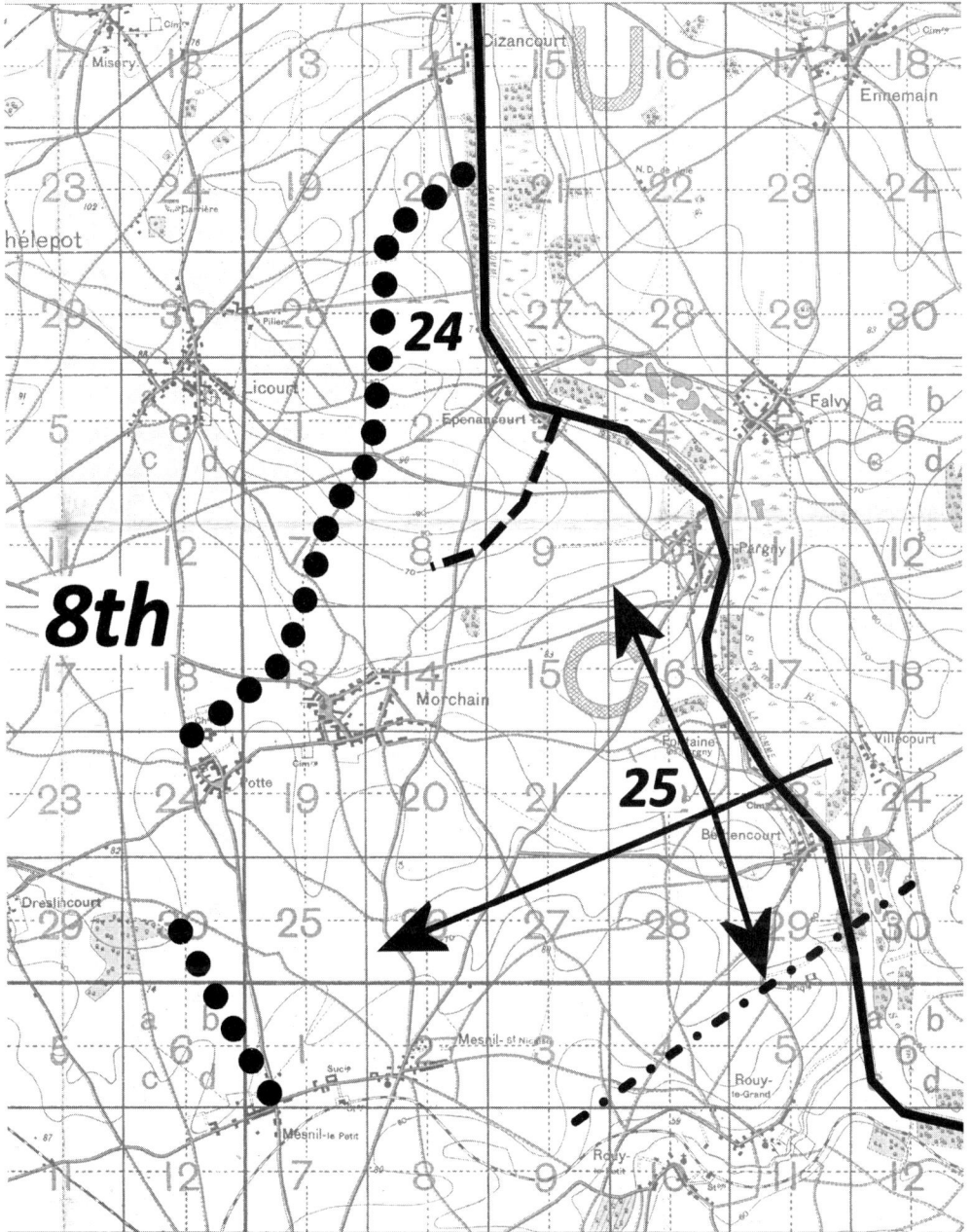

24 March: XIX Corps' south flank was pushed back from the Somme, compromising Fifth Army's line.

while Lieutenant Colonel Roberts managed to get the 1st Worcesters into a defensive flank at Épénancourt. However, Brigadier General Coffin had to order 25 Brigade to withdraw beyond Morchain as the Germans poured across the Somme.

Brigadier General Haig also ordered Lieutenant Colonel Latham's 2nd Northants and Worcesters to fall back, resulting in the gap widening on 8th Division's right. All Heneker could do was send his only reserve, the 22nd DLI, forward to keep contact with 20th Division around Dreslincourt.

Gough asked General Robillot to counter-attack with 24th Division the following morning after hearing of the crossing at Béthencourt. General Fayolle confirmed the French would, but reminded Gough that there were no French batteries in the area. Two staff officers returned from Robillot's headquarters during the night to report they doubted there would be an attack, so Watts cancelled 24th Division's plans.

XVIII Corps
Lieutenant General Maxse's left was still in a strong position along the Somme but his right flank had a deep re-entrant in it, where the Germans were pushing south of Ham.

<u>20th (Light) and 61st (2nd South Midland) Divisions, Along the Somme Canal</u>
The 2nd Scottish Rifles stopped the Germans scrambling over the damaged bridge at Voyennes while the 12th Rifle Brigade and the 12th KRRC stopped more crossing at Offoy. However, Major General Douglas Smith's flanks were under threat because the enemy were over the canal in 24th Division's sector, north of 59 Brigade, and they were at Grécourt behind 60 Brigade's right.

More crossed the canal on rafts and boats, overrunning the 11th Rifle Brigade on 20th Division's left flank. Brigadier Generals Hyslop and Duncan had to control a difficult withdrawal: 'the pursuing Germans came on in an imposing array, behind a line of skirmishers marched their infantry battalions in artillery formation and in the rear of these, all roads and paths were packed with transport.' They fell back behind the Canal du Nord where Lieutenant Colonel Wetherall was waiting with 184 Brigade.

Brigadier General Coffin VC marched 25 Brigade through Dreslincourt during the night because he thought 61st Division was going to occupy it. However, 183 Brigade came under fire from St Nicaise, so Brigadier General Spooner ordered his men to dig in around Mesnil instead. It left a gap in the line which the South Midland men failed to fill.

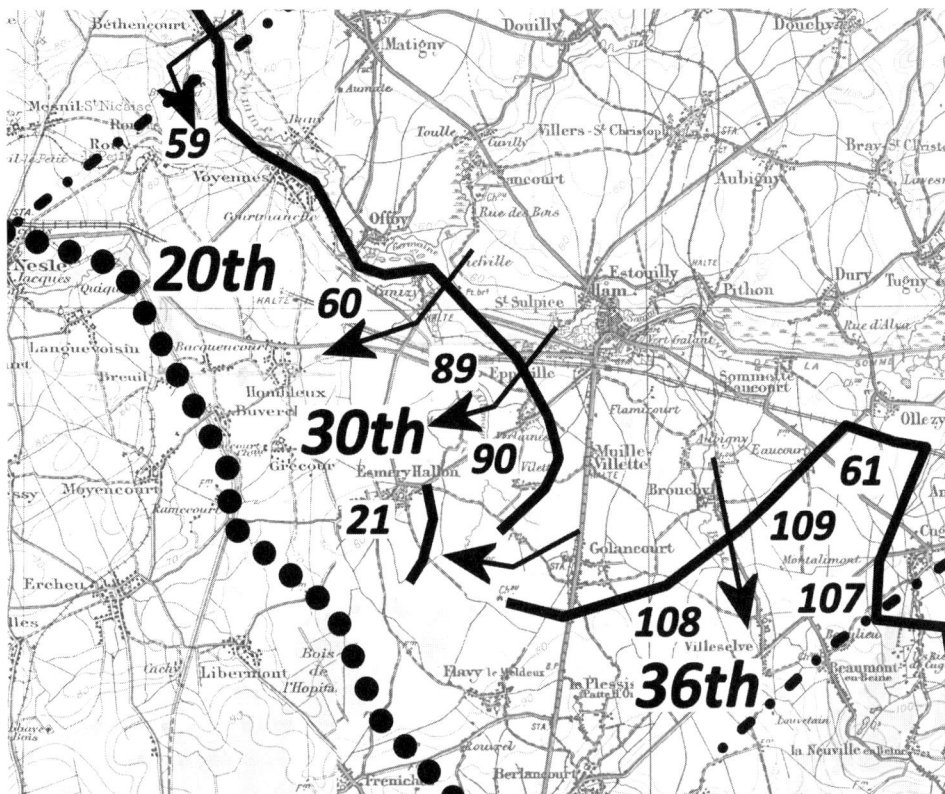

24 March: XVIII Corps' line disintegrated before the French were ready to meet the German onslaught.

30th Division, West of the Ham Bridgehead

The Germans used pontoons and boats to cross the Somme around Canizy and Eppeville, on 89 Brigade's front, in the mist. They rushed the 23rd Entrenching Battalion, the 11th South Lancashires and the 1/5th DCLI and they all fell back south-west across the Canal du Nord. During the retirement, Corporal John Davies stood firing on the parapet to keep the Germans' heads down while the 11th South Lancashires escaped across a stream. He would be awarded the Victoria Cross.

Lieutenant Colonel Poyntz was holding the west side of the Ham re-entrant with 90 Brigade. Major General Williams did not know the Germans had advanced two miles from the canal until the 2nd Bedfords' patrols encountered them at Golancourt in the morning mist. The Germans then forced the 2nd Bedfords and 2nd Scots Fusiliers to rally back on the 17th Manchesters and Captain Green's 2nd Green Howards around Esmery-Hallon. Further attacks forced both 90 and 21 Brigade to retire across the Canal du Nord near Moyencourt. There they deployed between 20th Division and the French.

36th (Ulster) Division, the Brouchy and Cugny Salient
Major General Nugent's men were south-east of Ham in 'two thin lines of men, literally back to back, with one mile between them'. They had been in action for seventy-two hours and while they were supported by British cavalry and French infantry, they had little artillery. The Germans spent the early hours reorganising and probing 36th Division's line in the mist. Unfortunately, the parties of 14th Division holding the east side of the salient with the Ulstermen withdrew after being told they were being relieved by the French.

The 7th DCLI and 7th Somersets withdrew from the railway but the Germans were close behind and the salient 'suddenly caved. From all sides the semi-circle fell back...' as both 109 and 108 Brigades fell back onto the French. 'The whole line was being driven back... There was much confusion, as it appeared at the time that a general rout was on.' Captain Thompson was killed as the 2nd Irish Rifles and some of the 12th King's fought on, unaware everyone else was retiring. The order to leave never reached them and it was too late by the time they realised they were cut off. Captain Bryans decided to make a stand near Cugny and when the final attack came 'many had only their bayonets left. Rather than wait for the end, they jumped from their entrenchments and met it gallantly. It was an unforgettable sight.' Over one hundred died in the frenzied hand-to-hand struggle before the rest were overpowered.

3rd Cavalry Division, Counter-attack from Collézy to the Forêt de Beine
Major General Harman's Detachment was south of Villeselve when they heard 36th Division was being driven back so Lieutenant Colonel Paterson was instructed to disrupt the German advance. He took 150 troopers of the 6 Cavalry Brigade to Collézy and then charged along three miles of the German line. Major Watkins Williams led the 'brilliant mounted charge which broke through the German line, taking over one hundred prisoners and sabering a large number of the enemy'. Seventy-three troopers had fallen by the time they rallied in the Forêt de Beine.

The sight of the cavalry cantering along the line restored the Ulstermen's confidence and they 'followed up the charge, cheering'. But the Germans soon recovered and both 108 and 109 Brigades fell back to Buchoire and Guiscard, becoming entangled with French units marching west to east. It would take Major General Nugent until midnight to re-establish control.

III Corps and the French
The Germans advanced out of the Bois de Frières in the dawn mist, and the French soon ran out of ammunition. They were soon falling back, 'and the two lines, relievers and relieved, had been rolled back before noon'.

18th (Eastern) Division, In Reserve
Major General Lee's men were dug in along the ridge between Beaugies and Caillouel, thinking they were three miles behind the French. They soon found themselves in the front line following a general withdrawal.

58th (2/1st) Division, Astride the Oise
The London men were separated from the rest of III Corps and they became even more isolated when the French fell back north of the Oise Canal, abandoning Chauny. Both the 2/4th London Regiment and the 1/4th Suffolk abandoned Condren and withdrew across the river when they ran low on ammunition. Major General Cator then instructed the engineers to blow up the bridges.

The survivors of 173 Brigade reorganised under Lieutenant Colonel Dann and then fell back through Chauny with the 6th Dismounted Brigade and the French. They would cross the Oise canal at Abbécourt and rejoin the rest of the division. The 175 and 174 Brigades formed a defensive flank around the Forêt de Coucy. Eighteenth Army would now ignore 58th Division, using the Oise to protect its flank.

Fifth Army's Summary
Haig sent his chief of staff, General Lawrence, on a tour of the front and his first impression was that Gough was being ambiguous about the situation on his right flank. So he visited General Fayolle and they agreed that Fifth Army would pass to French control. He then headed north to see Watts and heard that XIX Corps' position along the Somme was secure. However, Congreve's VII Corps was disintegrating as it fell back along the north bank of the Somme. Byng was Lawrence's last stop and they agreed VII Corps should come under Third Army's command, placing the army boundary along the Somme.

Lawrence returned to report that Third Army's left was safe and its right was falling back across the 1916 battlefield. Gough was reliant on French help but Pétain seriously doubted that Fifth Army would be able to hold on long enough to allow his divisions to deploy, while he was against sending

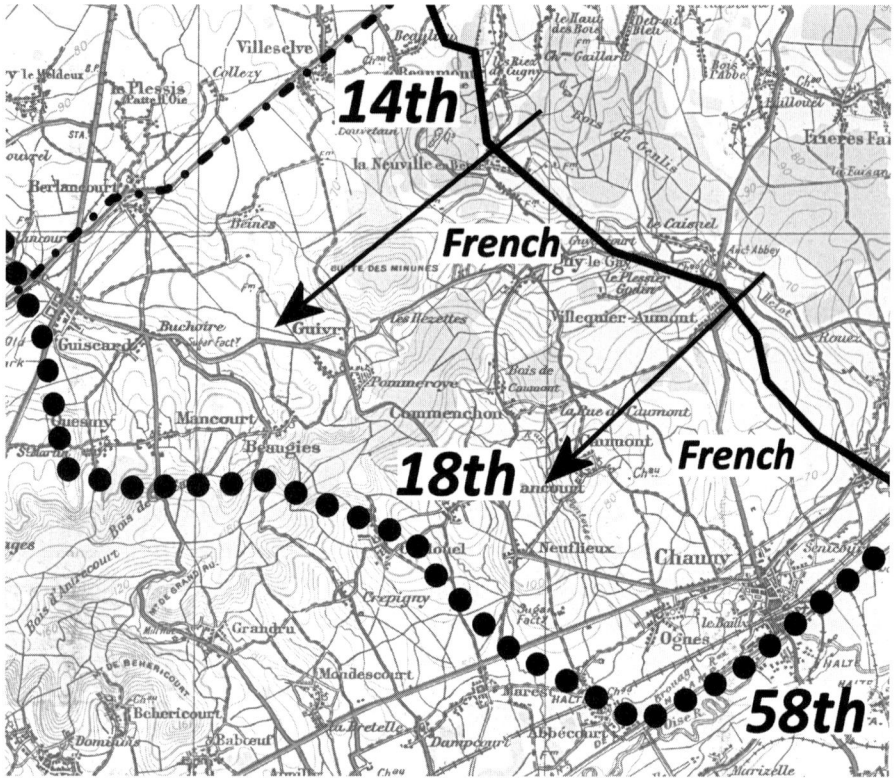

24 March: There was little left of III Corps to help the French hold the line north of the Oise.

them into the line one at a time. He had even instructed Fayolle to withdraw all his French troops in a south-west direction if Fifth Army collapsed.

The Second Army had been stopped along the Somme Canal but Eighteenth Army was across the waterway. It 'had become the spearhead, from which even still greater successes were expected, instead of carrying out its original task of protecting the left flank of the Michael attack'.

Chapter 12

At the Mercy of Rumours

Third Army, 25 March

Byng's left was secure but IV Corps had withdrawn up to five miles while V Corps had fallen back by double that distance. The line had gaps in it and the men were short of everything apart from rumours. Byng ordered a retirement from the 1916 battlefield during the evening so the Germans would have to deal with the maze of craters, trenches and entanglements behind their lines. While IV Corps headed back to the old British front line, V Corps would aim to cross the River Ancre. The problem was, Third Army had to withdraw from contact, often with insufficient notice. The men then faced a nightmare march along busy roads, lashed by hail and sleet, while fires lit the night sky.

Major General John Salmond wanted the Royal Air Force to give its maximum support so he handed over one hundred planes from GHQ and First Army to help Third Army. The pilots had instructions 'to bomb and shoot up everything they can see on the enemy's-side of the line. Very low flying is essential. All risks to be taken.' They would swoop low over the battlefield shooting at targets, only returning to their airfield for more ammunition. It was dangerous work and there would be many casualties.

VI Corps

31st Division, St Léger to Ervillers

To Brigadier General Lord Ardee's annoyance all attempts to widen the gap in the line north-east of Ervillers were stopped by accurate artillery. 'So successful indeed were the gunners that the 4 Guards Brigade complained that the excellence of their shooting prevented the infantry from taking its full toll of the advancing Germans with its rifle and machine-gun fire.' A final attack against the 13th York and Lancasters and 15th West Yorkshires to the west of St Léger also failed.

42nd, 59th and 40th Divisions, Ervillers, Béhagnies and Sapignies

The 1/10th Manchesters stopped multiple attacks against 121 Brigade's front and Lance Corporal Arthur Cross, 40th Battalion, Machine Gun

Corps, recaptured two lost machine guns with just a pistol. He then made his prisoners carry them back and collected enough men to man the guns in time to stop the next big attack. Cross would be awarded the Victoria Cross.

The rest of the Manchesters had to throw their flank back as the 2/4th Leicesters, 2/5th and 4th Lincolns of 177 Brigade, 59th Division, fell back south of Ervillers. On 120 Brigade's front, both the 14th HLI and the 10/11th HLI were forced to retire towards Béhagnies. The 14th Argylls stopped the Germans reaching Sapignies but a company of the 12th East

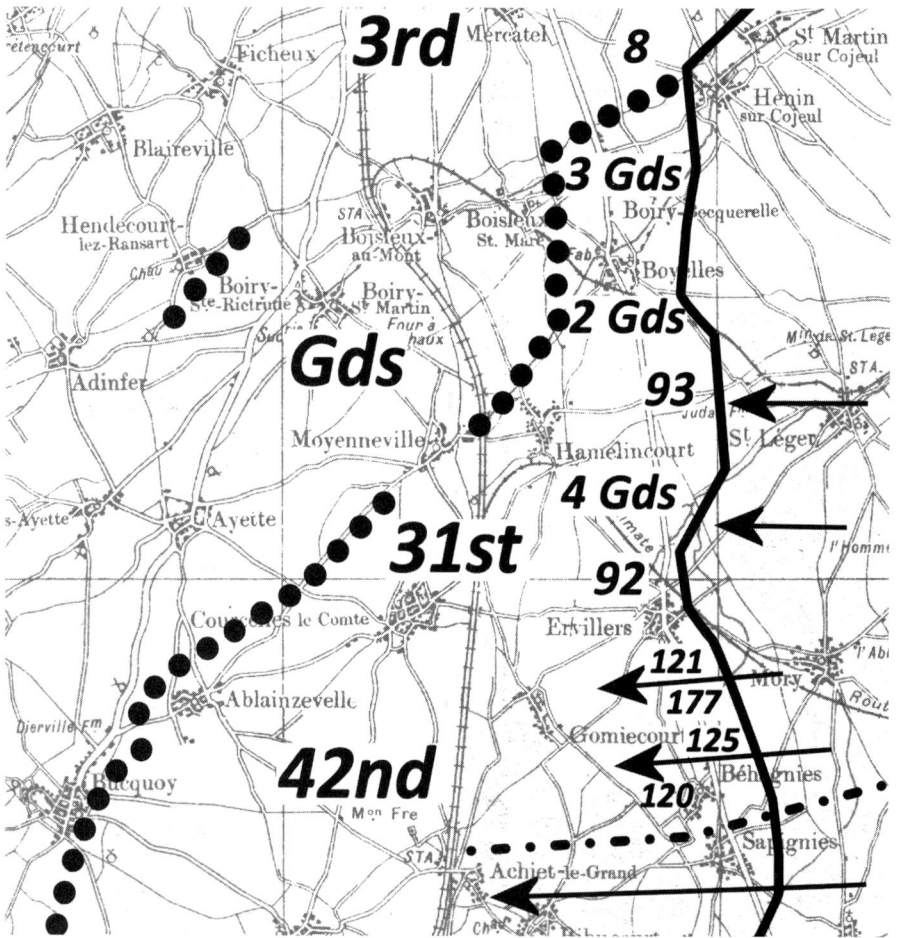

25 March: VI Corps right wheeled back to an old trench line, so the rest of Third Army could escape from the 1916 battlefield.

Surreys was overrun as the Germans pushed through the gap in IV Corps' line.

Brigadier General Fargus had secured the line around Béhagnies and Sapignies with three Lancashire Fusilier battalions. The Germans pushed past the flank of Lieutenant Colonel Holberton's 1/5th Lancashire Fusiliers' flank while Lieutenant Colonel Bird was wounded leading the 1/8th Lancashire Fusiliers in 'a dashing counter-attack'. But the Germans kept coming until Holberton made another counter-move. On the left, Lieutenant Colonel Brewis's 1/7th Lancashire Fusiliers 'had a very gruelling time, fighting many ding-dong battles.' All along the line junior officers and NCOs made sure their men fought on, sometimes 'practically surrounded and enfiladed'.

By the early afternoon the Germans had taken Béhagnies to their north and Bihucourt, two miles behind their south flank. The 1/7th and 1/8th Lancashire Fusiliers broke contact and assembled at Gomiécourt but Captains Gray and Tickler's companies of the 1/5th Lancashire Fusiliers were overrun. Major General Solly-Flood rushed his two brigades forward to reinforce the line and Brigadier General Seymour's 126 Brigade made a counter-attack to hold the line around Ervillers.

VI Corps Summary

After hearing about the loss of Béhagnies and Sapignies, Lieutenant General Haldane ordered 31st Division to throw back its right flank to Bucquoy. Major General Feilding also wheeled his right flank back behind the Cojeul stream, to Moyenneville. The exhausted men found plenty of food and ammunition in abandoned canteens and dumps before spending the night digging new trenches. All was going well until a shell-shocked staff officer told two of 93 Brigade's battalions to fall back to Hendecourt, resulting in a gap around Moyenneville.

However, 40th and 42nd Divisions had the furthest to go and some companies had to fight off the enemy before joining the chaotic withdrawal. Units were 'very scattered and communications between battalion headquarters and their companies broke down, so they were at the mercy of rumours of cancelled orders and reports of retirements on their flanks'.

IV Corps

Lieutenant General Harper was worried about the four-mile gap between Puisieux and Beaumont Hamel and he was waiting for 62nd Division to help extend his flank. Major General Walter Braithwaite's men were on their way: 'Packs dumped, ammunition issued and off the columns move in artillery formation to their various positions, laughing and joking like schoolboys. They stepped along cheerily to the tune of Colonel Bogey.' But they faced 'roads in a terrible state of confusion, blocked by all sorts of transport, and it was almost impossible to get along'.

<u>41st and 25th Division, North of Bapaume</u>
The thin line of men stayed 'dug in and held the enemy in large numbers' north of Bapaume throughout the morning. Eleven tanks helped to stem the tide for a time but the Germans were soon moving past their flanks, so everyone fell back towards Biefvillers. All along the line, commanders 'handled the withdrawal admirably, holding on tenaciously and inflicting heavy casualties on the enemy but not hanging on long enough to let the battalion be gripped'.

The Germans outflanked their line when 19th Division fell back from Grévillers to the south, so 41st and 25th Division had to withdraw through Bihucourt, compromising 40th Division's position north-east of the village. Brigadier General Henley's 127 Brigade and seven of 10th Battalion's tanks emerged from Achiet-le-Grand, to stop the enemy pushing beyond Bihucourt on the right flank.

<u>19th (Western) Division, Withdrawing from Grévillers to the Ancre</u>
Brigades were smaller than a company while battalions had just a few dozen men: for example 58 Brigade had only thirty-four officers and men while Lieutenant Colonel Smeathman had just eight men of the 9th Welsh under his command. The first attack against 57 and 58 Brigades failed and the German officers paraded one battalion 'in mass in full view but out of rifle range' so they could reprimand them. The British infantry could not contact the artillery in time to tell them about such a tempting target.

The next attack pushed past the 1/4th Shropshires' south flank and Brigadier General Glasgow's 58 Brigade followed them back. Brigadier General Cubbitt also allowed 57 Brigade to evacuate Grévillers because they had run out of ammunition. What was left of 19th Division fell back through 51st Division's line between Loupart Wood and Warlencourt while the 10th Warwicks formed a rearguard near Grevillers.

Soon afterwards, Major General Jeffreys heard that the Germans had reached Courcelette, some two miles to his south-west. He decided to head in the same direction and sent all the stragglers and details back to dig in along the Ancre between Achiet-le-Petit and Miraumont.

Both 56 and 58 Brigades crossed the river during the evening after a fight led by Lieutenant Colonel Sole and the 10th Worcesters near Loupart Wood. Eventually 57 Brigade and Major Croft's 6th SWBs (Pioneers) joined them after stopping the Germans advancing north of the wood. The pioneers were proving they 'could also be good infantry and could handle

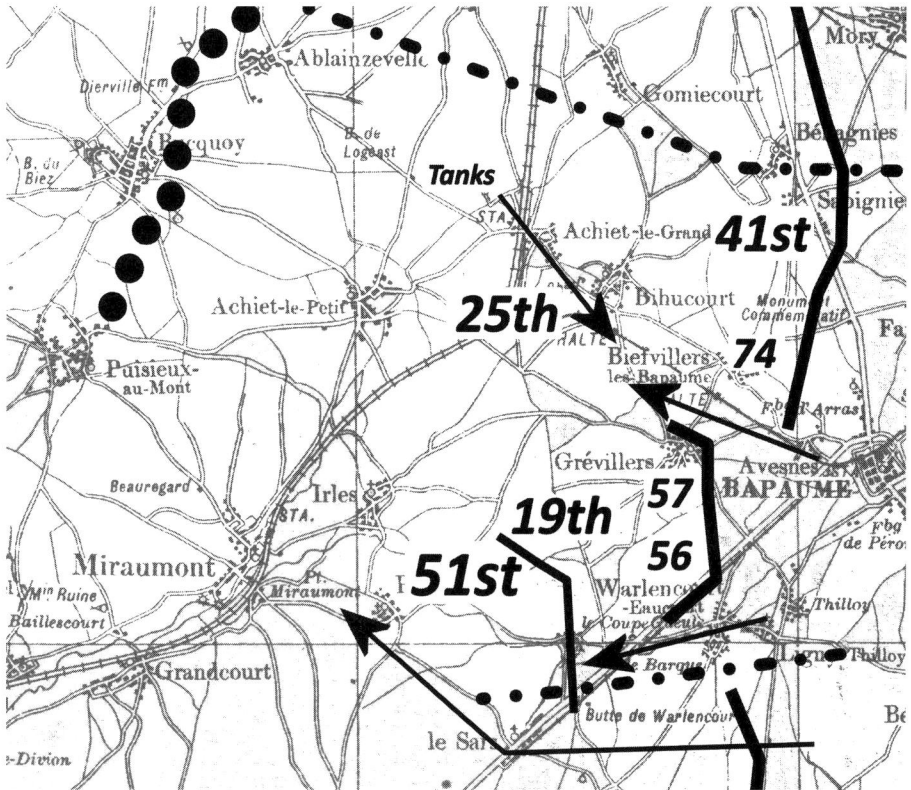

25 March IV Corps: The premature destruction of the Miraumont bridge meant IV Corps headed north-west to escape the 1916 battlefield.

a rifle and bayonet no less effectively than a pick, shovel or axe'. The whole division, or rather what was left of it, headed for Hébuterne during the night. Men were 'split into small parties, separated, lost, they plodded on, by chance in the same direction and then came together again'.

<u>51st (Highland) Division, An Escape through Irles and Across the Ancre</u>
Major General Carter-Campbell's men were in support between Loupart Wood and the Butte du Warlencourt 'when they heard a fresh division was coming up (joyous news) and we must hold on. This gave us fresh strength.' But the Scots saw 19th Division withdraw to the north and 2nd Division retiring to the south during the morning. The Germans discovered the gap on Brigadier General Buchanan's right by midday and they were soon moving past 154 Brigade, heading for Pys.

Brigadier Generals Beckwith and Burn had deployed everyone they could find in a shallow trench. They came under artillery and machine-gun fire and then 'like one man moved back' when the German infantry closed in. They were chased through Irles while a group of Royal Fusiliers from 2nd Division helped 154 Brigade hold back the Germans until the Scots escaped across the Ancre. While Carter-Campbell's men had escaped, casualties had been high; some of the 6th Seaforths were cut off and captured, Lieutenant Colonel Gemmel of the 8th Royal Scots was killed and Lieutenant Colonel Long of the 5th Gordons was wounded. It was estimated that only 1,500 out of 5,400 infantry had survived the gruelling five-day battle.

IV Corps Summary

The divisions had formed a new line by dusk and while 42nd Division wheeled its right back to Gomiécourt, 62nd Division extended the line south-west to Achiet-le-Grand. Harper also ordered 19th and 25th Divisions to form a defensive flank back to Puisieux.

Harper had been 'shaken by the plight of his old division, the 51st' and he wanted his tired divisions to withdraw and break contact. But 62nd Division was already withdrawing towards Bucquoy by the time his orders were sent out, while 42nd Division had to fight around Gomiécourt into the night before it could withdraw. Harper's main concern was his right flank where the premature demolition of the bridge at Miraumont had forced V Corps to cross the River Ancre at Beaucourt. It had left a three-mile gap between Bucquoy and Beaumont Hamel.

V Corps

Lieutenant General Fanshawe's men were tired after a long night marching across the old battlefield. Four battered divisions were deployed in a ragged line east of the Butte du Warlencourt, Eaucourt l'Abbaye, Martinpuich, High Wood and Bazentin-le-Petit. There was a shortage of ammunition until the brigade staff officers found dumps along the Albert road and they made sure it was distributed along the front line. Third Army's order to withdraw reached the divisions around 9.30 am and Lewis gun teams made the Germans 'shy of taking risks' as the infantry started another long march west.

2nd Division, Crossing the Ancre at Beaucourt

It took time to find 5 and 6 Brigades because they had withdrawn too far during the night, leaving the 10th DCLI (Pioneers) to cover the gap around le Barque. Major General Pereira had received the withdrawal order by the time he found them and he sent them to Pys and Courcelette to form a rearguard. Brigadier General Kellett could see IV Corps heading back on his north flank, so he ordered 99 Brigade to withdraw back through 6 and 5 Brigades, heading for Miraumont.

The 17th Royal Fusiliers had been chosen to cover the road through Pys and Brigadier General Buchanan told Lieutenant Colonel Weston to stay in his position until his 154 Brigade (51st Division) had escaped across the Ancre. He only had a few dozen men with him, so he recalled a company of the 2nd Royal Fusiliers to help him. Captain Aylmer and Second Lieutenant Panting helped him deploy around 200 men in shell holes and they soon faced the onslaught. 'They were gallant fellows those Germans but they were faced by men whose courage had been so often tried and not been found wanting.'

The few survivors fell back when they ran out of ammunition only to find the Miraumont bridge had already been blown up, so they headed west along a road 'full of officers and men from different units'. They all crossed the Ancre at Beaucourt, where staff officers were waiting to direct them onto the Beaumont Hamel ridge. It had been a close-run thing and 'the men were by now greatly exhausted; they could scarcely drag themselves along and the want of food and sleep added to their sufferings. The shortage of ammunition had become almost acute while the heavy losses sustained in officers made reorganisation difficult, though the NCOs worked grandly, and the men were not anywhere near out of control.' As Pereira toured his command he found that his brigadiers and staff 'were voiceless from the effects of gas and the intense fatigue they had undergone'.

63rd (Royal Naval) Division, Across the Ancre at Thiepval
Major General Lawrie saw 99 Brigade pulling back to Le Sars and then 47th Division fell back towards Contalmaison, so he too ordered a withdrawal. The Hawke and Drake Battalions lost heavily escaping from High Wood but Lieutenant Blackwell and sixty volunteers of the 4th Bedfords had stopped the enemy overrunning them, only leaving when they had no bullets left.

The 50, 188 and 189 Brigades assembled south of Courcelette, alongside 2nd Division, only to find there was no one in Pozières. So Lawrie ordered a second withdrawal to the old German trenches around Thiepval, as 2nd Division headed for Beaucourt on the Ancre.

Brigadier Hutchinson formed a rearguard and Lieutenant Colonel Kirkpartrick's Anson Battalion helped 190 Brigade keep the Germans at bay. As the skies grew dark the 7th Royal Fusiliers, 4th Bedfords and 1/28th London Regiment headed to the Ancre bridgeheads around Mesnil

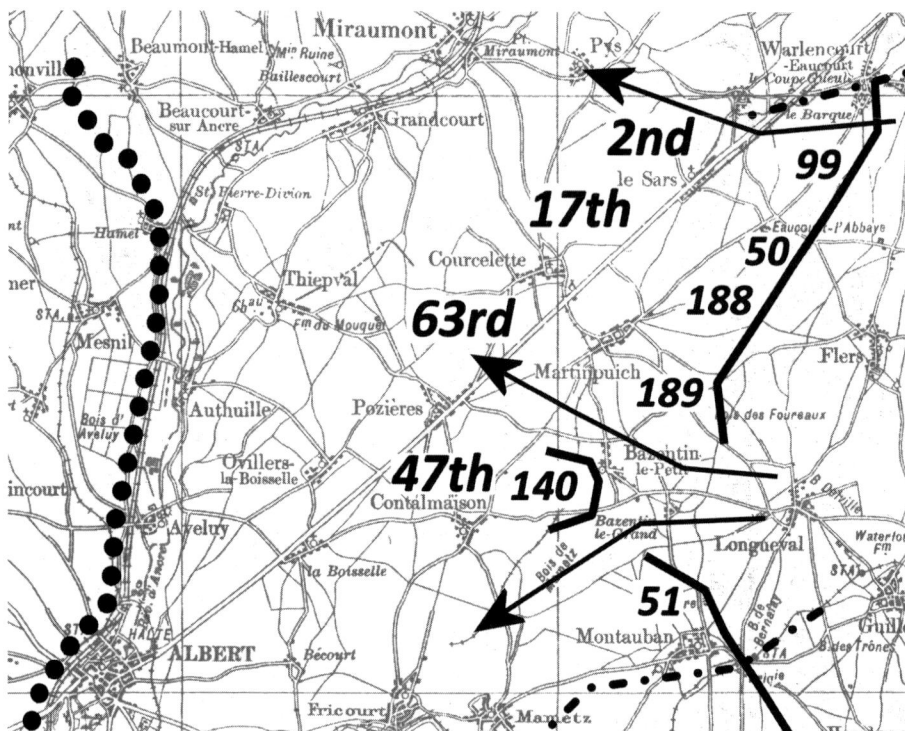

25 March V Corps: A rapid withdrawal left V Corps on the west bank of the Ancre but there was a huge gap on its left flank.

and Authuille. Major General Lawrie was able to report that he had lost contact with the enemy and while he was in touch with 2nd Division at Hamel, he had still not contacted 47th Division at Aveluy. Lieutenant Colonel Boraston recalled how the men referred to the rapid retreat as the 'Pys to Pas', Point to Point.

47th (2nd London) Division, Across the Ancre at Aveluy
At dawn Major General Gorringe told his brigadiers that they would defend La Boisselle with the few hundred Londoners still standing until 12th Division arrived. Only their column of buses was stuck in a traffic jam, 'all hurrying due west. Lorries filled with the luxurious furniture of a corps headquarters, troops without helmets or rifles, rumours of the most fantastic nature flapping from mouth to mouth like flames of fire…'

Brigadier General Kennedy could find no one on his flanks and decided 140 Brigade had to leave Bazentin wood before it was overrun. But the final company of 1/21st London suffered considerable casualties fighting its way back to Contalmaison. Gorringe had received the order to retire across the Ancre late and was about to leave when a column of men trudged up the Albert road to La Boisselle; 12th Division had arrived. They had marched over fifteen miles along roads 'crowded like Fulham Road after a football match', only to learn that 47th Division was about to withdraw. Gorringe asked them to counter-attack Pozières, so his men could leave, but patrols found no one. Both 47th Division and 12th Division then headed back to Albert to join the rest of V Corps.

17th (Northern) Division, Across the Ancre at Albert

Major General Robertson's command had splintered during the long retreat and while 50 Brigade had retired with 63rd Division, 52 Brigade was in reserve at Martinpuich. However, it was the 600 men of 51 Brigade covering the gap on V Corps' right who had the biggest problem. They came under attack around Bazentin-le-Grand when 9th Division retired from Montauban.

Brigadier General Bond prolonged 47th Division's right flank as far west as Fricourt Wood while Brigadier General Eden moved 52 Brigade west of Fricourt, in support. But they all headed for Albert when the Germans pushed through Mametz Wood. Major Cubbon collected around one thousand stragglers along the main Bapaume road, organised them into three battalions, and then marched them through Albert, where they found 12th Division digging in. Robertson's exhausted men withdrew into reserve after five days of fighting and twenty-five miles of marching.

V Corps Summary

For the second day running, General Fanshawe's V Corps had fought and then withdrawn a long distance across the 1916 battlefield before crossing the Ancre. Casualties had been heavy but the stragglers joined the first unit they saw and followed them. One officer recorded: 'What remains in my memory of this day is the constant taking up of new positions, followed by constant orders to retire, terrible blocks on the roads, an inability to find anyone anywhere; by exceeding good luck almost complete freedom from shelling, a complete absence of food of any kind except what could be picked up from abandoned dumps.'

But as Fanshawe's men began digging in, there was a rumour that enemy armoured cars had crossed the river. The sighting turned out to be some new Whippet tanks, a faster and more manoeuvrable model than the Mark IV. Few had seen one before because it was the first time they had been deployed.

VII Corps

Lieutenant General Watts was out of contact with V Corps on his left around Bazentin but his right flank was anchored along the River Somme.

9th (Scottish) and 35th Divisions, North of the Somme

Major General Franks of 35th Division controlled all of VII Corps' front and he had Brigadier General Kennedy's 26 Brigade from 9th Division and the 2nd and 9th Composite Cavalry Brigades covering Montauban on his left flank. Lieutenant Colonel Lawrenson reported the Germans were trying to force their way past the 8th Hussars but they held their position with the help of the 19th Northumberland Fusiliers (Pioneers).

The 18th HLI's line was overwhelmed and Captain Mower stopped the Germans while Major Gooderson rallied the stragglers until Lieutenant Colonel Stevens and the 19th Durhams counter-attacked south of Bernafay Wood. Lieutenant Colonel William Anderson rallied the 12th HLI after the

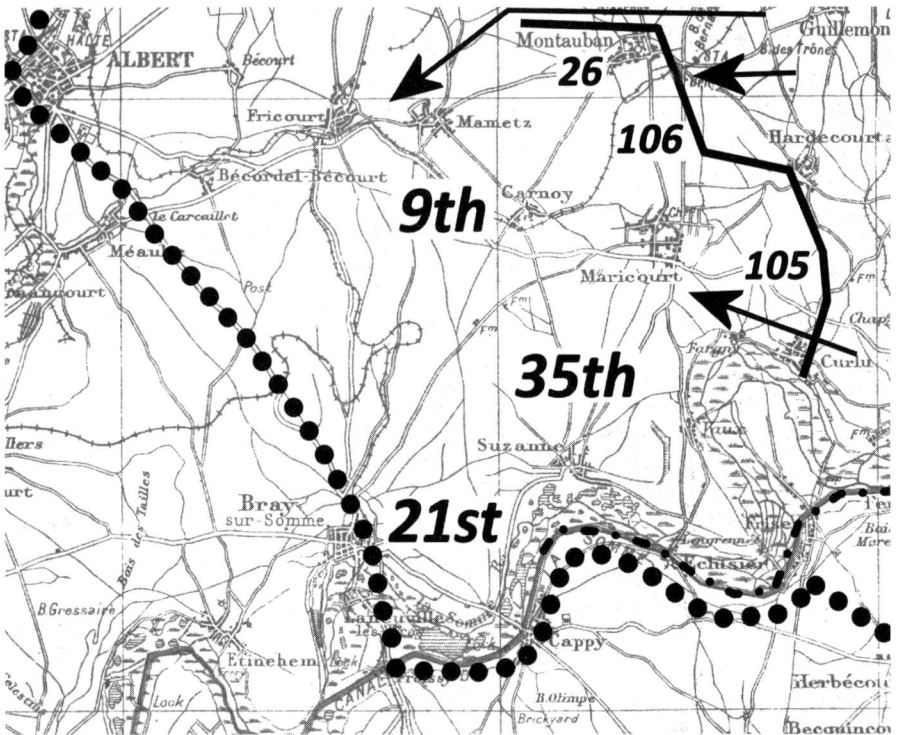

25 March: A crumbling VII Corps fell back quickly along the north bank of the Somme.

Germans captured part of Bois Favières and led a charge to restore the line. Both the 15th Sherwoods and the 15th Cheshires held on until the 17th Royal Scots were forced back from Curlu next to the Somme. Only then did 35th Division's line start to crumble because 'it appeared probable that the survivors of the front line would be overwhelmed by the sheer weight of numbers.'

By midday the Germans were closing in on Maricourt where the 17th and 18th Lancashire Fusiliers were involved in confused fighting in which there was a large 'amount of shouting amongst the German troops. It was remarked afterwards that it appeared as if they had all gone mad.' Both 105 Brigade and part of Hunt's Force fell back along the bank of the Somme until Brigadier General Marindin stopped the 'mob of retiring troops' and 'hastily organised and placed them in position'.

The brigade staff organized a counter-attack which stopped the Germans reaching Maricourt while Lieutenant Colonel William Anderson was 'quite fearless' as he was killed leading the 12th HLI through Maricourt Wood; he was posthumously awarded the Victoria Cross. By mid-afternoon Brigadier General Headlam of 64 Brigade had gathered around 1,500 men of 21st Division and deployed them north of the Somme.

The way to Amiens had been blocked but that evening Lieutenant General Congreve told Major General Franks to retire to a new position between Albert and Bray on the Somme. His men marched through the night, picking their way through 'the now familiar spectacle of hopeless congestion, civilian carts, guns, tanks, transport, wounded soldiers, civilians and leaderless men, all struggling westward.'

Chapter 13

They Came Back with their Tails Straight Up over their Heads

Fifth Army, 25 March

All three corps had been put under French control but General Watts continued to receive XIX Corps' orders from General Gough, so he could coordinate with Third Army across the Somme.

XIX Corps

Lieutenant General Watts had been holding the Somme for two days and the Germans were now ready to cross. VII Corps was several miles behind his left flank and XVIII Corps would withdraw on his right flank.

39th Division, Along the Somme West of Biaches

Major General Feetham's men lined out along the south bank of the Somme between Biaches and Frise. They shot at the German troops following up VII Corps across the river until they were ordered to withdraw.

16th (Irish) Division, Along the Somme

Major General Hull's original orders were to face north across the Somme to protect VII Corps' rear, on Third Army's right flank. Later in the day he was instructed to cross the river and face south, to cover XIX Corps' rear.

66th (2nd East Lancashire) Division, Along the Somme Facing Péronne

The 2/5th East Lancashires prevented the Germans leaving Péronne but the 2/5th and 2/7th Manchesters could not stop them crossing the La Chapelette railway bridge. They contacted their second bridgehead, south of the hamlet, so both 199 and 197 Brigades withdrew east onto 149 Brigade around Assevillers. The 1/1st Cambridge Regiment then formed the rearguard while 198 Brigade escaped to join the rest of the division.

25 March: Withdrawals to the north and south meant XIX Corps' left had to retire from the Somme.

8th Division, Withdrawal from the Somme astride the Amiens Road

Major General Heneker had gathered most of his men near Licourt, on his right, ready to drive the Germans back across the Somme, with the help of three Durham battalions of 50th Division. But the Germans had other ideas.

Brigadier General Grogan's 23 Brigade was stretched along the Somme and the enemy first crossed north of Éterpigny, pushing the

1/7th Durhams (Pioneers) back to Barleux. Twenty-year-old Captain Alfred Toye escaped with a handful of the 2nd Middlesex, counter-attacked with seventy of the Durhams and then held on along the river until the 2nd West Yorkshires arrived. Toye was wounded twice as the Middlesex fell back onto the 1/6th and 1/5th Northumberland Fusiliers but he had held the river line for most of the day; he would be awarded the Victoria Cross.

Lieutenant Colonel Page did not get the order to abandon the bridge at Brie and Captain Robertson continued firing his Vickers machine gun as the Germans advanced towards the 2nd Middlesex. Page eventually told his men to fire five rounds rapid and then escape down an old communication trench; many did not hear his instruction and they were captured.

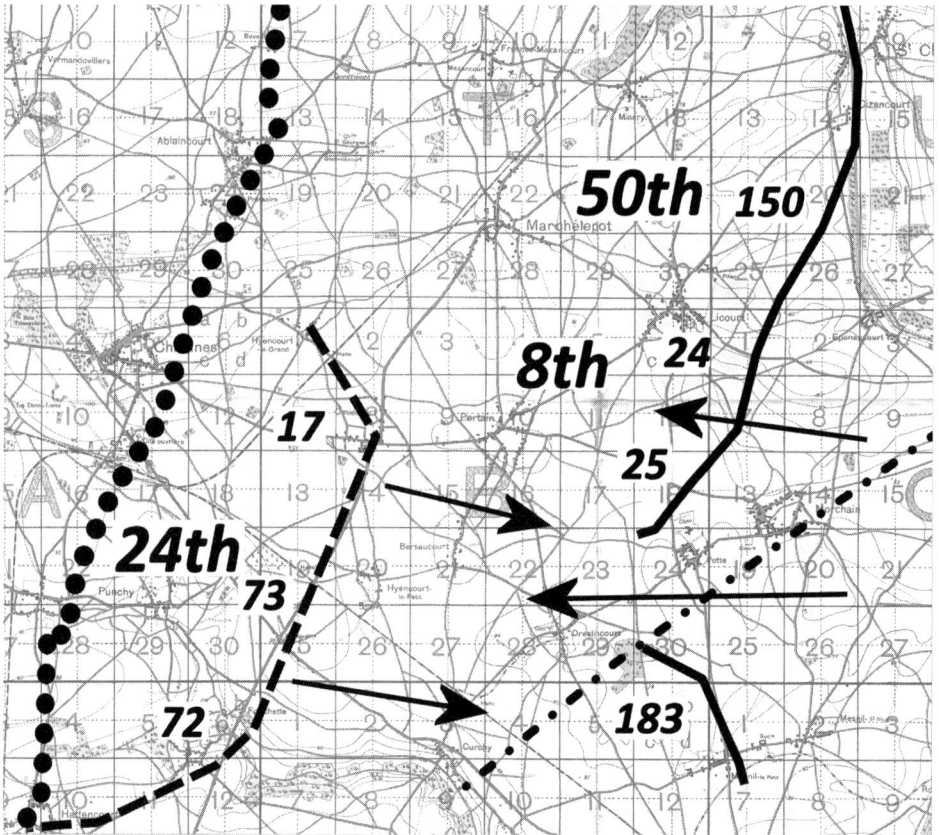

25 March: The Germans pushed past 8th Division's flank as XIX Corps abandoned the Somme.

Lieutenant Colonel Cope left one platoon behind to defend the bridge at Happlincourt as the rest of the 2nd Devons made a run for it. Captain Thuiller was killed leading a bayonet charge through the Germans in Misery but Lieutenant Tindal got the rest of the men to safety. It left the 1st Sherwoods at St Christ and their complaint was, 'had it not been written in the divisional orders that the line of the Somme will be held at all costs and there will be no retirement from it?' Lieutenant Colonel Moore made sure his men picked up their wounded and made a run for Marchélepot after realising the Germans were around his flanks. 'They came back with their tails straight up over their heads, but alas, with only half the number of effectives they started with.' On the right, the Germans had quickly driven 25 Brigade back to Pertain. The 2nd Rifle Brigade, 2nd East Lancashires and 22nd Durham Light Infantry fell back west onto 17 Brigade at Omiécourt.

The 4th West Yorkshires and 4th East Yorkshires had crossed the Somme at Licourt from 50th Division's front to join 25 Brigade's survivors. They were waiting for armoured cars to arrive when the Germans struck. Lieutenant Hepton's company was overrun and Licourt was lost so Lieutenant Colonel Thomson withdrew the rest of the 1/5th Green Howards. Lieutenant Colonel Wilkinson used stragglers from the 1/4th and 1/5th Green Howards to form a rearguard with his 1/8th Durhams in the running battle that followed.

The 1st Worcesters and the 2nd Northants fell back towards Misery where they were joined by the 1st Sherwood Foresters who had been clinging to the Somme around Cizancourt. They found 151 and 150 Brigades waiting but Brigadier General Haig gave instructions to withdraw because 'the flank was in the air, no orders had been received and repeated demands for ammunition had met no response.'

24th Division, Counter-attack towards Dreslincourt

Major General Daly's men advanced from Omiécourt and Fonchette, expecting the French to join them. However, the 8th Queen's and the 1st Royal Fusiliers found German troops deployed around Dreslincourt in the mist. Meanwhile, the 9th Sussex and 7th Northants came under fire from where the French should have been. Brigadier General Dugan sent a staff officer to find what the French intentions were and he returned with bad news: they were unable to help.

Eventually both 17 and 73 Brigades found the Germans around their flanks and Brigadier Generals Stone and Dugan were falling back when the retirement order came from XIX Corps. Daly's men also had to withdraw to cover Chaulnes and Hallu.

XVIII Corps

Lieutenant General Maxse had a mixture of British and French troops, some covering Nesle and others lined out along the Canal du Nord.

20th (Light) and 61st (2nd South Midland) Divisions, Canal du Nord

Major General Douglas Smith's men held the canal between Quiquery and Breuil, with their left flank in the air. Brigadier General Spooner galloped across to find 183 Brigade, hoping they could cover the gap opening around Mesnil-le-Petit on his left flank. But the Germans had already pushed through and were heading for Dreslincourt. Only rapid action by Captain Paulin and some of the 9th Royal Scots stopped the Germans going any further. Many of the Scots were captured but the rest fell back onto the French troops covering Nesle.

Elsewhere the Germans had been probing the canal position. They shelled it, sprayed it with machine gun fire and then tried to cross. Both 60 and 184 Brigades drove them back with rifle and Lewis gun fire. Observers later noticed infantry massing for another attack so the artillery were notified and they scattered them.

Brigadier General Wetherall of 184 Brigade was wounded during the exchange of fire and Lieutenant Colonel Lawson's first order was to withdraw from the canal at dusk along a road 'indescribably congested with troops, guns, limbers and wagons'. The highlight of the day was when 2/5th Gloucester found a large stock of good champagne. The merry soldiers dug in between Billancourt and Cressy only to be told to march through the night to Roye, to break contact.

30th Division, Canal du Nord

The French on Major General Williams' right withdrew from the canal into the Bois Hospital when German cavalry approached. Lieutenant Colonel Carus-Wilson was killed leading a company of the 1/5th DCLI, 61st Division's pioneers, which helped the 2/6th Warwicks defend the Buverchy bridge. Their last stand allowed 30th Division to escape to Roye, seven miles to the west.

XVIII Corps Summary

Two French divisions had been asked to cover XVIII Corps' position but they only had half their guns. The infantry had little ammunition and so they kept retiring whenever the Germans appeared, abandoning the high ground between Roye and Noyon. They had hoped they could break contact during the hours of darkness but the Germans followed by moonlight. They were all moving in a south-west direction, increasing the gap between the

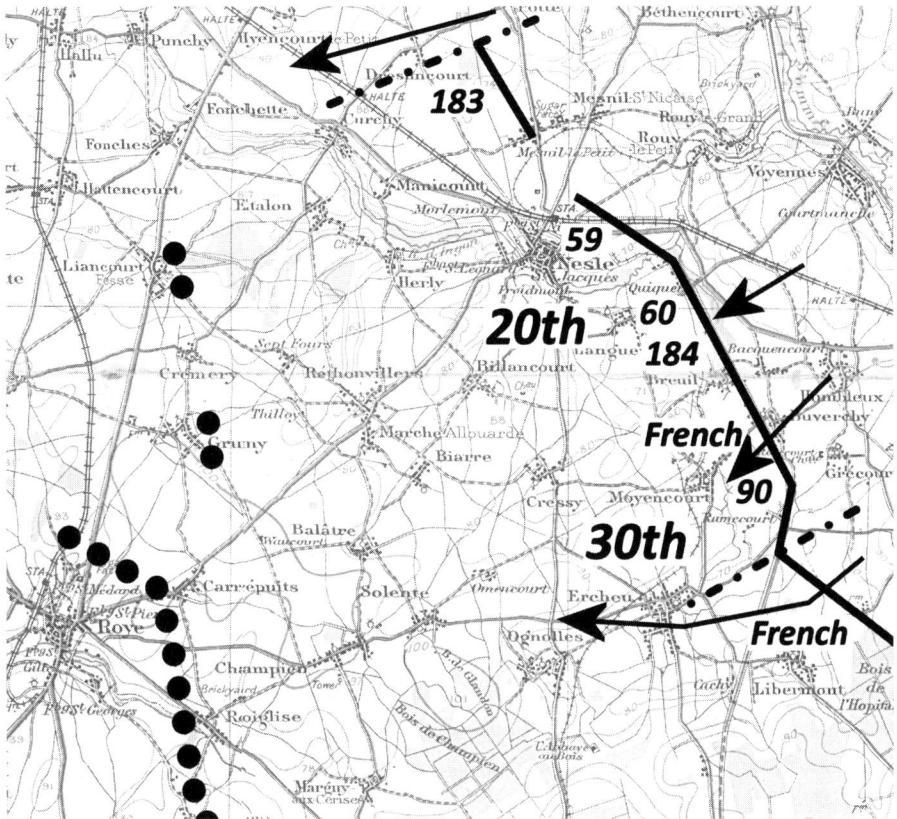

25 March: XVIII Corps had to abandon the Canal du Nord when the French fell back.

French and the British. They marched along roads 'filled with a solid mass of exhausted and retreating troops and reached Roye before dawn'. The four divisions had less than 1,000 rifles each while their artillery was supporting the French.

III Corps

Lieutenant General Butler's command had disintegrated and all that was left were scattered groups of tired infantry and gunners helping the French. French reinforcements continued to reach the area north of the Oise but they had little ammunition and found it difficult to arrange artillery support with the British gunners. They were soon falling back across Canal du Nord to the west or Oise Canal to the south. The uncoordinated withdrawal resulted in a large gap in the French line and the Germans passed through it to capture Noyon, at the junction of the two canals.

2nd Cavalry Division, Noyon and the Canal de l'Oise

Major General Harman's Detachment started the day in reserve behind the French troops facing Guiscard. They soon found themselves under fire as the French withdrew to the Canal du Nord at Noyon. Meanwhile, Brigadier General Pitman had deployed one thousand dismounted troops along the Canal de l'Oise, east of Noyon.

14th (Light) Division, Canal du Nord

Major General Greenly withdrew his men across the Canal du Nord at Beaurains only for the French to follow them with the Germans in hot pursuit. The battered division was withdrawn into reserve after dusk.

18th (Eastern) Division, Bois d'Autrecourt

Major General Lee organised a withdrawal from the east side of Bois d'Autrecourt across the River Oise. Brigadier General Sadleir-Jackson organised a counter-attack to stop the Germans following and the 7th Bedfords and 11th Royal Fusiliers captured over 200 prisoners in Baboeuf 'with surprising ease because the Germans were reaching the end of their tether'. Sadleir-Jackson's men escaped across the Oise via the ruined bridge at Varesnes after the French had hauled away their guns.

Fifth Army's Summary

Third Army was four miles behind XIX Corps' left flank along the river and there was another four-mile gap to the French on the right. Lieutenant General Watts wanted his divisional commanders to hold on but they were allowed to fall back if they felt they were in danger. Anyone who saw the soldiers could see that they were nearing the end of their endurance:

> *Men's faces were deeply marked by overwhelming fatigue and lack of sleep. Some moved in a sort of trance, stumbling forwards, oblivious to their surroundings; in some cases their boots had given out. Many company officers dispensed with the regulation halts because they found it almost impossible to get their men on their feet again after them. They lay like logs and had to be violently shaken before they could be recalled to consciousness.*

The civilians were suffering too during the rainy night: 'here and there a woman sobbed, a man cursed his chance. Their big wains would be piled high with their household possessions, with perhaps the old grandmother holding the youngest baby, perched perilously on top. The children trudged mile after mile at the cart trail or driving the cattle which became mixed up in the British transport.'

The Chief of the Imperial General Staff, General Henry Wilson, visited GHQ to learn that the half-dozen French divisions interspersed along Fifth Army's line were short of ammunition and relying on British artillery. Haig wanted Wilson to ask the French for more help before the Germans broke through. Later that day Haig met Prime Minister Clémenceau, Lord Milner and General Maxine Weygand, Foch's Chief of the Staff, at Abbeville and he again asked for French help.

Yet again, everything was not going to plan for the Germans. There had been less progress against the British while the French had fallen back further than expected. General von Kuhl was told to keep forcing the British back while planning to launch Operation Mars towards Arras on 28 March. Operation Valkyrie, an attack towards the Lorette ridge, would be made the following day. However, the plan to attack across the Lys would be scaled down and maybe even dropped if everything else went to plan. The name was also changed from Operation George to Operation Georgette.

Chapter 14

Everyone Agreed, it had been a Top-Hole Day

Third Army, 26 March
Byng warned his corps commanders to withdraw if the Germans pushed through the gap at Puiseux. The left flank would be anchored on XVII Corps around Arras while the rest fell back to a new trench line which was being prepared. It meant that reinforcements could reach the gap before the Germans pushed any further through it. The Cavalry Corps was positioned ready to cover VII Corps right flank along the Somme.

VI Corps
Guards Division
The Germans had slowly pushed men through Boiry-Becquerelle and Boyelles and were preparing to attack 2 Guard Brigade when Major General Feilding asked Haldane to move some heavy artillery batteries forward. An intense bombardment of the area dispersed the enemy.

31st Division, Moyenneville
Major General Bridgford discovered the gap in the line at Moyenneville at dawn. Lieutenant Colonel Taylor extended the left of the 15th West Yorkshires as far as he dared with the help of a company of the 2nd Irish Guards while the 13th York and Lancasters and 18th Durhams marched forward. But they found the enemy had reached Moyenneville first. The village was captured and Sergeant Albert Mountain's group of West Yorkshiremen stopped around 200 of the enemy re-entering it. He then rallied his men and held off another 600 while his company withdrew from Moyenneville. Mountain's surrounded group then held on for another twenty-four hours; he would be awarded the Victoria Cross.

IV Corps
The effects of the early demolition of the bridge at Miraumont were still being felt along IV Corps' line. It had pushed Lieutenant General Harper's

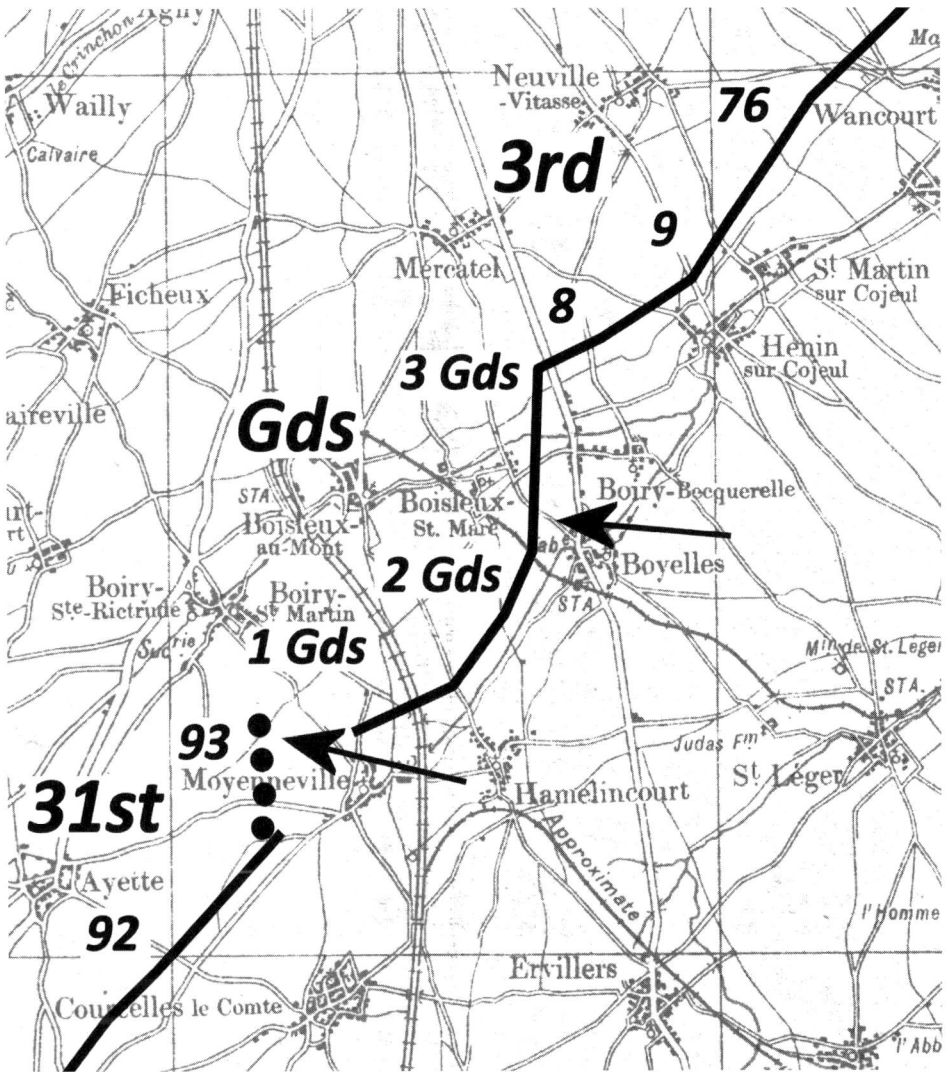

26 March: VI Corps' line was steady and being reinforced, except where a mistake had left Moyenneville unguarded.

men north-west to Bucquoy and Hébuterne, leaving a four-mile gap around Puisieux and Serre on the right flank. Harper decided against telling his subordinates about Byng's early morning warning order in case it unsettled them. He was anxious to hold on to Bucquoy until the 4th Australian Division and New Zealand Division arrived.

42nd (East Lancashire) Division, East of Bucquoy
Major General Solly-Flood's men covered the line between Ablainzevelle and Bucquoy.

62nd (2nd West Riding) Division, South West of Bucquoy
Several prisoners were taken during the night and they 'were well clothed, well fed and most optimistic; quite certain that the war was now over and that they had won. Unfortunately, there happened to be someone even more optimistic than he was – the Yorkshireman!'

Major General Braithwaite's men were digging in between Bucquoy and Rossignol Wood (Nightingale Wood) when waves of Germans advanced towards them through the mist. Lieutenant Colonels Waddy and James made sure the 2/5th and 8th West Yorkshires stopped them and one German account said, 'the name Bucquoy brings painful remembrances.' It was a painful day for the 8th West Yorkshires too because James was killed. The 2/7th and 2/5th Dukes held on with the help of Major Wilson's 1/9th Durhams (Pioneers) until Lieutenant Colonels Thackeray and Walker saw the enemy moving past their flank.

Braithwaite welcomed the huge commandant of the Machine Gun School, Lieutenant Colonel Edmund 'Tiny' Ironside: 'Have you any use for one hundred of the best machine gunners in the world?' The reply was, 'Have I not!' They reinforced Lieutenant Colonel Blacker's 2/4th York and Lancasters and stopped the attacks on Rossignol Wood with the help of eleven tanks of 10th Battalion.

> *It was amazing to see how cheerful all ranks were in this time of strain, partly because they knew what depended on them sticking and partly because they could see the damage they were doing. But mainly because of the sporting spirit in them; the more difficult and desperate the circumstance, the more cheery and self-reliant they became.*

The Rumours about Hébuterne
As usual there were 'the never ceasing rumours of an alarming nature; rumours which as a rule, turned out to be false or a too intelligent anticipation of events.' The rumours increased the traffic on the roads as refugees and soldiers tried to squeeze pass each other. One report said, 'the road was greatly congested while the inhabitants of Bienvillers were now in flight, having heard a rumour that the enemy had broken through at Hébuterne with cavalry and armoured cars.'

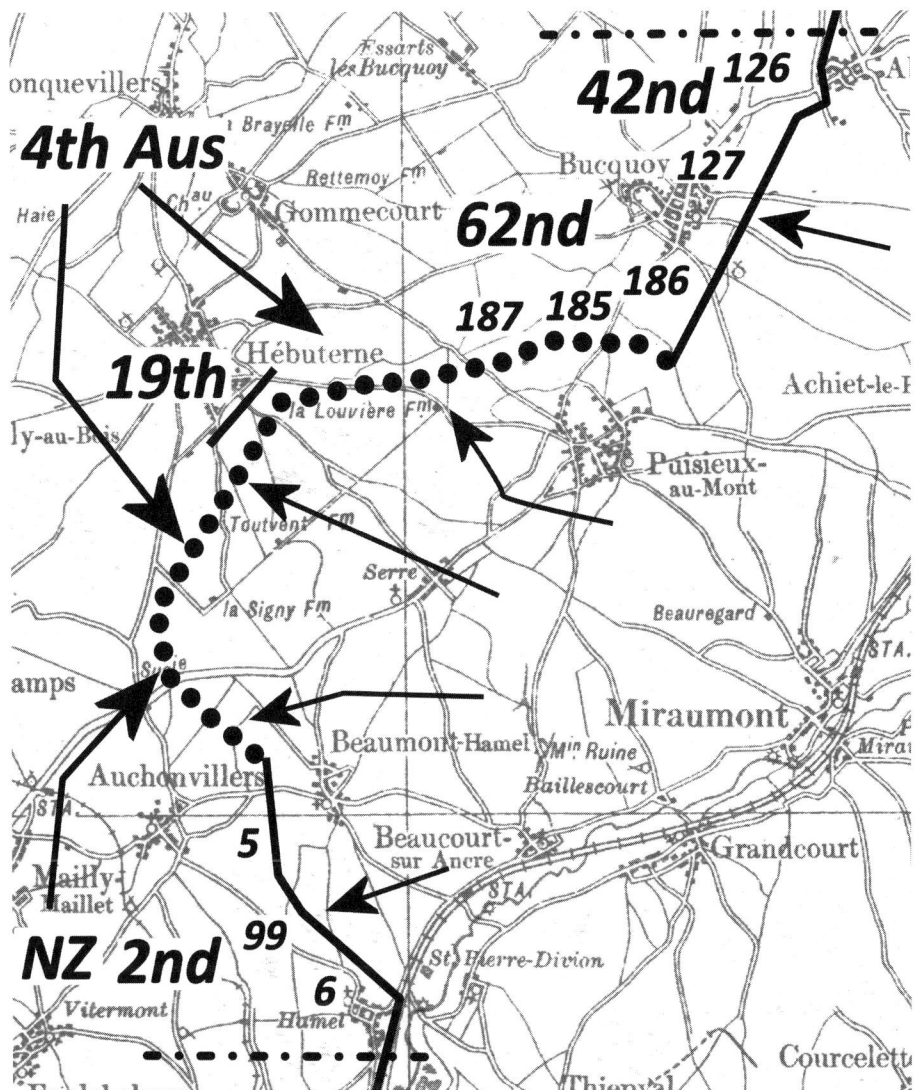

26 March IV Corps: The arrival of 4th Australian Division and the New Zealand Division covered the gap between Hébuterne and Beaumont Hamel.

A staff officer of IV Corps then called 25th Division headquarters to say the Germans were in Hébuterne and it had to abandon Foncquevillers; he was wrong. General Haldane sent out staff officers to check the situation while Lieutenant Colonel Occleston deployed IV Corps' reinforcements to sort out the traffic. Major General Bridgford was also instructed to deploy his men to collect and organize all the stragglers.

19th (Western) and 4th Australian Divisions, Hébuterne

Early in the morning Major General Jeffreys and his staff trotted to the east side of Hébuterne, 'only to turn about and gallop back as they had ridden right into a party of the enemy'. Brigadier General Willan rounded up 250 men of 56 Brigade and they 'fixed bayonets and doubled in fours down the main streets.' The Germans fled at the sight of Lieutenant Colonel Bowen's men.

After hearing German armoured cars were moving forward, the message was flashed to 4th Australian Division to 'do your utmost to block the roads'. Lieutenant Colonel Murray ambushed what turned out to be the French Agricultural Corps driving their tractors and ploughs to the rear. Again a cavalry patrol had spotted some of the new Whippet tanks and reported them as German tanks, starting a confusing chain of messages. The reported enemy cavalry turned out to be mounted patrols checking out the British line.

Meanwhile, patrols led by Brigadier Generals Glasgow and Cubitt returned having seen enemy troops moving west from Serre. The brigade battalions were in the process of driving them out of the village when they were 'unexpectedly relieved by a battalion of Australians who marched up boldly in fours'. The 4th Australian Division had arrived.

Lieutenant General Harper had told Major General Ewen Sinclair-Maclagan to occupy the high ground near Hébuterne, behind IV Corps line. By dusk, 4 Australian Brigade was digging in and Brigadier General Brand's officer patrols reported that the rumours of a breakthrough were false; the village was still in British hands. Brand reported the news with the words, 'I have just ridden through the place we are to attack.' The Australians relieved 500 of 19th Division's exhausted men during the night; some 'broke down and wept when they learned that they were to be at last relieved'. They had been fighting and marching for five days without a break.

V Corps

The withdrawal had placed V Corps behind the Ancre between Hamel and Albert but the men had no trenches, no wire and no tools. They only had the ammunition they carried and were short of grenades and flares. The bridges over the Ancre were still standing and under fire, so the engineers could not reach them, even if they had explosives to blow them up. Meanwhile, the Germans could see what the British were doing across the valley and were using the old trenches to get to the river.

2nd Division, Hawthorn Ridge

Major General Pereira was forming a defensive flank on the high ground facing Beaumont Hamel. Lieutenant Colonel Pipon had just taken over from Brigadier General Bullen-Smith in command of 5 Brigade but the 24th Royal Fusiliers and the 2nd HLI had a huge four-mile gap on their left and the Germans were approaching Serre in the centre. Lieutenant Colonel Smith was relieved to welcome Lieutenant Colonel Stewart and told him to deploy the men of the New Zealand Rifles around his position, anchoring 2nd Division's open flank; it meant the New Zealand Division was near.

An attack from Beaucourt hit Lieutenant Colonel Winter's 99 Brigade but 'the position was splendid and ample small arms ammunition had now begun to arrive. The general outlook was very hopeful and "hang on" was the idea and kill the Boche… Some very fine sport occurred in Y Ravine.' The Germans also tried to push 6 Brigade back north of Hamel but 'time and again the German advance was brought to a standstill by a handful of resolute men. Even at the end of it all, when at last there was to be no more retiring, everyone agreed it had been a top-hole day. The one aim and object of all was to capture, kill or maim the enemy.'

The New Zealand Division Closing the Gap between Hébuterne and Beaumont Hamel

Byng had given Major General Sir Andrew Russell orders to close the gap in Third Army's line. The New Zealanders dumped their greatcoats and packs, filled their pockets with ammunition and marched ten miles through the night to the sound of guns. The plan was for Lieutenant Colonel Stewart's 3rd New Zealand Rifle Brigade to cover the gap between Hébuterne and Beaumont Hamel, so 1st and 2nd New Zealand Brigades could deploy and advance towards Puisieux.

The 1st New Zealand Rifles engaged the Germans around Lone Tree Hill, north of Auchonvillers, while Stewart made contact with Lieutenant Colonel Pipon, who was in command of 2nd Division's left flank. A battery of 2nd Division's field guns galloped into action and fourteen Whippet tanks of 3rd Tank Battalion drove out of Colincamps when the Germans tried to outflank the New Zealanders. Around 300 ran, while the rest surrendered. The crisis had passed and the two Canterbury Battalions cleared the ground north of Auchonvillers.

Major General Russell reported V Corps' flank was secure and he had relieved what remained of 2nd Division. His own men needed a rest after fighting and marching for thirty-six hours but there was still work to be done. The 3rd Rifles, the 2nd Otago Battalion and 2nd Wellington

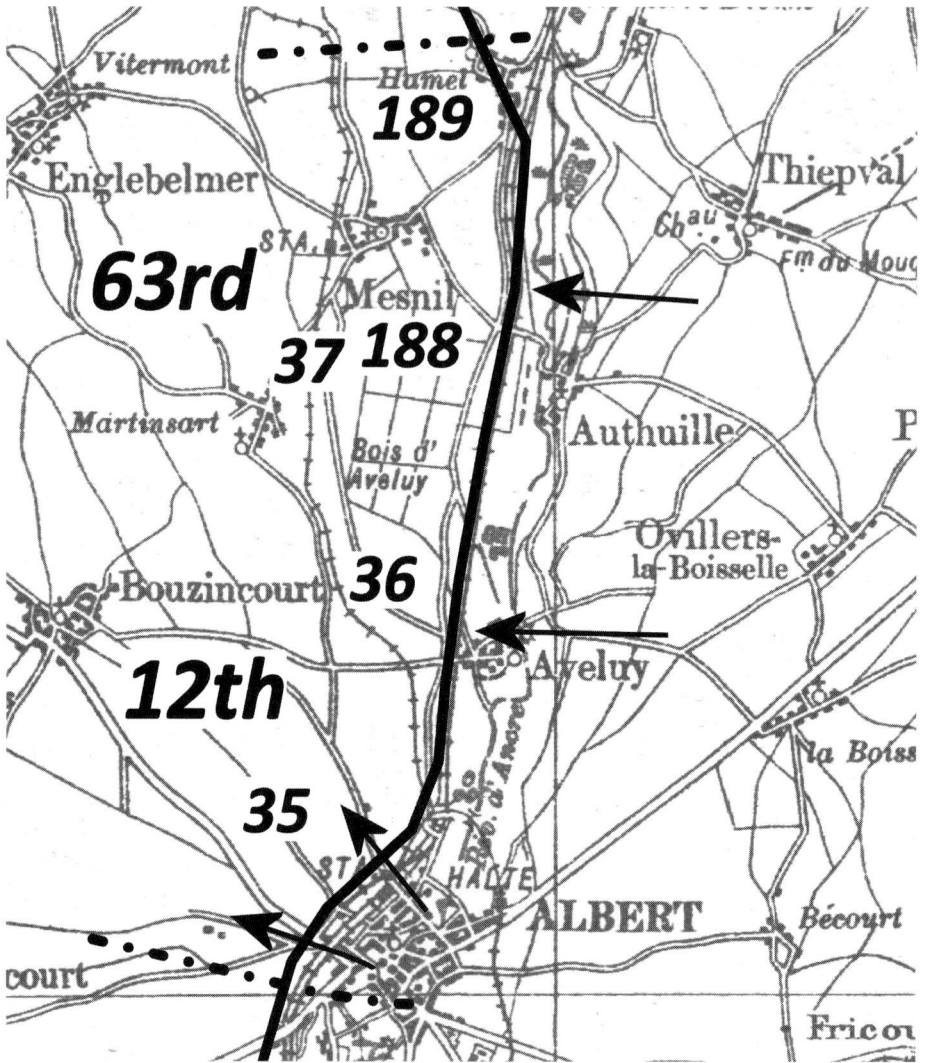

26 March: The Germans were unable to push V Corps back from the Ancre while a big attack out of Albert failed.

Battalion were the freshest, so they were organised into a composite brigade under Lieutenant Colonel Stewart. They advanced north-east of Colincamps in skirmishing order, finding 4 Australian Brigade outposts around Hébuterne. It meant the gap which had troubled Generals Byng and Gough for several days was finally being closed.

63rd (Royal Naval) Division, Aveluy Wood
Major General Lawrie had been reinforced by 37 Brigade along the Ancre. The 6th Queen's had joined the Drake and Hood Battalions of 189 Brigade around Hamel. Both the 1st Marines and the Anson Battalion stopped attempts to drive 188 Brigade back towards Mesnil, 'some moving in a sort of scattered, irregular crowd and others marching in fours down a road'. A night attack infiltrated the 7th Queen's Own in Aveluy Wood but the Anson Battalion helped Lieutenant Colonel Dawson's men drive them back across the river.

12th (Eastern) Division, Along the Ancre around Aveluy
Major General Arthur Scott's men were deployed along the slopes between Aveluy wood and Albert. Brigadier General Owen's 36 Brigade was in the centre while Lieutenant Colonel Impey's 7th Sussex held the south end of Aveluy wood. Meanwhile, Lieutenant Colonel Van Someran's 9th Royal Fusiliers were stopping the Germans crossing the Ancre at Aveluy.

Albert was 'in a sorry state as a result of the heavy bombing the previous night. The streets were choked up with broken transport vehicles, remains of buildings, dead men and horses. In spite of this a few of the inhabitants still remained.' The town was a shell trap, so 35 Brigade deployed on the western outskirts. The first attack during the evening fell back in the face of heavy fire but a night attack came close to breaking through Brigadier General Vincent's line.

Masses of German infantry charged Lieutenant Colonel Rees's 7th Norfolks on the Bouzincourt road on the north-west side of the town while Lieutenant Colonel Cooper's 7th Suffolks fought them to a standstill astride the Amiens road on the south-west side. Lieutenant Colonel La Terrière's 9th Essex and Lieutenant Colonel Trent's 5th Northants reinforced the line, helping them to stop two German divisions from leaving Albert. Their only success was to drive the 7th Suffolks back from the railway line, south of the town.

V Corps Summary
Fanshawe's men were safely across the Ancre and digging in. As the sky darkened, 'it was an awe-inspiring sight to see the whole of the Somme battlefield a mass of blazing dumps, huts and camps. The reflection of the flames in the moonlight caused a weird and ghostly glare to hang over Aveluy wood, increasing the eerie effect.'

VII Corps
Lieutenant General Congreve sent out instructions to hold on south-east of Albert as long as possible before withdrawing towards the confluence of the Somme and Ancre.

9th (Scottish) Division, Méaulte
Brigadier General Croft's 27 Brigade moved back to a short sector south-east of Albert with the Germans in close pursuit. The 12th Royal Scots stopped them reaching Méaulte during the afternoon, shooting up a battery as it galloped forward to support the infantry. Major General Blacklock would later withdraw the Scots behind the Ancre.

35th Division, North Bank of the Somme
Congreve instructed Major General Franks to continue the line south-east from Albert to Bray on the River Somme. He was to hold on until dusk if possible, to give the reserve divisions time to move up, but Franks was not to risk his infantry or guns. Brigadier General Pollard was given command of the troops at the front and he had instructions to withdraw by echelon. The two men then visited the front line, missing Congreve's visit to 35th Division's headquarters. His message to Franks' staff was that 'it was important to gain time for the removal of stores, but that units were not to become engaged so deeply as to prejudice their withdrawal.' The mist started clearing around 9.30 am but it was the afternoon before the Germans attacked the left flank.

Nine tanks from the 1st Battalion reinforced the area while the 17th Royal Scots made a fighting withdrawal. The rest of 35th Division followed soon afterwards, earlier than Franks wanted, because a British bombardment had driven Headlam's Force out of Bray. Brigadier General Sandilands instructed 104 Brigade to follow but Major Jewels' 18th Lancashire Fusiliers were cut off in the Bois des Tailles until Major Keenlyside's 17th Lancashire Fusiliers helped them escape. The rest of 35th Division followed, heading for Morlancourt 'in the most methodical manner' while the 12th and 18th HLI acted as their rearguard. Headlam's Force continued to withdraw past Étinehem.

During the afternoon General Congreve received two conflicting messages. The one from the front said the retirement had begun while the one from Third Army wanted to delay it until dusk. By the time General Franks forwarded the order 'that every effort must be made to check the enemy advance by disputing ground. It is to be distinctly understood that no retirement is to take place unless the tactical situation imperatively demands it', it was too late. Lieutenant Colonel McCulloch's force of 1,200 stragglers and rear area men were already withdrawing along the Somme when 106 Brigade's brigade major arrived to tell McCulloch to hold his ground. Most had already left but 500 men were told to stay and dig in next to 106 Brigade's rearguard between Morlancourt and Chipilly. It was dusk when the Germans attacked Morlancourt and both 106

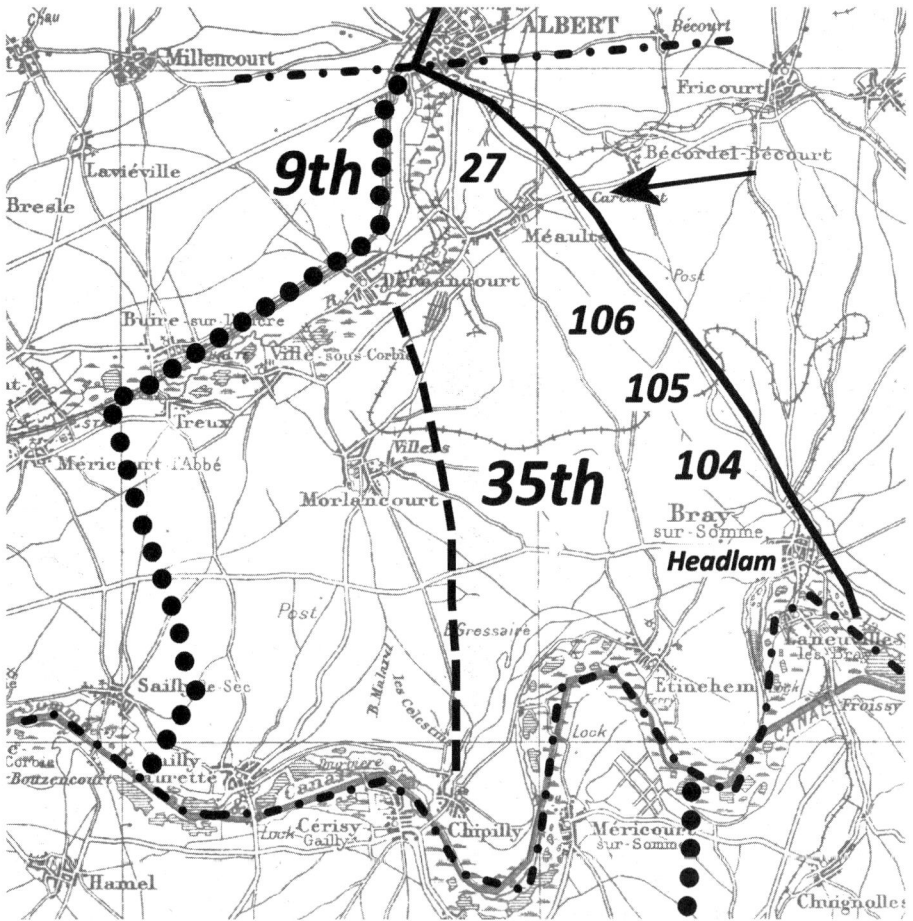

26 March: VII Corps made a disorganised withdrawal behind the Ancre, jeopardising Fifth Army's flank across the Somme.

Brigade and McCulloch had to withdraw because they had no artillery support.

The rest of the division had withdrawn behind the River Ancre around Ribemont and Heilly before Brigadier Generals Marindin and Headlam received their instructions to retake Morlancourt. Both brigades were tired and low on ammunition and they were all relieved when a staff officer from VII Corps arrived with revised orders. They only had to re-cross the Ancre and join 106 Brigade and McCulloch's men between Méricourt-l'Abbé and Sailly-le Sec. Unfortunately, the 4th North Staffords did not get the message and most were never seen again; the same happened to two officers sent to find them. The arrival of Major General Richard Mullens' 1st Cavalry Division meant that the road to Amiens, north of the Somme, had been closed.

Fifth Army, 26 March
XIX Corps
XIX Corps held a thirteen-mile sector south of the river under French command but there were large gaps on both flanks. Lieutenant General Watts had intended to slowly withdraw five miles but the Germans had penetrated his line at several points before the order reached the front. To make matters worse, his troops were retiring south-west rather than west.

16th (Irish) Division, Along the Somme
Major General Hull's men were deployed along the Somme behind XIX Corps' left flank. The infantry were digging trenches while the engineers prepared the bridges for demolition. Brigadier General Ramsey started withdrawing 48 Brigade from either side of Cappy first and then Brigadier General Leveson-Gower pulled 49 Brigade back from the Foissy area. They were all behind Proyart by the early afternoon but they had to retire again when they came under artillery fire at dusk. The problem was that Third Army had moved even further west, leaving 47 Brigade to cover the river crossings around Cerisy and Morcourt.

Lieutenant General Watts had expected to be reinforced by the 1st Cavalry Division but it had been ordered north, into Third Army's area. So the engineers were instructed to demolish most of the bridges before midnight while the 6th Connaughts, the 2nd Leinsters and the 1st Munsters kept a watch on crossings. Lieutenant Colonel Horn took a Canadian motor machine-gun battery and 350 men to the river to reinforce the Irishmen.

39th Division, South Bank of the Somme
The Germans captured Herbécourt from the 1/6th Cheshires in the early morning mist and then enfiladed the 1st Cambridgeshire Regiment to the north. Major General Feetham ordered everyone back through Dompierre to Proyart.

66th (2nd East Lancashire) Division, Withdrawal to Framerville
Major General Malcolm's command had been reduced to three composite brigade battalions of weary survivors. The early loss of Herbécourt forced 199 Battalion to retire through Dompierre where it came under fire from German troops moving from the south-east. Meanwhile, 198 Battalion

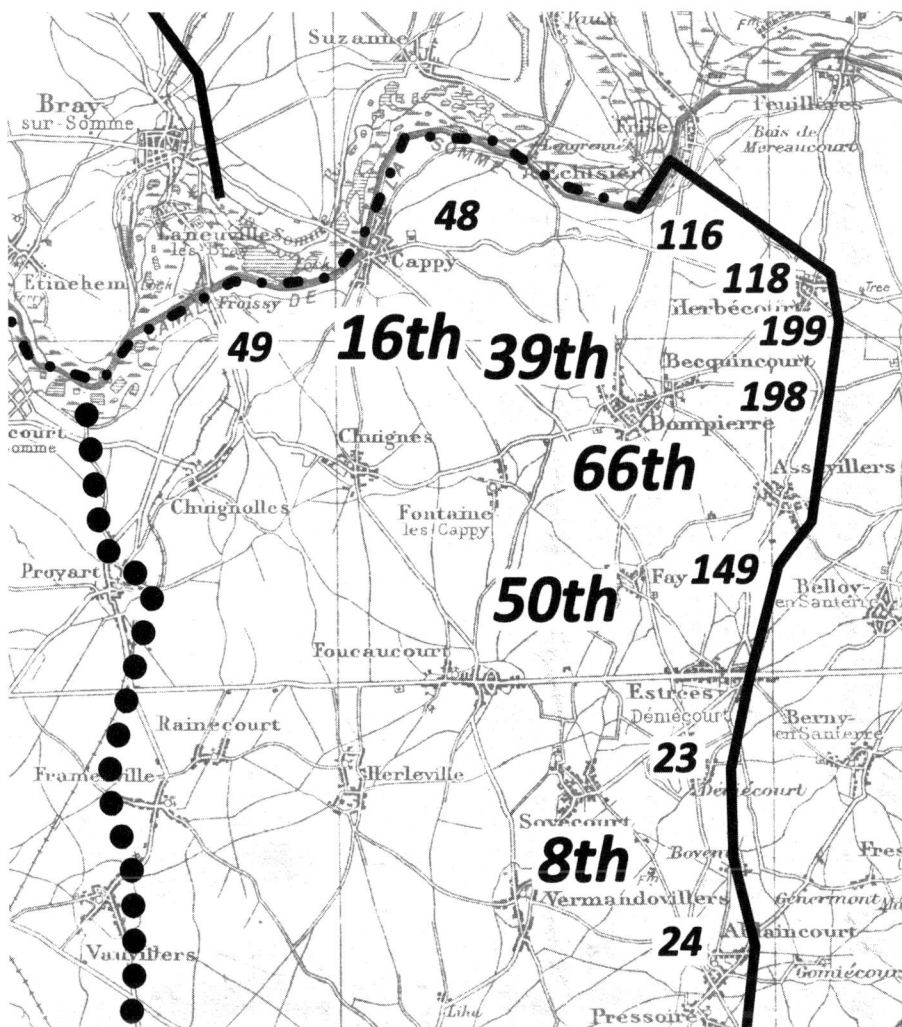

26 March XIX Corps' North Flank: The plan for an orderly retirement was disputed when the Germans broke, pushing XIX Corps' left to the south-west.

formed a rearguard at Foucaucourt on the Amiens road until barrage by British heavy artillery forced it to abandon Rainecourt and Framerville.

50th (Northumbrian) Division, Estrées Back to Vauvillers
The three Northumberland Fusilier battalions came under enfilade fire after 66th Division fell back. They first headed south-west across the Amiens

road, passing though Foucaucourt where 'huts and stores were blazing'. A military policeman waited until every last man had gone through, leaving for Vauvillers when the Germans were only 200 yards away.

8th Division, Ablaincourt through Lihons to Rosières

An early morning attack south of the Amiens road was stopped and then the division started to withdraw from the left. The 2nd West Yorkshires and 2nd Middlesex got away but some of the 2nd Devons were cut off. The 1st Worcesters and 2nd Northants were next to leave Ablaincourt, with 150 Brigade Battalion and two battalions of the 151 Brigade from 50th Division. Brigadier General Coffin kept 25 Brigade steady as they moved south-west through Lihons so they 'arrived gradually and in perfect order on their positions' in front of Rosières.

24th Division, Chaulnes to Fransart

Major General Daly planned to retire in echelon from right to left from Chaulnes to Fransart but 72 Brigade was pushed back at dawn. The 1st North Staffords and the 8th Queen's Own reached the prepared trench at Rouvroy but the 9th East Surreys were surrounded and captured south of Hallu. The 9th Sussex, 13th Middlesex and 9th Northants escaped to Rosières without a problem and while the 8th Queen's and 3rd Rifle Brigade escaped Chaulnes, the 1st Royal Fusiliers did not get the withdrawal order. It was late in the afternoon before they realised they had to escape.

XVIII Corps

Lieutenant General Maxse had four battered divisions to fill the gap on XIX Corps' right, north of the Avre. The plan was for General Watts' divisions to withdraw, while 30th and 36th Divisions advanced side-by-side to Le Quesnoy and Andechy.

30th Division, Le Quesnoy

The advance from Bouchoir came under fire around le Quesnoy so Captain Combe formed one hundred men of the 7th DCLI into a rearguard while the rest of the division fell back to Folies. The enemy were too close by the time the order to withdraw arrived, so Combe waited until it was dark before making his escape.

36th (Ulster) Division, North Bank of the River Avre

Major General Nugent had no artillery support but he told Brigadier General Withycombe to contact 30th Division. Lieutenant Colonel

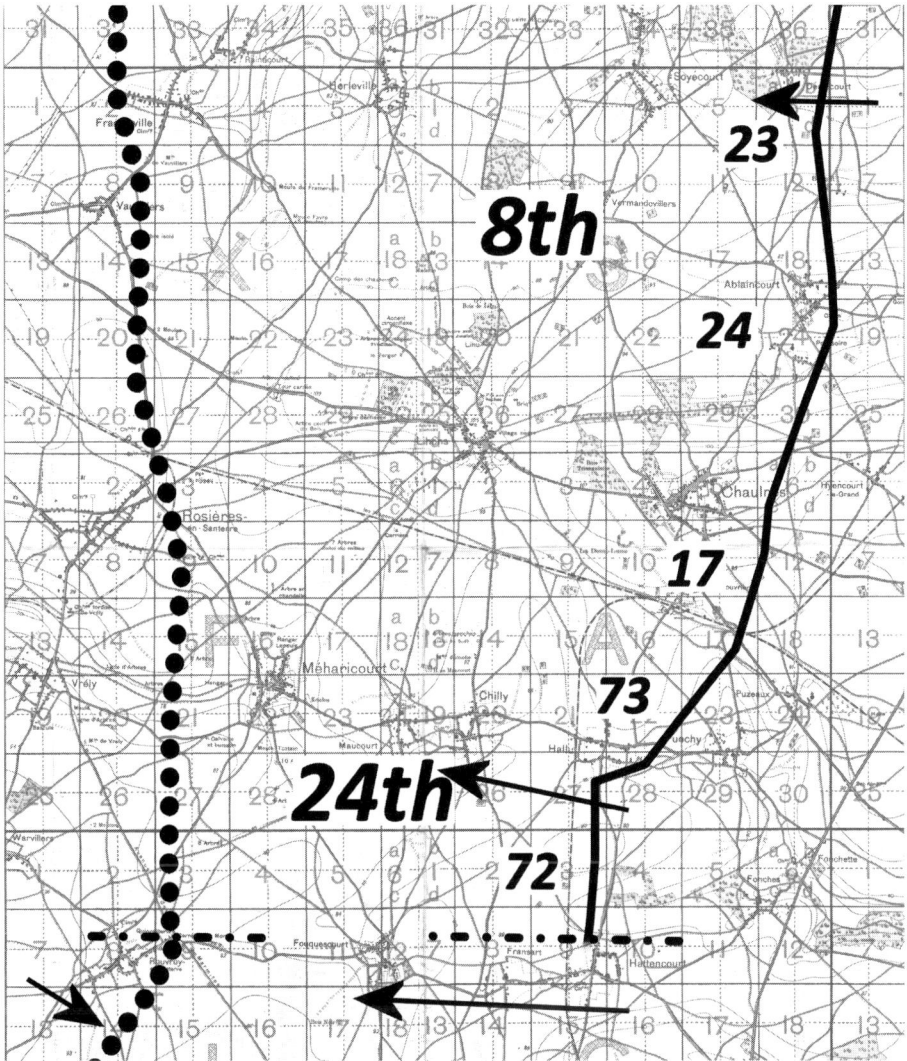

26 March XIX Corps' South Flank: Parts of XIX Corps' right withdrew in good order but some units were cut off.

McCarthy-O'Leary of the 1st Irish Rifles found them at Bouchoir, securing the left flank. The Germans already occupied Andechy so Brigadier Generals Hessey and Griffiths withdrew 109 and 108 Brigades to an old French trench west of the village. It left the Ulstermen holding a disjoined line with a large gap in the centre.

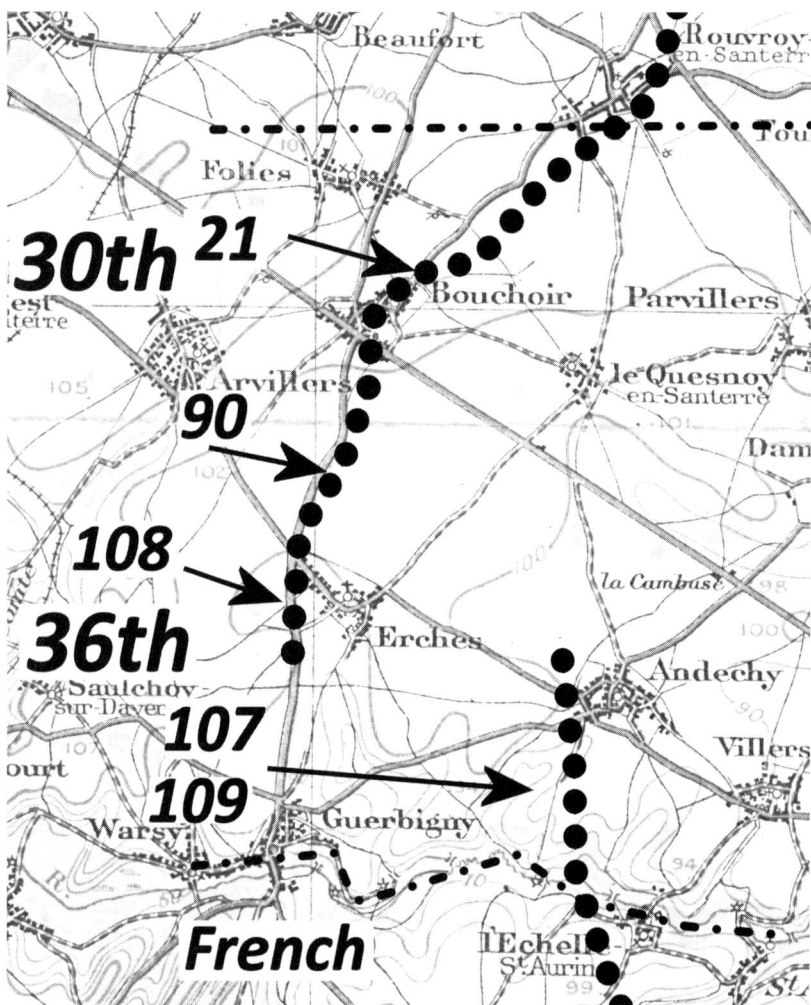

26 March: XVIII Corps struggled to form a line north of the River Avre.

The Germans engaged 108 Brigade headquarters at Erches and took a wounded Brigadier General Griffiths prisoner. The GSO1, Lieutenant Colonel Place, Lieutenant Colonel Furnell of the 1st Irish Fusiliers and Major Brew of the 9th Irish Fusiliers were ambushed and captured as they tried to escape in a car. Captain Miller's men of the 15th Irish Rifles stopped the Germans advancing any further but machine gun fire would stop the ammunition wagons reaching 109 and 108 Brigade.

Attempts to reach Guerbigny were stopped by Captain Densmore's few machine gun teams even though they too had little ammunition left. 'We were entirely surrounded, if only by Hun patrols, and we only knew hazily what direction to make for… I reckon the Boche should have wiped out our party at Erches but we turned on him severely enough to persuade him to let us go quietly.'

After a week of fighting and withdrawing, Major General Nugent's depleted command finally trudged back into reserve. The men were relieved to see lines of buses waiting for them and the fitter men dumped their kit before helping their hobbling comrades on board.

26 March Summary

Third Army was able to make use of trenches dating back to 1916 on its left and the River Ancre on its right. Byng had also been given eight of the nine divisions and the crisis on his front had ended when the Australians and New Zealanders closed the gap in its centre. Byng's problem now was the four-mile gap along the Somme, where VII Corps had fallen back too far. He sent Brigadier General Marindin to replace Franks in command of 35th Division because he 'had misinterpreted the verbal instructions and orders issued in the morning of the 26th.' Byng was sure he had made it clear 'that no retirement should have been made from the Bray–Albert Line'.

Meanwhile, the rest of 4th Australian Division was marching south through the night to the threatened area on Fifth Army's front. The men had been instructed to travel light and picquets were posted because they were so close to the battle front. Lieutenant Colonel Leane summed up the problem to the officers of 48th Australian: 'Gentlemen, we do not even know that the road is clear or whether we can beat the enemy to Albert. We must protect our flanks and be ready for anything.'

Fifth Army had no old trenches to occupy or river line to hide behind. The French had built a defensive position around fifteen miles in front of Amiens in 1915 but it had been cleared away after the Germans withdrew to the Hindenburg Line in the spring of 1917 so the land could be farmed.

Gough needed a new line and Major General Philip Grant, Chief Engineer of Fifth Army, spent the day collecting nearly 3,000 men including army troops, training staff and all types of engineers. They were reinforced by Lewis guns from the army Gun Park and Vickers guns provided by the Canadians. Major General Sandeman Carey took command as they dug a new line twelve miles east of the city. Lieutenant Colonel Horn covered the south bank of the Somme, Lieutenant Colonel Graham was astride the Amiens road and Lieutenant Colonel Irwin deployed on the north bank of the Lucre.

Meanwhile, the Germans had not achieved 'what the events of the 23rd, 24th and 25th had encouraged us to hope for,' and they had another new problem to deal with. They were struggling to move their artillery, ammunition and food across the two devastated areas: the twenty-mile-wide area where they had applied a scorched earth policy in 1917 and then the ten-mile-wide crater field belonging to the 1916 Somme battlefield. As one German commentator said, 'the Somme desert had spoken its last inexorable and mighty word.' The slowing up of the advance over the past twenty-four hours brought about a change in attitudes. After the triumph of the early stages of the advance, German morale was declining while British morale was increasing. Ludendorff was disappointed to hear the Second Army 'was already complaining of the old shell holes, it could not get further than Albert'.

The Doullens Conference
President Raymond Poincaré, Prime Minister Georges Clémenceau, General Foch and member of the War Cabinet, Lord Alfred Milner, had met at General Phillipe Pétain's headquarters on 25 March. They arranged to meet again the following morning at the British Advanced GHQ in Dury, south of Amiens, unaware it was occupied by Fifth Army Headquarters, so alternative arrangements had to be made.

Field Marshal Douglas Haig was planning to meet Generals Horne, Plumer and Byng at the Hotel de Ville at Doullens the following morning. The politicians agreed they could meet immediately after the generals. Major General Archibald Montgomery would act on behalf of General Rawlinson while he was representing the British at Versailles.

Starting at 11 am on 26 March, Haig heard how Byng was satisfied his men had fought the Germans to a standstill. He promised to give Third Army reserves to hold Arras but he also wanted Third and Fifth Armies to cover Amiens while giving the French time to deploy.

As the generals talked, Poincaré and Clémenceau welcomed their Minister of Armaments, Louis Loucheur, and Generals Foch and Pétain. Lord Milner and CIGS, General Henry Wilson, also arrived. They talked in separate groups before the meeting and Pétain was adamant he did not want to be placed under Haig's command. He was also expecting the British to be defeated in front of Amiens and was still planning to withdraw the French divisions to the south-west when it happened. Foch was more optimistic and wanted to keep in touch with the British. Meanwhile, the British representatives and generals agreed there was no plan to abandon Amiens.

President Poincaré took the chair at midday and while he was concerned about Third Army's situation around Arras, he was even more worried about Fifth Army. Pétain believed Fifth Army 'no longer really exists, it is broken,' and was then rude about Gough's soldiers. Wilson objected, saying that he was influenced by General Fayolle's negative reports.

Then came the arguments over who was the most committed to the battle. Haig said the BEF was fully committed and that he had no more reserves left. Pétain countered that twenty-four French divisions were either engaged or about to be and that more were en route. Foch interrupted to say, 'we must fight in front of Amiens. We must fight where we are now. As we have not been able to stop the Germans on the Somme, we must not now retire a single inch.'

After a brief recess, Clémenceau suggested making Foch responsible for the battle in front of Amiens. But both Haig and Pétain agreed Foch should be made responsible for all the Western Front. After Clémenceau and Milner signed the agreement on behalf of their respective governments, Poincaré declared, 'I think, gentlemen that we worked well for the victory.' Lord Milner asked Haig's Chief of Staff, General Herbert Lawrence, how the War Cabinet could help the generals win the war. Lawrence's answer was simple; they should leave them to get on with fighting the war.

Foch told Pétain to get as many divisions into the battle zone as quickly as possible. He then visited the French generals and told General Fayolle's Chief of the Staff to support the British. He finally saw Gough and asked him to hold on at all costs. The Doullens conference made sure that the Allies would work together and that the French would do their utmost to support the British in front of Amiens. Pétain cancelled his order to fall back south and promised to send General Fayolle another ten divisions.

Chapter 15

Bomb and Bayonet were Frequently Used

27 March

The temperature had dropped which meant the morning mist cleared faster than normal. Third Army's line was continuous and General Byng had plenty of reserves but it was a different matter south of the river. The Germans were about to exploit the six-mile gap between VII Corps and XIX Corps. There was another weak spot where XVIII Corps was struggling to stay in contact with the French along the River Avre.

Third Army, 27 March

The artillery fire against XVII Corps and VI Corps line around Arras increased, suggesting an attack was imminent. Third Army was holding a strong position along the 1916 front line and the Ancre but its right flank was six miles behind Fifth Army's along the Somme. Byng's midday order reminded everyone to hold their ground while corps commanders were told it was 'undesirable to constantly withdraw corps headquarters. The effect on the troops is not good.'

VI Corps

The artillery stopped the initial large attacks, so the Germans withdrew to try another approach. Infantry moved forward in ones and twos and then they rushed forward in small groups.

Guards Division, Boisleux St Marc to Moyenneville

The 2nd Scots Guards stopped an attack directed at Boisleux, on the 3 Guards Brigade front. Major General Feilding wanted to pull back the 1st Grenadier Guards on his exposed left flank but he was promised 97 Brigade was on its way to reinforce the area.

31st Division, Ayette

An attack was launched from around Courcelles-le-Comte and 'it resembled an encompassment of werewolves. They slouched forward while men rubbed tired eyes, in twos and threes, at no point offering any definite target and yet in some wizard fashion, always thickening and spreading, while our guns from the rear raged and tore uselessly at their almost invisible lines.'

They eventually penetrated between the 11th East Yorkshires and 11th East Lancashires 'after more than five hours' fighting, in which the line swayed to and fro while bomb and bayonet were frequently used'. A rumour that the enemy had broken through was dispelled when the divisional artillery dispersed two battalions of infantry assembling ready to attack.

The evening mist prevented signalling so Major General Bridgford let the battalion commanders retire to a new position around

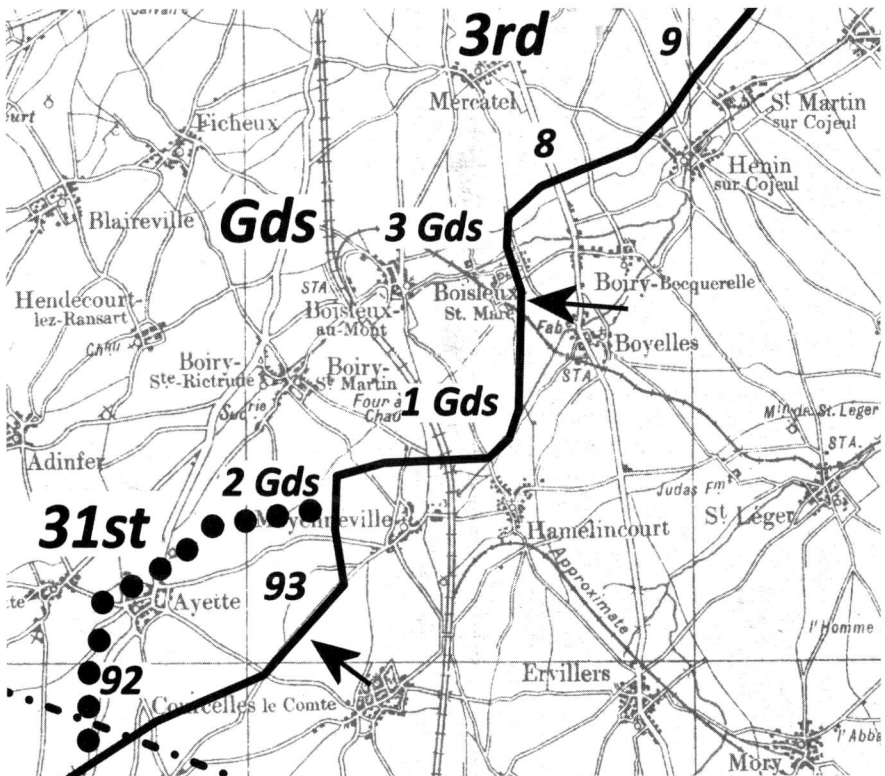

27 March: VI Corps' right withdrew because no one could see the signals from the front line through the mist.

Ayette. The 3rd Grenadier Guards closed the gap on the left with the 1/10th Manchesters around Ablainzevelle. A wounded Second Lieutenant Basil Arthur Horsfall had refused to leave the 11th East Lancashires because the three other officers in his company had been killed and he made sure everyone left when a withdrawal was ordered. He was killed soon afterwards and would posthumously be awarded the Victoria Cross.

IV Corps
Australian and New Zealand reinforcements had filled the gap in IV Corps' line. Seventeenth Army faced Bucquoy and Hébuterne while Second Army faced the south side, around Beaumont Hamel; there was little coordination between their attacks.

42nd (East Lancashire) Division, Ablainzevelle
The 1/10th and 1/6th Manchesters stopped the Germans pushing past the north side of Ablainzevelle while the 1/6th and 1/7th Manchesters held on the south side.

62nd (2nd West Riding) Division, Rossignol Wood
The first attack against the east side of Bucquoy was broken up when Lewis gunners emerged from shell holes to open fire. An artillery barrage called for by the 2/7th West Yorkshires then came down 'like a blanket', scattering the survivors. The Germans regrouped for a second bombing attack along old trenches while field guns, trench mortars and low-flying planes gave covering fire. They too made no progress. Braithwaite sent out a message: 'men are doing splendidly and I know how tired they are but we have got to stick it,' and stick it they did.

Major Perry's 2/4th KOYLIs were driven out of the Rossignol Wood after running out of bombs. Major General Braithwaite's order to counter-attack never reached Brigadier General Burnett but he and Lieutenant Colonel Watson organised one on their own initiative. The 5th KOYLIs advanced from the direction of Biez Wood and the Germans withdrew when four tanks approached. German bombers returned along abandoned trenches to infiltrate the wood and they took four companies of KOYLIs prisoner; Watson was killed and two tanks were knocked out. A misunderstood order meant that the rest of the Yorkshiremen retired and German machine-gun teams based themselves in the two broken-down tanks and held them off until dawn.

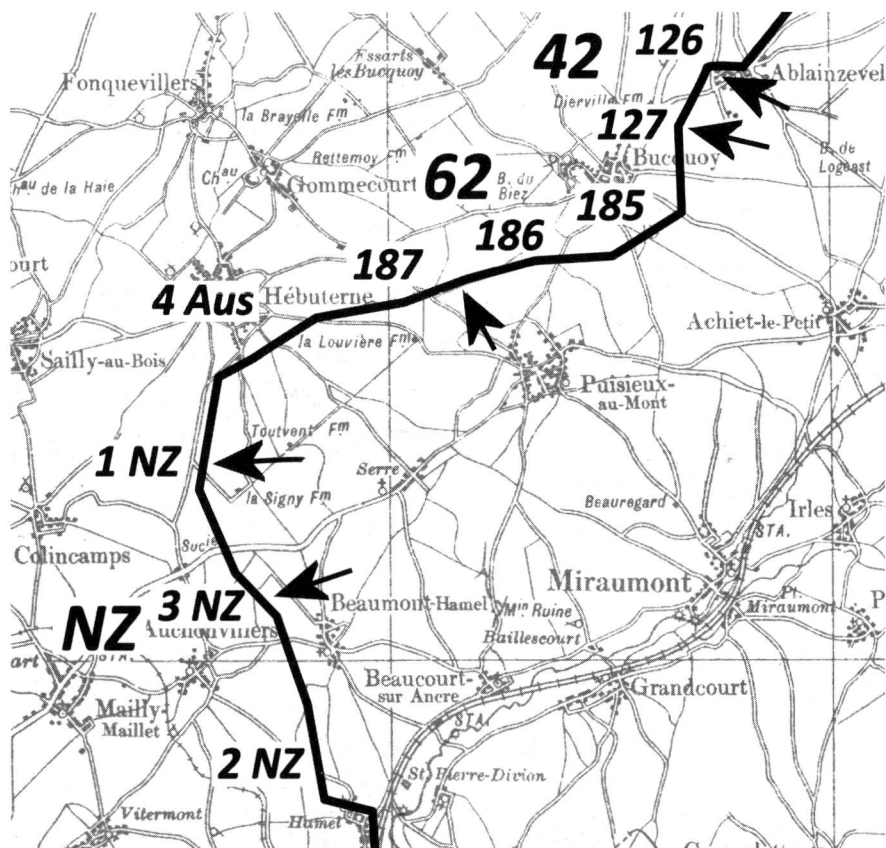

27 March IV Corps: With its centre sealed by 4th Australian Division and the New Zealand Division, IV Corps was able to stop all attacks.

4th Australian Division, Hébuterne

The Australians had marched all night long: 'the column moved through almost empty villages, the last of the fleeing inhabitants looking silently out upon it. Dawn found it still marching, 108 paces to the minute, with ten-minute halts in each hour… None knew where the enemy was, and by the time the trip was half over no one really cared much, as everyone was too utterly weary.'

The Australians had covered over eleven miles to reach the danger point and then Brigadier General Brand told them, 'it is to be distinctly understood that no retirement from our present position is permissible.' As luck would have it, the German attack was directed towards the New Zealanders so 15th and 13th Australian Battalions poured enfilade fire into their flank. A night attack by Captain McKillop and Lieutenant White captured the cemetery, securing the flank with 62nd Division.

New Zealand Division, Hébuterne and Ancre
The 3rd Rifle Brigade and the 2nd Wellington of Lieutenant Colonel Stewart's composite brigade had closed the gap in the line south of Hébuterne during the early hours. The 2nd and 1st Auckland Battalions occupied the centre of the division's line while the 2nd and 1st Canterbury Battalions took over the trench facing Beaumont Hamel.

Machine-gun fire stopped the early German probes as they located the New Zealanders' line in the mist. Then 'attack followed attack, for once beaten back at one point the enemy's infantry was remorselessly launched at another.' SOS flares called down previously arranged barrages onto the old British trenches, dispersing the Germans every time they assembled. A rumour that the enemy had pierced the line south of Hébuterne turned out to be untrue.

V Corps
12th (Eastern) Division, Aveluy Wood
The 6th Queen's were instructed to evacuate Le Hamel next to the river because it was a shell trap. The 6th Buffs were in reserve around Mesnil, further up the slope, when Brigadier General Incledon-Webber heard that enemy patrols had been spotted in Aveluy Wood. The Buffs dealt with them but 188 Brigade headquarters then heard that Mesnil had been captured. Brigadier General Coleridge ordered Commander Buckle's Anson Battalion from reserve to advance from Martinsart and retake it. A 'friendly fire' incident followed as 'quite a lively fight between the two raged, each under the impression that the other force was German.' One observer heard the Anson Battalion had been 'having its rum ration at the time of the breakthrough, so it was doubtless in good fettle'.

Brigadier General Owen's 36 Brigade was under attack around Aveluy and the Germans captured the bridge, cutting off some of Lieutenant Colonel Van Someren's 9th Royal Fusiliers on the far side of the Ancre. Captain Baudains escaped after Lieutenant Colonel Nicolls sent some of the 5th Berkshires to retake the bridge. Lieutenant Colonel Impey's 7th Sussex lost the south end of Aveluy Wood but Lieutenant Commander

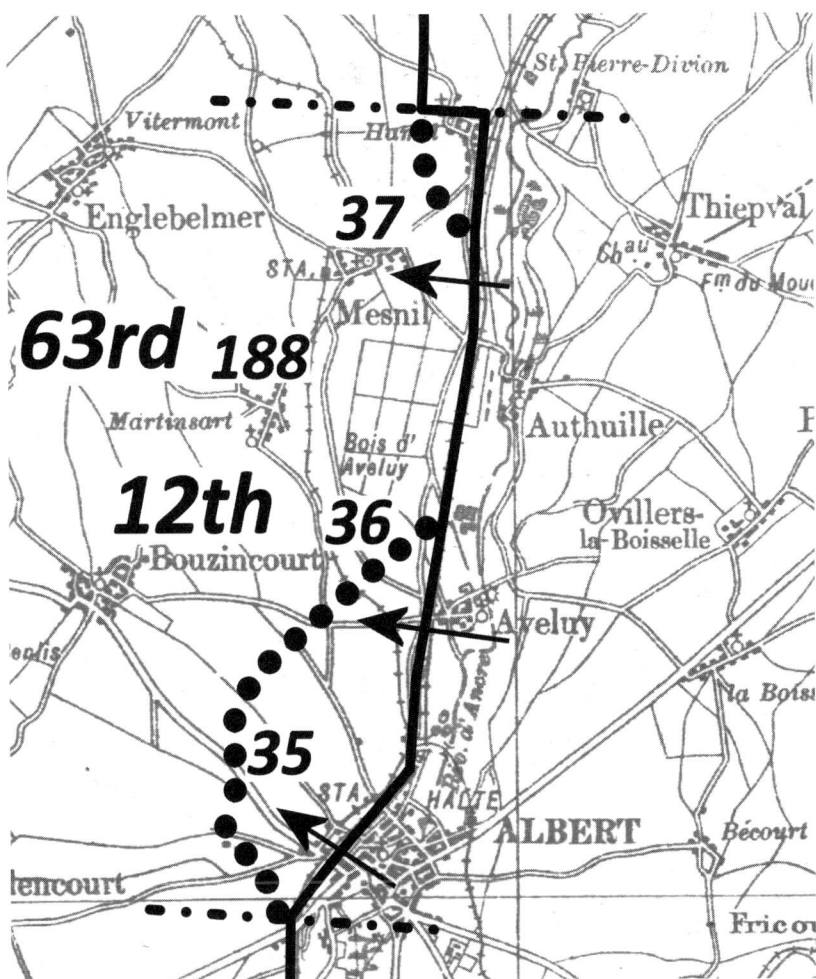

27 March V Corps: The Germans pushed V Corps' line back south of Aveluy Wood.

Coote's 2nd Marines were able to turn 'on their pursuers and drive them before them like chaff'.

More attacks drove the 7th Suffolks back north of Albert and Second Lieutenant Comber's company of the 9th Essex alone fired 15,000 rounds to stop them penetrating any further. All the headquarters staff armed themselves with a rifle to hold the position while Impey burnt the battalion's paperwork before grabbing his revolver and 'turned the tide of the fight like some leader of old'. Lieutenant Blackwell of the 5th Northants was killed helping the 7th Norfolks and while Lieutenant Colonel Rees retook the railway line, he was captured during a second attack. Men from 17th Division and 63 Division helped Brigadier General Vincent's 35 Brigade hold its ground around the town.

63rd (Royal Naval) Division, West of Albert

Early in the morning Brigadier General Hutchison's 190 Brigade advanced from Bouzincourt towards Albert, just as the Germans launched their own attack out of the town. The 4th Bedfords, 7th Royal Fusiliers and 28th London Regiment found themselves in the middle of a desperate battle in which the Germans got the upper hand. Lieutenant Colonel John Stanhope Collings-Wells called for volunteers to help the 4th Bedfords and they held on for nearly two hours, stopping all attacks until their ammunition was running out. Collings-Wells then shouted for his men to follow him in a desperate counter-attack, 'knowing they were nearly dead beat after six days of fighting with very little sleep'. A mortally wounded Collings-Wells 'continued to cheer his men on until he fell'; he would be posthumously awarded the Victoria Cross. Lieutenant General Fanshawe had to concede that he had to abandon the river bank north of Albert and he gave instructions to withdraw onto the high ground covering Martinsart and Bouzincourt.

VII Corps

9th (Scottish) Division and 4th Australian Division, Dernancourt

There were rumours the Germans had broken through from time to time but the Scots 'repulsed the massed attacks with great slaughter'. Major Campbell was mortally wounded silencing a machine gun firing on the 11th Royal Scots from the south side of Albert. Major General Blacklock told Brigadier General Kennedy to evacuate Dernancourt and 35th Division sent Lieutenant Colonel Heathcote's 17th Royal Scots to man a line around the shell trap.

Blacklock welcomed the arrival of Brigadier General Gellibrand during the afternoon and his 12th Australian Brigade moved towards the sector south of Albert late in the afternoon to be greeted by the panorama of battle.

> *A grey mist over the place, red shell bursts, and the smoke of many fires. Shells were bursting all over the landscape.*

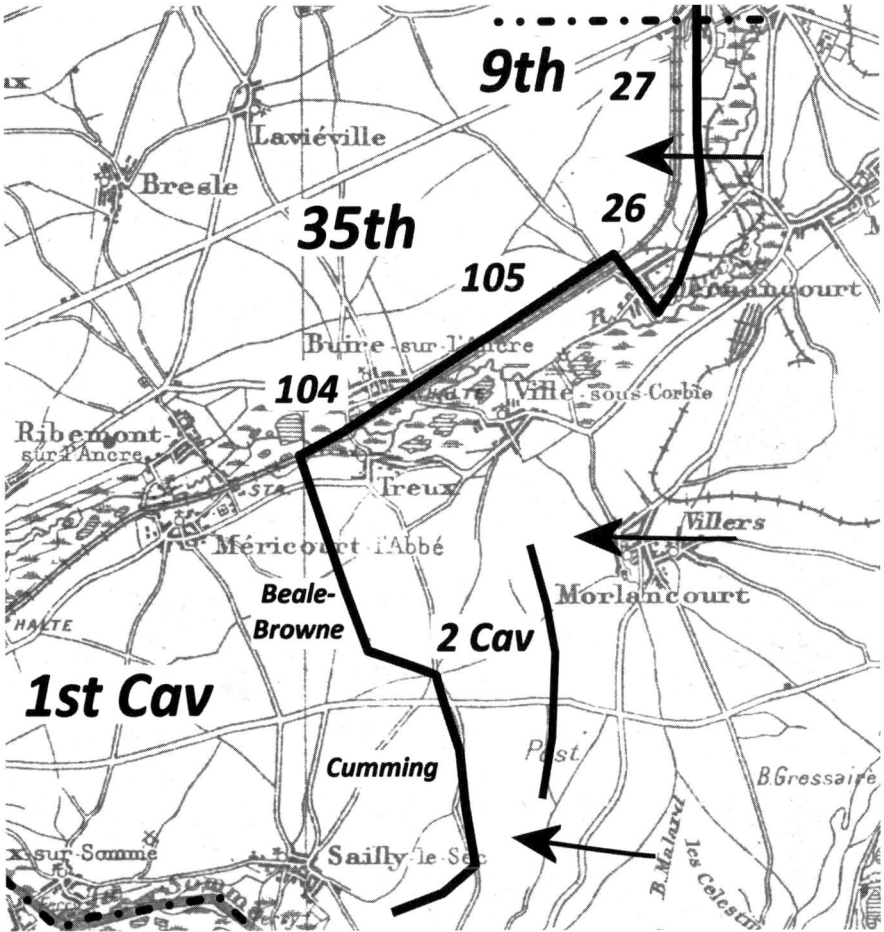

27 March VII Corps: VII Corps' line steadied between the Ancre and the Somme.

Batteries of artillery were firing, limbers galloping in and out. Albert lay in the hollow, hazy with the smoke of burning houses, the cathedral tower rising high above the roofs, and the well-remembered gilt figure of the Virgin still diving as in 1916 over the street. Our guns blazing like Hell. Mounted men dashing all over the landscape. Wounded dribbling wearily back; Red Cross motors tearing along the road.

> *Shells bursting down all the roads. A full-dress battle was in*
> *progress.*

35th Division, Dernancourt to Méricourt

Weak battalions were lined out along the west bank of the Ancre between Dernancourt and Méricourt waiting to be relieved. As luck would have it the Germans attacked elsewhere.

1st Cavalry and 3rd Australian Divisions, Between the Ancre and the Somme

Brigadier General Beale-Browne had deployed the 9th Lancers and the 15th Hussars in front of the main line and they stopped the Germans making any progress towards Corbie. The 4th and 5th Dragoon Guards also made sure they did not cross the Somme at Sailly Lorette.

Trains had brought the 3rd Australian Division to Doullens the previous afternoon and the Diggers had marched through the night to join VII Corps. Lieutenant General Congreve welcomed Monash with the words, 'thank God, the Australians at last'. He then explained the situation south-west of Albert and the current German tactics, saying, 'the situation was so serious that Amiens may go if we fail to hold this line.'

Monash took over responsibility for the front between the Ancre and the Somme during the afternoon, believing his men were entering 'the fight of their lives'. The 10 Australian Brigade relieved McCulloch's Force of cavalrymen while 11 Australian Brigade took over from 21st Division's men serving under Brigadier General Cumming. They soon learnt that rumours that Dernancourt and Sailly Lorette had been lost were untrue.

There had been little aerial combat over the battlefield during the retreat across the Somme because there had been so many lucrative targets on the ground. Pilots concentrated on strafing the crowds of military traffic on the roads rather than engaging other planes. But it was dangerous flying so low through a hail of bullets and shrapnel and even the slightest loss of concentration could result in a crash.

A few pilots went in search of enemy planes to engage, like Canadian pilot Lieutenant Alan McLeod of No 2 Squadron of the Royal Flying Corps. On 27 March he had shot down four planes during a prolonged dog fight over Albert when his luck ran out. Both pilot and observer were injured and the fuel tank was on fire, so he put his Armstrong Whitworth FK8 into a steep dive to keep the flames away from Lieutenant Hammond. McLeod crashed in no man's land and then dragged Hammond from the burning wreckage before carrying him to the safety of the British trenches. Sadly, he died of Spanish Influenza in a Canadian hospital only a few days before the Armistice; he was only 19.

Fifth Army
XIX Corps, 27 March
Lieutenant General Watts' men were holding a thin line between the Somme and Rouvroy. Most had been in action since the battle started and they were nearing the end of their endurance. Third Army was six miles behind their left flank; he was unsure about the French situation on his right. All Watts had in support was a Carey's Force, a thin line of 3,000 engineers, American railway troops and other rear area men. His order stated that he wanted 'all ranks to make one more supreme effort and maintain to the last the magnificent fighting qualities and endurance already displayed'.

16th (Irish) Division, South Bank of the Somme
The 1st Munsters were driven back so Brigadier General Gregorie had to tell the 6th Connaughts and 2nd Leinsters to abandon Proyart. Brigadiers Generals Ramsay and Leveson-Gower told 49 and 48 Brigades to follow. Captain McConnochie was killed and Major Then was captured as the 11th Hampshires (Pioneers) covered the withdrawal.

General Watts was alarmed to hear that aerial observers had seen German troops crossing the Somme at Cerisy and Morcourt. A staff officer sent to investigate reported hundreds of enemy soldiers advancing towards Villers-Bretonneux, behind his flank. The 7/8th Inniskillings, 2nd Irish Regiment and 7th Irish Regiment also came under machine-gun fire from the river bank, confirming the problem. Watts sent another staff officer to collect 'all and sundry and dig in where he stood' at Warfusée-Abancourt and he was joined by Colonel Walden with the Connaughts, the Hampshires and 66th Division's engineers.

Captain Peirson, 48 Brigade's brigade major, led 400 men towards Cerisy but they were too few to stop the masses of Germans crossing the Somme. Neither the 2nd Munsters, 2nd Leinsters nor the 1st Dublin Fusiliers got the message to withdraw and 200 men had to escape along the canal when it was dark. They used a German password to trick the sentries guarding the tow path and eventually reached Carey's Force. The Germans were close behind and some even entered Warfusée-Abancourt forcing 61st Division's headquarters to make a run for it.

39th Division, Withdrawing astride the Amiens Road
The Germans pushed past the left flank when 16th Division withdrew from Proyart. Brigadier General Bellingham pulled back 17th KRRC and

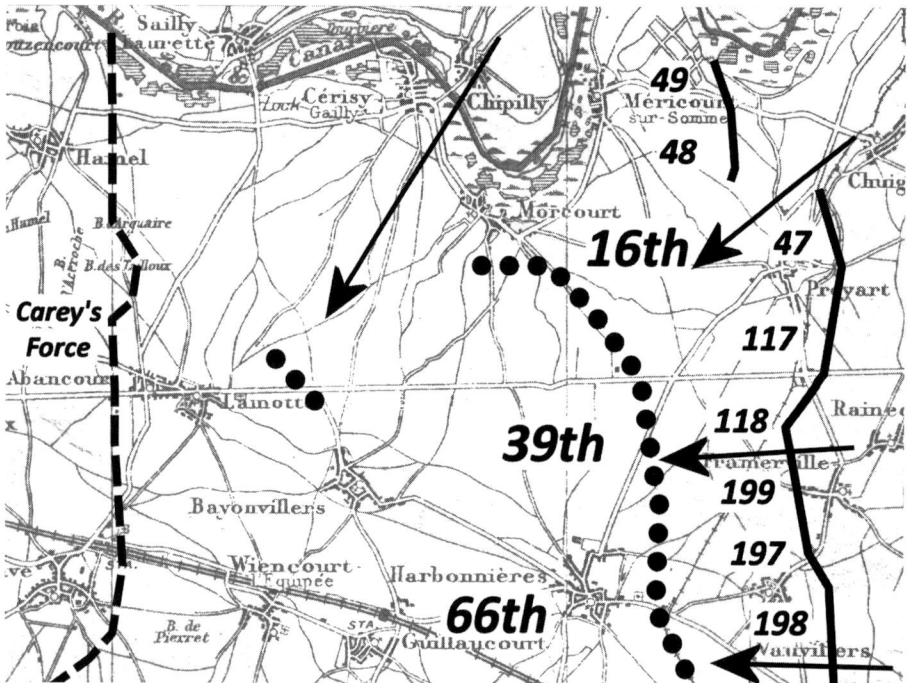

27 March: The Germans crossing the Somme at Cerisy pushed behind XIX Corps' north flank, resulting in a difficult withdrawal to the south-west.

the 16th Sherwoods and Brigadier General Armytage did the same with the 4/5th Black Watch, 1/6th Cheshires and 1st Cambridge astride the Amiens road. Major General Feetham moved the 11th and 13th Sussex, the 1st Hertfords and the 13th Gloucesters (Pioneers) forward, extending the flank to overlook Morcourt but the Germans could still cross at Cerisy.

By evening it was clear the division was in danger of being cut off from Carey's Force and the three brigadiers met during the night to discuss withdrawing south. However, Feetham's message told them to hold on because he was arranging a counter-attack for the morning.

66th (East Lancashire) Division, Framerville to Vauvillers
Major General Malcolm had two weak brigade battalions in line south of the Amiens road. First 50th Division was driven from Vauvillers to the south and then Little's Force was overwhelmed to the north. The East Lancashire men withdrew via Harbonnières towards Carey's Force during the night.

50th (Northumbrian) Division, East of Harbonnières

Major General Jackson issued a warning order to prepare to retire just after midday, after hearing that 66th Division was falling back. Unfortunately, the 5th and 6th Northumberland Fusiliers thought it was an executive order and they began withdrawing from Vauvillers and Rosières. The 1/4th Northumberland Fusiliers stood fast at Vauvillers but the 1/5th Durhams thought they had to retire and most of Brigadier General Riddell's men were soon falling back.

Colonel Ainsty galloped up with new instructions but 'there was no panic and we watched the counter-attack with interest.' The 7th Durhams (Pioneers) and 22nd Entrenching Battalion attacked on the left and Brigadier General Riddell made sure the Northumberland Fusiliers joined in, 'pushing on platoon by platoon and section by section in the old field day style, the men firing freely at the Germans....' They charged the last stretch and 'the effect was magical; our foes trooped away like crowds on a race course.'

Men from the 2nd East Lancashires, 1st Sherwoods, 2nd Berkshires and 2nd West Yorkshire helped as both Lieutenant Colonel Robinson and Captain Armstrong were wounded leading the Northumberland Fusiliers on the right. Between them, they drove back as many as nine waves of infantry beyond Vauvillers. However, 149 Brigade expended all its ammunition in the counter-attack and had to retire; casualties had been heavy and the 1/6th Northumberland Fusiliers had been reduced to just twenty men.

8th Division, Rosières and Harbonnières

The first attack drove the 6th DLI back south-east of Rosières but Lieutenant Colonel Moore's 1st Sherwoods restored the line. However, the problem was the breakthrough at Proyart, which was threatening to roll up XIX Corps' line from the north. Lieutenant General Watts told Major General Heneker he had sent his reserve north to counter-attack to restore the situation. Lieutenant Colonel Cope led the 2nd Devons, the 22nd Durhams (Pioneers) and the 151 Composite Battalion north, via Harbonnières, where he found 'things were in utter confusion; guns and limbers were moving rapidly back and men were straggling in disorder.' Captain Cargo led 'a very gallant and successful counter-attack' which drove the enemy across Amiens road and captured a battery of field guns. Cope and Cargo's men then helped 39th Division hold their line.

Attention then shifted back to the right flank, where the 6th Durhams were once again in trouble. For a second time the 1st Sherwoods went

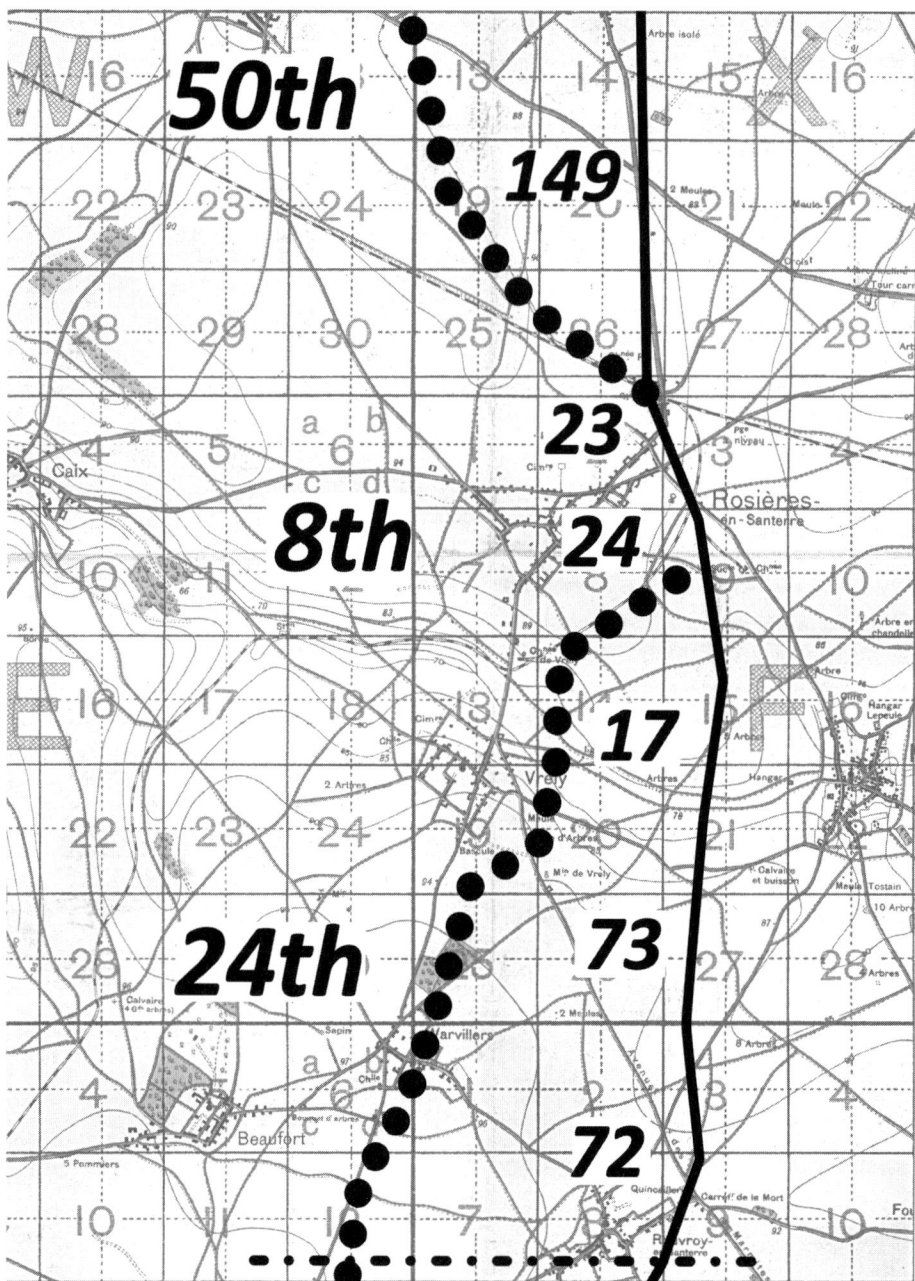

27 March: XIX Corps' centre was under threat of being rolled up from the north while the right was in danger of the same from the south.

forward, taking all the headquarters personnel, engineers and trench mortar crews they could find in a bayonet charge, and restored the line south-east of Rosières.

24th Division, Vrély, Warvillers and Rouvroy

A mixture of engineers, entrenching battalions and men from training schools were driven from Rouvroy on the division's right flank. Brigadier General Morgan's 72nd Composite Battalion briefly recaptured the village but they too had to retire to Warvillers when they ran out of grenades. Major General Daly ordered Brigadier Generals Stone and Dugan to withdraw 17 and 73 Brigades to Vrély after hearing XVIII Corps had retired on his right.

61st (2nd South Midland) Division, Marcelcave

Late in the afternoon, Major General MacKenzie was directed to move his men from support around Le Quesnel to the north-west, to join Carey's line at Marcelcave.

Another Withdrawal

Major Generals Heneker, Jackson and Malcolm met Lieutenant General Watts at midnight to tell him that their divisions were in danger of being cut off. Watts asked Gough, he spoke to Foch and they all agreed that XIX Corps' left had to withdraw onto Carey's Force as soon as possible. Events were moving fast on XIX Corps' right too, where the French had fallen back over six miles. There was nothing else to do but withdraw everyone to Carey's line.

It was around 4 am before Watts told his divisional commanders to fall back yet again, even later before the men at the front line heard. No one ran or marched any more, they were too tired; they just shuffled along until their officer told them to stop.

> *After some days and nights of constant fighting, they were blessed with two hours rest and then had to stagger up again to march; to line some scratch trench, to march again; and again to call on the last reserves of human endurance and face the enemy with rifle and bayonet.*

The only saving grace was that the Germans were equally exhausted and they would stop whenever the British soldiers laid down and took aim.

XVIII Corps
<u>30th Division and 36th (Ulster) Division, Bouchoir, Erches and Andechy</u>
Major General Nugent was worried because his line was broken, with 107
Brigade in front of Erches and the rest near Andechy, two miles in front.
The first attack nearly captured 108 Brigade headquarters and Brigadier
General Griffith was wounded while the GSO1, Lieutenant Colonel Place,
and two battalion officers were taken prisoner. It meant a lot of men did not
get the message to retire. The Germans drove the 15th, 1st and 2nd Irish
Rifles back to Arvillers and the 1st, 2nd and 9th Inniskillings followed
when they saw the French retreating south of the River Avre. That left
108 Brigade isolated at Andechy and the 1st and 9th Irish Fusiliers were
overrun.

After fighting to hold Bouchoir, the 2nd Bedfords and 2nd Scots
Fusiliers fell back when 36th Division lost Erches around midday and
the 17th King's, 11th South Lancashires (Pioneers) and 19th King's
retired to keep in line. The Germans then pushed south-west through
the gap heading for Montdidier while 90 and 89 Brigades rallied round
Folies.

Fifth Army's Summary
Fifth Army was still fighting on under French control but the time had come
to replace General Gough. He had commanded the Fifth Army (Reserve
army before 30 October 1916) through the Somme campaign and then
followed up the German withdrawal to the Hindenburg Line before the
difficult battle at Bullecourt. Gough had then been sent north to Flanders
to fight his way through the entire Third Ypres campaign. But Wilson now
needed a scapegoat and he blamed the reverses on the Somme on Gough,
to appease Lloyd George's government.

Gough's failure to build enough defences and the loss of the Somme
and Crozat Canals had caused many problems, particularly for the French.
The new Military Secretary, Major General Harold Ruggles-Brise visited
Fifth Army headquarters in Dury and in Gough's words, 'told me as nicely
as he could' he had been sacked. His replacement was General Sir Henry
Rawlinson, who had been serving as the British Military Representative
for the Supreme War Council. Gough's staff officers offered to help
Rawlinson's staff take over and the headquarters would be renamed Fourth
Army on 2 April.

Foch's order of the day had called for 'a supreme effort' and Pétain
had been told that 'not a yard more of French soil must be lost.' But the
plan to stay in contact with Fifth Army was severely tested when First
Army's line collapsed south of the Avre, exposing XVIII Corps' right. The

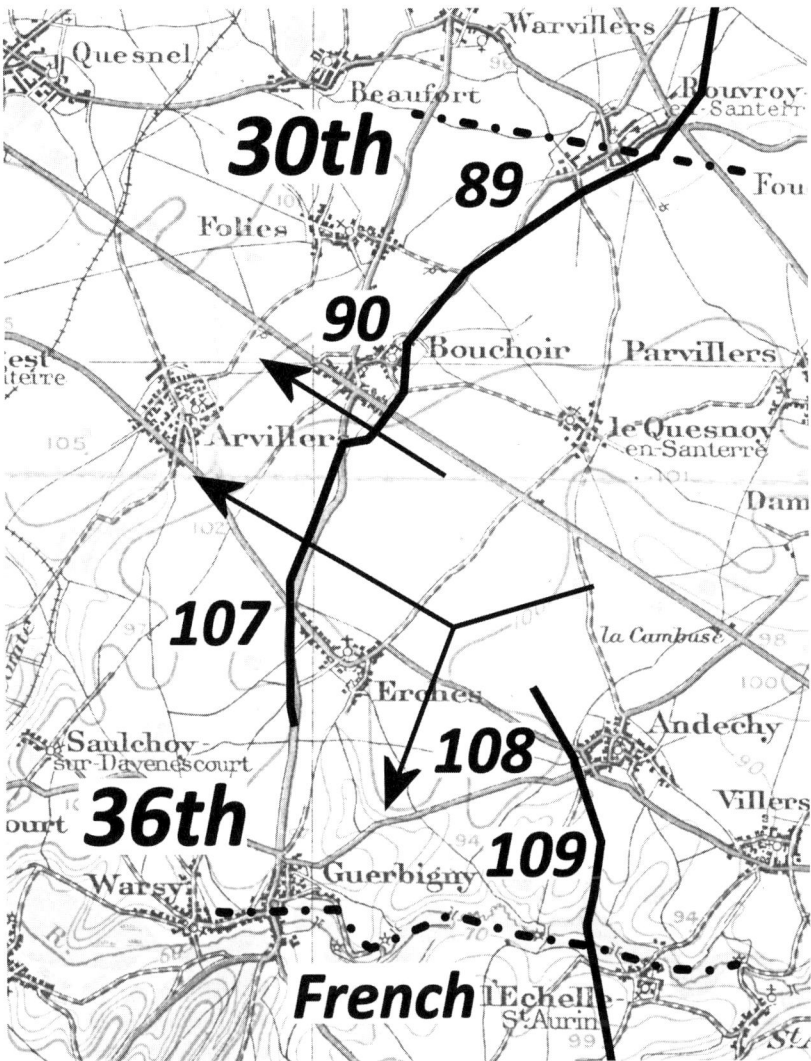

27 March: The gap in 36th Division's line resulted in the collapse of XVIII Corps' line.

French troops fell back up to fifteen miles, abandoning Montdidier. It was a worrying reverse because Amiens was a similar distance behind Fifth Army's line.

The Germans were as exhausted as the British and the French while the failure to make progress against Third Army was undermining morale.

OHL's refusal to send three divisions to Seventeenth Army resulted in an angry Crown Prince Rupprecht shouting, 'then we have lost the war.' The next day would test his theory because Operation Mars was to be launched towards Arras at dawn. Operation Valkyrie would be launched north of Arras the following day.

Chapter 16

Here They Are, Right on Me!

Operation Mars, 28 March

Eighteenth Army's progress towards Amiens was slowing down while it had almost stopped elsewhere. The plan was to launch Operation Mars towards Arras, kick-starting the advance elsewhere. General Otto von Below's Seventeenth Army would extend the attack front north by another seventeen miles astride the River Scarpe, mainly across the area of the Arras 1917 battlefield.

The attack would come as no surprise to GHQ and Third Army. Many of the preparations were rushed and working parties had been seen working around the clock. Aerial observers spotted the heavy howitzers used during Operation Michael moving north and they were then busy registering targets. A prisoner even suggested the attack would start on 25 March. Rumours were rife and one resulted in the following message: 'In view of possible appearance of enemy agents, warn all ranks against the use of the word RETIRE. Any person using this word before or during an attack to be shot.'

The bombardment used a similar timetable to that used on 21 March and 'the infantry in the front line soon realised that they were for it.' The heavy guns smothered the British battery positions with a mixture of gas and high explosive shells while the field guns shelled targets in the Forward Zone. The British guns retaliated and many guns hit no man's land, causing havoc amongst the assault troops assembled in craters.

Trench mortars added to the rising crescendo of shell fire and in many cases the British front line was 'blotted out'. A few minutes before zero hour 'a glistening line of bayonets, those of the Germans ready to go over the top, rising as it seemed out of the morning mist'. Then at 7.30 am nine divisions advanced against First Army's right and Third Army's left. Artillery commanders listened closely to the enemy bombardment and responded accordingly when they heard the creeping barrage moving forward. Their counter-barrage landed in no man's land as the German infantry, 'advancing in dense masses, made a determined attack.'

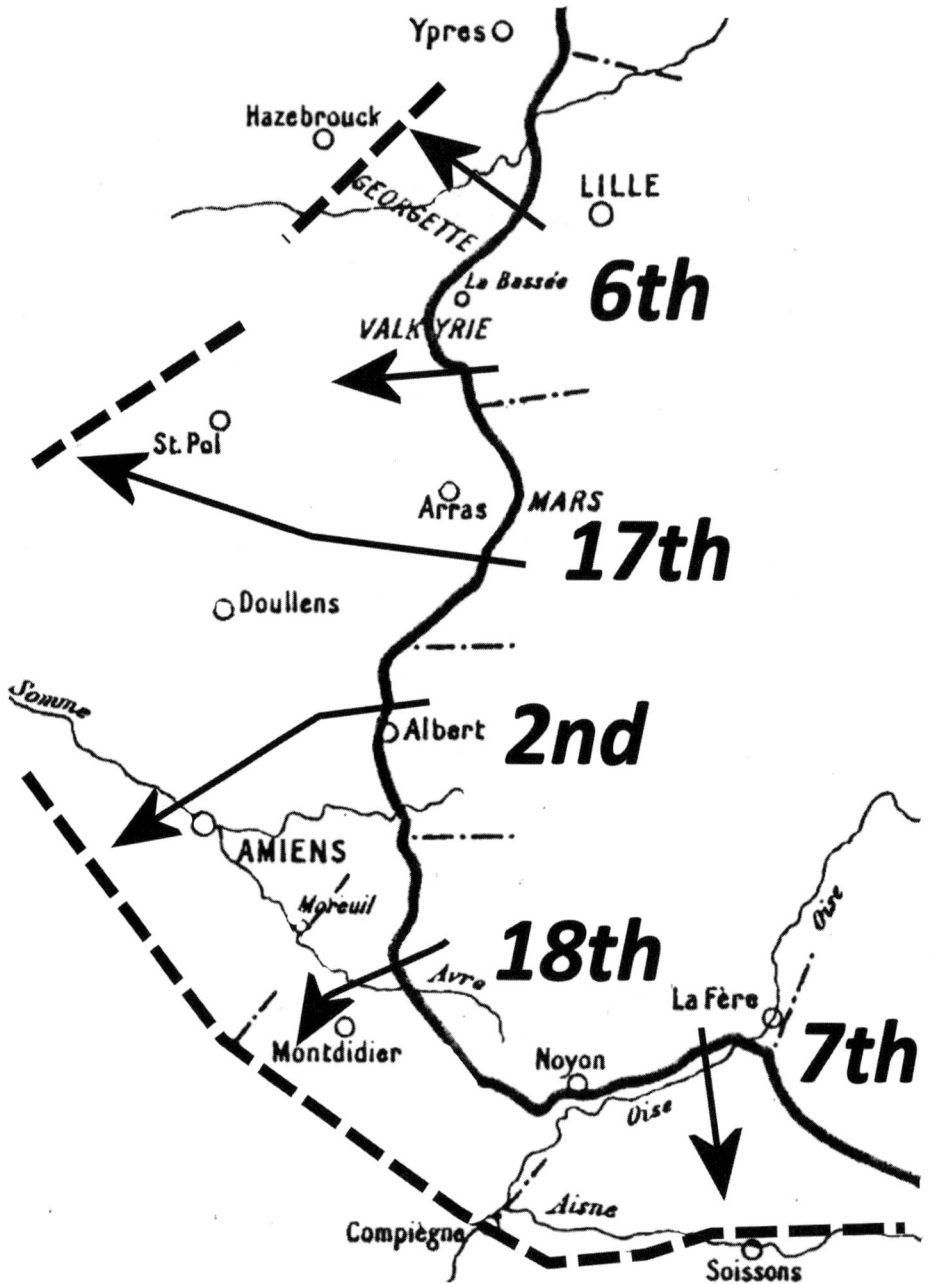

Operation Mars was designed to smash Third Army's left and take Arras.

First Army, 28 March
Vimy Ridge overlooked the area north-east of Arras and while the high ground was useful for observation, it was too far behind the front line to help the gunners.

XIII Corps
<u>56th (1st London) Division, Arleux and Gavrelle</u>
First Army had treated the Forward Zone as an outpost line and it had concentrated on improving the Battle Zone. However, 4th Division was going to hold the front line in strength and so 56th Division had to do the same, to present a continuous front to the enemy. The outpost garrisons stood no chance in the early morning mist and the last message from one post was, 'The Germans are on the wire. We'll do our best.'

The assault teams could not keep up with the creeping barrage as they crossed no man's land and they then struggled to get through the maze of wire and trenches between Arleux and Gavrelle. The delay gave the London machine-gun teams time to emerge from their dugouts and meet the onslaught. The barrage called down by the SOS flares scattered the waves of infantry that were following.

Brigadier General Loch's 168 Brigade was in the process of a relief when the German bombardment began and a few men of the 1st Canadian Rifles were still holding Sugar Post at zero hour. The 1/13th London Regiment held onto Arleux Post and Tommy Post, south-east of Arleux. Oppy and Beatty Posts were overrun on the 1/4th London Regiment's flanks but Wood Post held on in the centre. Major Phillips counter-attacked with twenty details, giving Lieutenant Hudson time to form a defensive line in Marquis Trench. The German assault teams were forced below ground but they then used trenches to work around the 1/4th London Regiment's flank.

Brigadier General Coke's 169 Brigade held Marine Trench and Naval Trench, covering Gavrelle. The 1/5th London Regiment had been hit so hard that the enemy infantry 'simply walked into the front line and rushed the few men at the blocks'. They had to abandon Bird Post, Bradford Post and Mill Post as the enemy infiltrated Gavrelle and then withdrew onto the 1/2nd London Regiment in the Battle Zone. Lieutenant Colonel Glazier made the 1/16th London Regiment form a flank and Gavrelle Post poured enfilade fire into the advancing Germans.

British howitzers firing short destroyed a trench block and then 4th Division withdrew on the right, so Towy Post had to be abandoned. Captain Lowndes was the last man to leave but the Londoners fought on in the many shell holes and communication trenches. Some of the Germans 'threw their rifles forward into a shell hole, held up their hands and advanced, only to drop by the side of their arms, which they immediately proceeded to use'. The Londoners stopped them.

The Germans reorganised for a second attempt, using smoke to hide the limbers hauling field guns forward. They were knocked out as soon as it cleared and the Londoners held on until Major General Frederick Dudgeon ordered everyone back to the Battle Zone. Lieutenant Colonel Marchmont watched the withdrawal through his binoculars: 'it was carried out in a very steady and orderly way, the men leaving in groups of about a dozen. Although exposed to heavy fire, they made excellent use of the ground and suffered very few casualties. The men of the reserve company met the survivors returning and covered their retirement.'

Third Army, 28 March

XVII Corps
Lieutenant General Sir Charles Fergusson's men were deployed east of Arras. The concern was that the Germans would infiltrate across the spurs and valleys alongside the Scarpe. North of the river, 4th Division held the Forward Zone while 15th Division held the Battle Zone to the south-east of Arras.

<u>4th Division, North of the Scarpe</u>
Major General Torquhil Matheson's men were trained to evacuate the front line by day and returned at night to reduce the number of casualties. The German bombardment caught his men in the front line and there were many casualties as trenches were flattened and posts were blown in.

A marshy area divided 56th and 4th Divisions, south of Gavrelle, and it was too exposed to hold. The bombardment tore gaps in the wire and knocked out the 2nd Essex's posts detailed to watch the area. The assault teams then moved across it quickly before turning behind the Essex and only thirty-five men escaped back to the battalion headquarters.

Lieutenant Colonel Watkins had warned the 2nd Lancashire Fusiliers to 'man their battle stations' north of Fampoux and he told them 'not to yield an inch'. They did not and the Lewis gunners 'mowed down the Germans time after time' while 'officers and men could be seen lying on the parapet shooting as fast as they could handle their rifles.' Second Lieutenant Bernard Cassidy 'moved up and down Humid Trench, cheering his men'. He could not retire because the ground behind was open but he kept Watkins informed by telephone. Then came the words, 'here they are, right on me,' and the line went silent. Only six men of his company escaped. Cassidy was posthumously awarded the Victoria Cross for saving 4th Division's left flank.

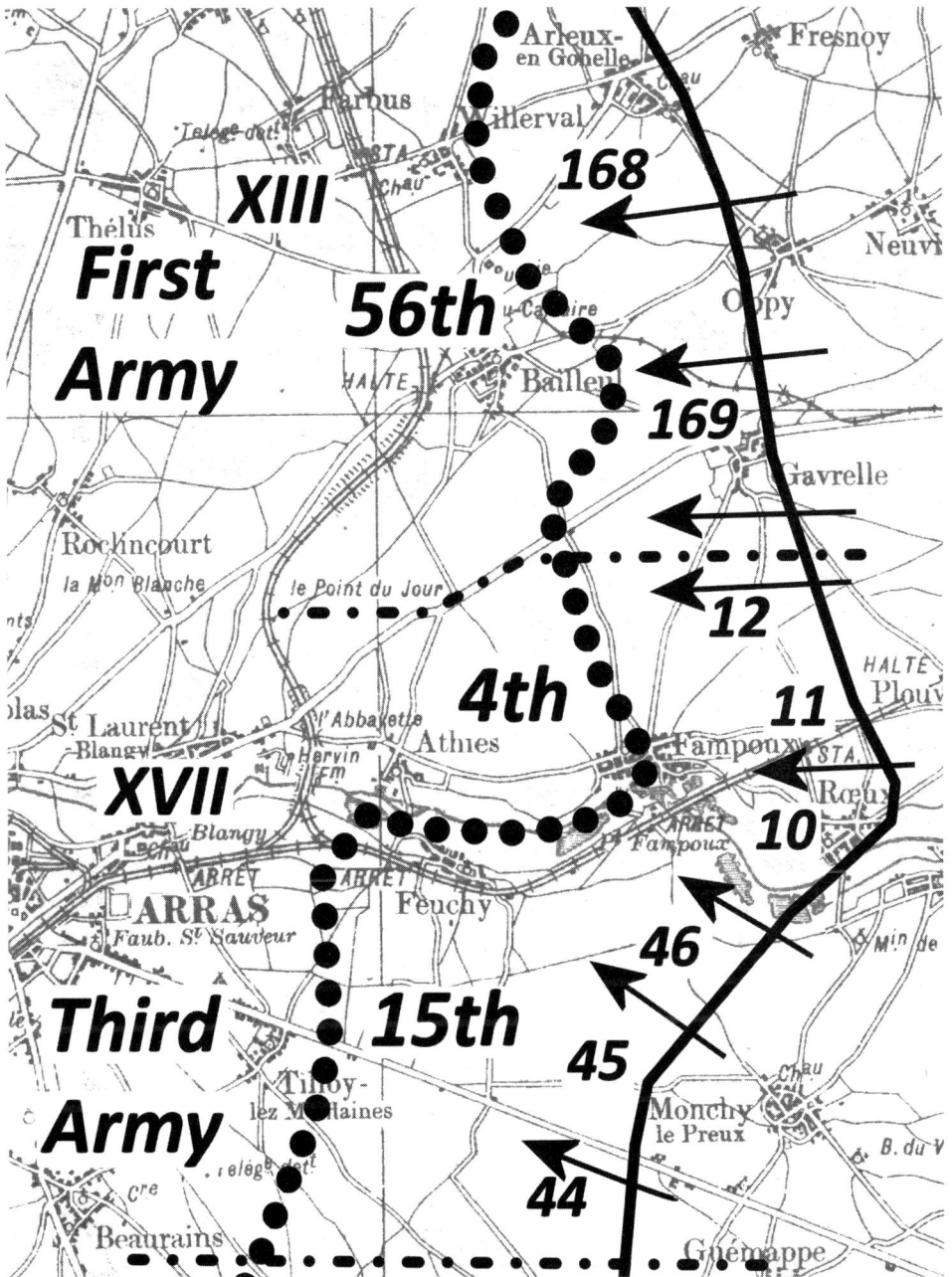

28 March XIII Corps and XVII Corps: Heavy attacks resulted in deep penetrations, so there was a withdrawal into and beyond the Battle Zone.

Lieutenant Colonel Armitage's 1st Hampshires were driven back along Calico Trench, on 11 Brigade's front, north of Roeux, while Lieutenant Evans kept the Germans at bay. The 1st Somersets then formed a defensive flank along the north bank of the Scarpe after the 2nd Seaforths abandoned Roeux. The clearing mist forced the Germans to advance along trenches and their attacks 'now lacked punch and vigour,' but the 2nd Seaforths became isolated when the railway bridge across the river was demolished.

Both 12 and 11 Brigades made a fighting withdrawal to the Battle Zone during the afternoon and the attacks died down. A counter-attack at dusk by 10 Brigade and some of 15th Division secured Fampoux and the north bank of the Scarpe.

15th (Scottish) Division, Astride the Cambrai Road

The attacks hit Major General Reed's line in succession from right to left, with the first one against 44 Brigade at 6 am. Brigadier General Hilliam was able to report that only one trench was lost and only after a company of Lieutenant Colonel MacLeod's 7th Camerons had been reduced to twelve men. The mist had cleared by the time 45 Brigade's line was hit but the 13th Royal Scots were overrun leaving Captains Kelly and Considine isolated on Orange Hill. Both brigades retired to the back of the Battle Zone but Lieutenant Colonel Hannay and the 13th Royal Scots' staff held on around Feuchy Chapel until his men had fought their way back. The third attack drove Major Binnie's 9th Black Watch out of Jerusalem and Cromarty Trenches on 46 Brigade's front, leaving the 7/8th KOSBs cut off on the south bank of the Scarpe.

Green flares told the German gunners when and where to fire while the infantry advanced after a pre-agreed length of shelling. Major General Reed was so concerned that he ordered his artillery to fall back after telling the infantry to hold the Green Line at all costs. Unfortunately, his message was misinterpreted and there was a withdrawal to the Green Line while rearguards detonated mines to stop the Germans following.

A call for reinforcements resulted in General Fergusson sending the corps cyclist battalion and as many men as could be spared from the wagon lines forward to reinforce the line. He also directed a tank battalion to Telegraph Hill, behind 15th Division's right flank. They were enough and by dusk all three brigades were digging in 600 yards in front of the Green Line.

Fergusson's message ran, 'I knew you could be relied upon to stick it out to the end. Well done. There are fresh troops in support of you now but I want the honour of holding Arras to be yours.'

VI Corps

3rd Division, Neuville-Vitasse

The Germans assembled on the west bank of the Cojeul stream during the night, ready to attack 9 Brigade at dawn. The British artillery did not see the SOS signals in the morning mist so one group pushed past the 1st Northumberland Fusiliers and the 13th King's and headed for Neuville-Vitasse. Captain Lawrence and both Lieutenants Rose and Turnbull were hit in quick succession but Lieutenants Burton and Allen 'set a magnificent example by their energy and determination'. The Fusiliers stemmed the tide for a time but many were forced to surrender when their ammunition ran out. Most of the 13th King's 'were last seen standing on the parapet of their trench engaged in a gallant but hopeless fight. None returned.'

Captain Chipper found chaos when he went forward, so he organised everyone he could find into a defensive line and this time the gunners saw the SOS flares. The two lieutenant colonels divided command of the front between them, with Moulton Barrett organising the front line while Lawrence coordinated the support line. Brigadier General Potter sent Captain Lord forward to form a flank with the 4th Royal Fusiliers but Major Buckle had to take over the front line when Moulton Barrett was wounded.

The Germans kept coming and 'the hillside teemed with field-grey figures in coal-scuttle helmets dodging from shell hole to shell hole… Further away were columns of infantry advancing down the valley apparently unopposed.' Another group bombed along the trenches in 8 Brigade's sector, driving back Major Johnston's 7th Shropshires and Lieutenant Colonel Gordon's 1st Scots Fusiliers. The Scots were overwhelmed when they ran out of grenades and Captain Hadden was just one of over 360 casualties. Brigadier General Tanner had no option but to withdraw the rest of 8 Brigade to the back of the Battle Zone.

The mist had cleared when a later attack hit 76 Brigade's line. Both the 1st Gordons and 8th King's Own held on until the Germans pushed past their flanks and engaged Lieutenant Colonel Likeman's 2nd Suffolks. Men helped manhandle the guns forward so they could knock out the German machine guns but the German infantry kept coming. Captains Simpson and Baker were cut off and surrendered when they ran out of ammunition but the Germans had to stop to regroup because they had suffered so many casualties.

Green flares signalled the start of a new bombardment and the infantry again advanced after a pre-agreed time. Major General Deverell gave the same messages about holding the Green Line around Neuville-Vitasse but they were again misinterpreted and everyone abandoned the Battle Zone, carrying all the wounded with them.

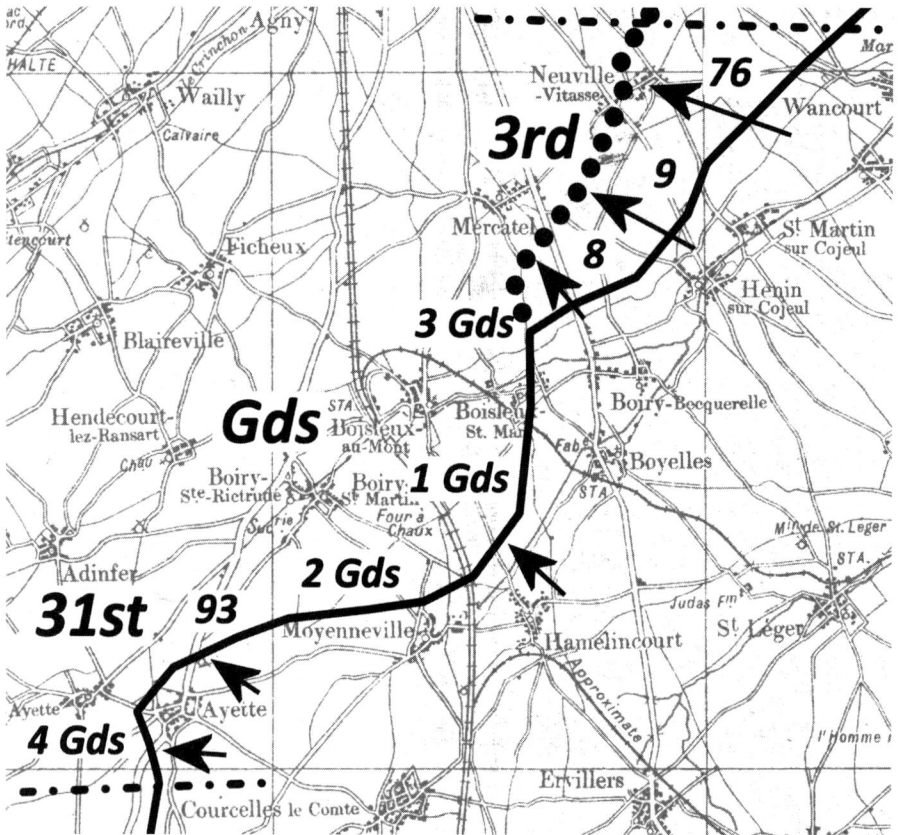

28 March VI Corps: Misunderstood orders resulted in a withdrawal to the Green Line and the loss of Neuville-Vitasse.

It was some time before the Germans followed up but a local attack in the afternoon drove the 8th King's Own out of the Green Line. The loss of Neuville-Vitasse brought a long day's fighting to an end but the men faced a miserable night. The officers had to organise their men while they dug a new trench in the rain. No one quite knew where they were and one convoy of supply wagons nearly drove straight into the enemy lines before making a quick about turn under fire.

Guards Division, Boisleux St Marc to Moyenneville
The 1st Welsh Guards were pushed back around Boisleux St Marc, on 3 Guards Brigade's left, due to the attack on 3rd Division. Patrols of the 1st Irish Guards and the 2nd Grenadier Guards spotted the German infantry

dribbling across the Cojeul stream on 1 Guards Brigade's front but the artillery made sure the 'attack was nipped in the bud'. The 3rd Grenadier Guards and the 13th York and Lancaster stopped the only attack on 1 Guards Brigade's right flank.

31st Division, Ayette

Major General Bridgford's men stopped three attacks either side of Ayette during the morning. A few Germans entered Ayette and the 2nd Irish Guards and the 3rd Coldstream Guards covered the exits by fire rather than try to retake the village. Lieutenant Colonel Alexander requested a barrage when masses of troops in marching order appeared in the distance and they were soon scattered.

IV Corps

42nd (East Lancashire) Division, Ablainzevelle

The Germans advanced from Ablainzevelle and Logeast Wood towards General Solly-Flood's line on three occasions. A few penetrated the line only to be killed or captured by the 6th and 8th Manchesters. Many others were shot down and the troops sometimes stood on their parapets to get better targets.

62nd (2nd West Riding) Division, Rossignol Wood

The Germans wanted to drive Major General Braithwaite's men from Bucquoy because it had commanding views of Third Army's rear. They attacked the village and Rossignol Wood, sometimes in 'six waves of German troops, advancing shoulder to shoulder,' but they came to grief as 'time after time they advanced up the open slope, only to fall and melt away.' Eventually, they entered Rossignol Wood between Lieutenant Colonel Perry's 2/4th KOYLIs and Lieutenant Colonel Blacker's 2/4th York and Lancasters.

Lieutenant Colonel Oliver Watson led what remained of the 5th KOYLIs forward only to find his men were badly outnumbered. He ordered his men to retire, staying behind to cover the withdrawal until he was killed; he was posthumously awarded the Victoria Cross. The 8th West Yorkshire would clear the wood during the night.

Private Thomas Young acted as a stretcher bearer for the 9th Durhams (Pioneers) during 62nd Division's time around Bucquoy. He rescued nine men under fire and would be awarded the Victoria Cross.

4th Australian Division, Hébuterne

The Germans 'made several half-hearted attempts to attack,' doing nothing more than keeping the Australians 'busily firing all day long at easy targets'.

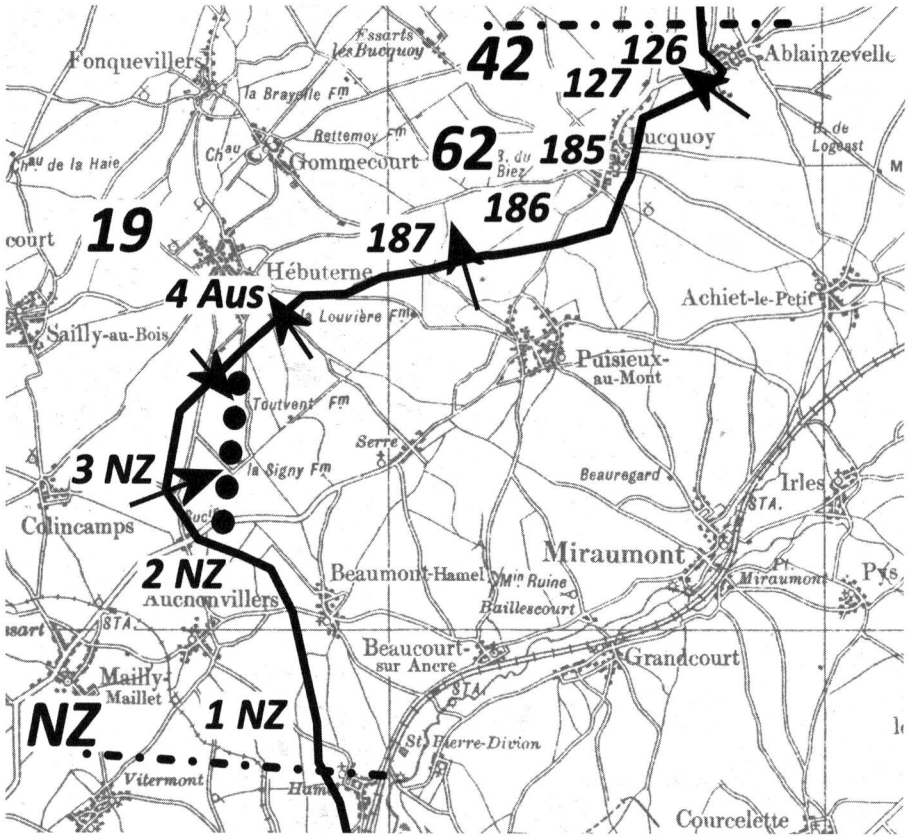

28 March IV Corps: Half-hearted attacks against IV Corps' line were all stopped.

The 15th and 13th Australian Battalions stopped all attacks aimed at Hébuterne but the 14th Australian Battalion lost Nameless Farm. The Germans eventually abandoned the area because 'the old trenches were too deep in mud.'

New Zealand Division, Colincamps to Beaumont Hamel
Having secured the line, the New Zealanders struck back, looking to improve their position between Hébuterne and the Ancre. Major Bell's 3rd Rifle Brigade captured a valuable observation post south of Hébuterne but the 4th Rifle Brigade were unable to make progress towards La Signy Farm. The German bombing teams used the old British trenches leading from Beaumont Hamel as cover but the two Auckland battalions of 1 New Zealand Brigade stopped them all. The Germans did not try to dislodge

the two Canterbury Battalions of 2nd New Zealand Brigade from around Y Ravine.

V Corps

12th (Eastern) Division, Aveluy Wood

Major General Scott's battalions had reinforced 63rd Division along the Ancre. The 6th Queen's stopped an attempt to capture Hamel but Lieutenant Colonel Dawson's 6th Queen's Own lost ground north of Aveluy wood. Lieutenant Colonel Impey's 7th Sussex and Lieutenant Colonel Nicolls' 5th Berkshires were digging in when enemy planes dropped flares marking their trenches for the artillery. Then the infantry attacked, resulting in bitter fighting in which it was difficult to distinguish between friend and foe because so many Germans were wearing British helmets taken from the dead. Major Osborne eventually counter-attacked with some of the 9th Essex, driving the enemy out of the wood.

17th (Northern) Division, Albert

It should have been straightforward to assemble troops under cover of the ruins of Albert and then advance down the Amiens road. However, the German officers were experiencing problems because their men were more interested in getting drunk than fighting. 'It is practically certain that the reason we did not reach Amiens was the looting in Albert.' The town which had been 'captured fairly easily, contained so much wine that the divisions, which ought properly to have marched through them lay about unfit to fight in the rooms and cellars.' Discipline had collapsed and men were staggering about, carrying loot or dressed up in 'comic disguise' and they were ignoring their officers.

VII Corps

4th Australian Division, South of Albert

Before dawn 200 Germans headed for the 47th and 48th Australian Battalions in the mist but 'the sound of bayonet scabbards flapping on the thighs of marching troops' gave them away. Sergeant Stanley McDougall shot many down with his Lewis gun but around fifty still crossed the railway. He turned his weapon on them and then killed seven with his bayonet before the rest surrendered. McDougall took over thirty prisoners and would be awarded the Victoria Cross.

35th Division, Along the Ancre

The Germans occupied an abandoned Dernancourt opposite 106 Brigade during the night and then surged out of it at dawn against the 19th

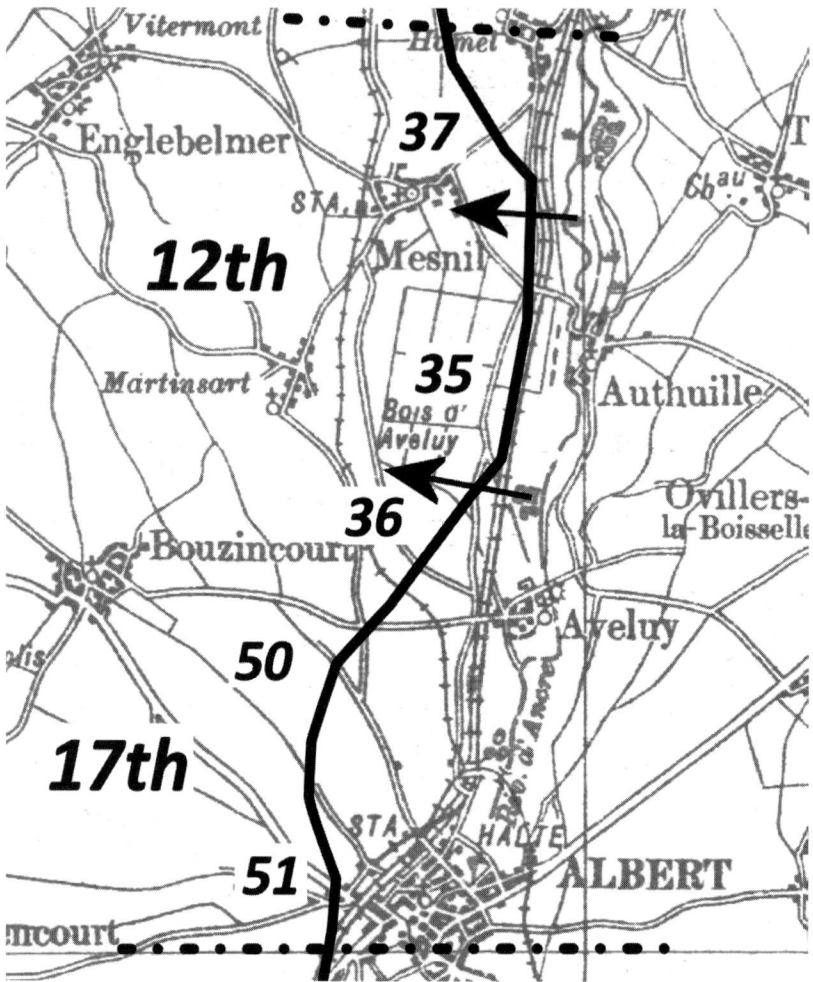

28 March: V Corps managed to contain the German bridgehead west of Aveluy.

Northumberland Fusiliers. Corporal Dodds' Lewis gun team accounted for many while an injured Lieutenant Colonel Foord 'decided that the best defensive is the offensive'. A bayonet charge by one hundred Fusiliers recaptured Dernancourt and Major Gooderson's 18th HLI reinforced the position. The third of three attacks drove the 18th Lancashire Fusiliers out of Treux and the 19th Durhams out of Marett Wood in 104 Brigade's sector.

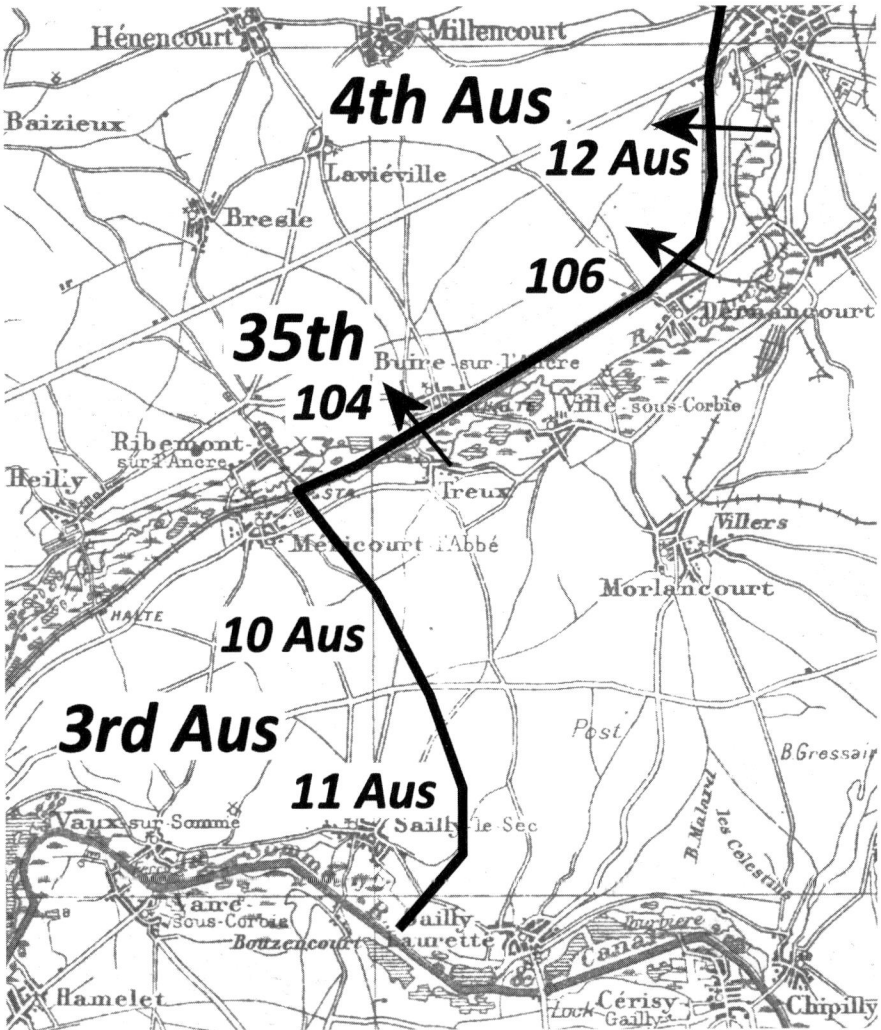

28 March VII Corps: The arrival of 3rd Australian Division stopped the Germans getting any closer to Amiens.

3rd Australian Division

The Germans made no progress against the fresh Australian troops digging in between the Ancre and the Somme.

Fifth Army, 28 March

After a long week, General Gough's command had been reduced to seven battered divisions holding a thin line south of the Somme. He also had a mixture of stragglers and support troops deployed astride the Amiens road under Major General Carey. The left flank was under threat because the Germans had been crossing Cerisy bridge and moving behind 39th and 66th Divisions all night long. It was dawn before the order to withdraw was sent out but Feetham's and Malcolm's men were under attack by the time they got it. Some runners would be hit en route while others could not find the battalion and company commanders in time. It meant Gough's plan to retire onto Carey's Force turned into a chaotic retreat.

XIX Corps

<u>39th Division, Amiens Road to Bayonvillers to Cayeux to Démuin</u>
Major General Feetham's three battered brigades were attacked astride the Amiens road. First 116 Brigade and then 117 Brigade fell back in a south-west direction through Bayonvillers to Wiencourt-l'Équipée. Brigadier General Bellingham and his brigade major were captured as 118 Brigade formed the rear guard. The whole division, or what was left of it, fell back across the Luce stream to Cayeux as heavy rain blinded the enemy. They then withdrew behind Carey's Force when it was dark.

<u>66th (2nd East Lancashire) Division, Guillaucourt back to Carey's Force</u>
The Germans pushed behind the three brigade battalions after 39th Division fell back and they too were soon falling back to Guillaucourt. A counter-attack by 39th Division kept the enemy at bay long enough to escape in the heavy rain which fell during the afternoon. They ended up around Ignaucourt on the Luce stream, alongside Cary's Force. The Lancashire Fusiliers had found food in Démuin but they were unimpressed when Brigadier General Borrett 'asked them if they did not infinitely prefer a war of movement to life in the trenches'. We can only imagine what they thought when he was wounded a couple of days later.

<u>61st (2nd South Midland) Division, Counter-Attack towards War-fusée-Abancourt</u>
The plan was for 61st Division to stage a counter-attack towards the main Amiens road, to clear the Germans from behind XIX Corps' left flank. Major General Mackenzie protested he had too few men while Brigadier Generals Spooner and Pagan said their two brigades were too tired to attack at dawn. So they advanced at midday with no artillery or machine gun support, just a lone plane strafing the enemy position. The Germans

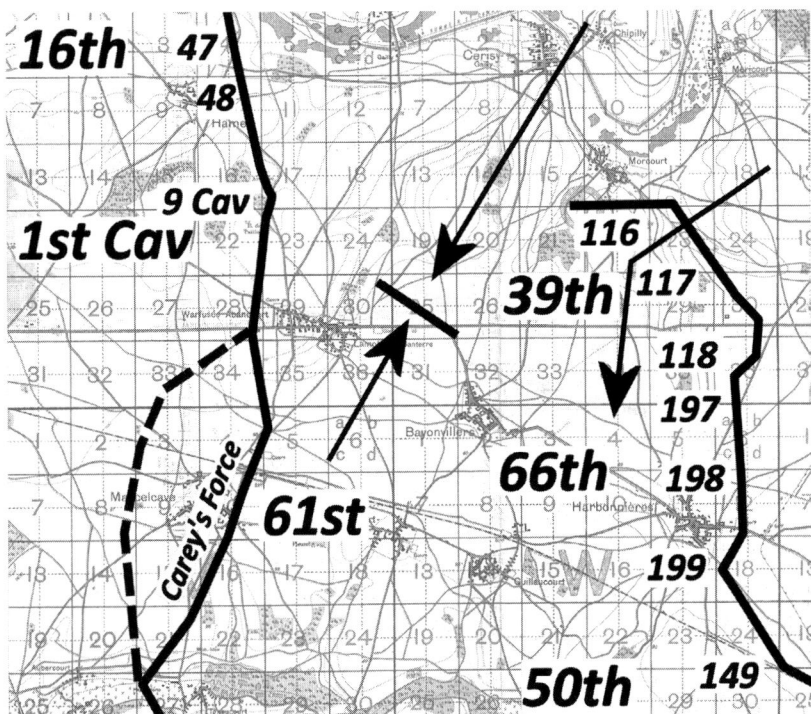

28 March XIX Corps North: Attempts to restore XIX Corps' north flank failed and a difficult retreat onto Carey's Force followed.

waited until the South Midland men were only 200 yards from their line around Warfusée-Abancourt and then opened fire. The 2/5th Gloucesters alone suffered over 200 casualties.

50th (Northumbrian) Division, Harbonnières to Marcelcave

A surprise attack from a wood drove the 7th DLI (Pioneers) back south of Harbonnières, exposing 149 Brigade's left. Brigadier General Riddell wanted the 22nd Entrenching Battalion to counter-attack but the Germans reached them before the order did and they were forced to abandon their dinner and fall back towards Guillaucourt. The 4th and 6th Northumberland Fusiliers and the 5th Durhams followed but they made a stand north of Caix until dusk. Major General Jackson's men then withdrew behind Carey's Line around Marcelcave as heavy rain hid their movements from the Germans. The Northumbrian men were tired, hungry, cold and wet but they had not been beaten.

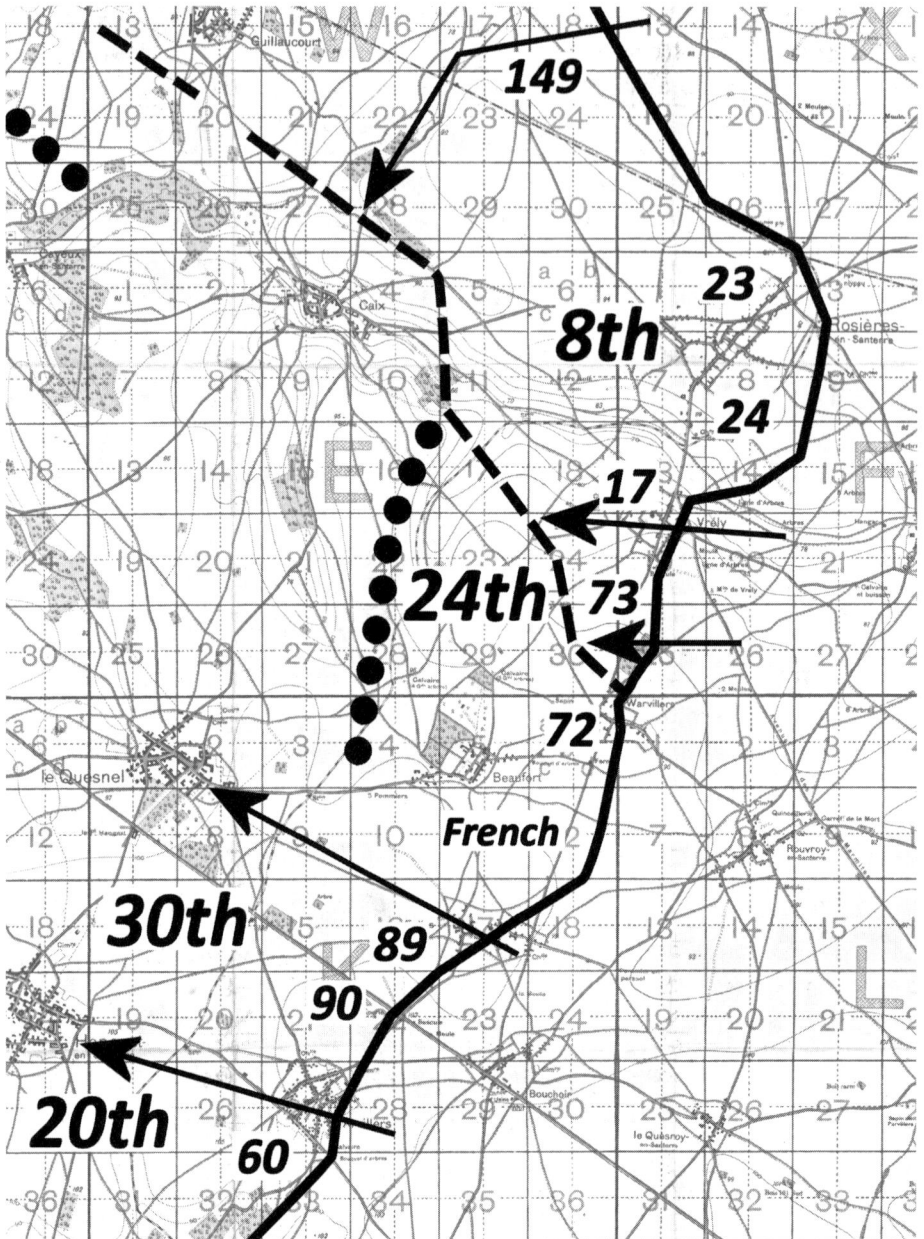

28 March XIX Corps South: The collapse of XIX Corps' left wing resulted in a withdrawal of the right onto Carey's Force under cover of a torrential rain storm.

8th Division, Rosières

Brigadier General Coffin VC rode around giving his men encouragement as they withdrew behind Rosières. The Germans were in Caix behind 23 Brigade by the time Brigadier General Grogan received another order to withdraw. Unfortunately, his brigade major was wounded, so the 2nd West Yorkshires and 2nd Middlesex never got the message and they were surrounded. Lieutenant Colonel Lowry sent the West Yorkshires back in small groups, in the hope they could escape but he was taken prisoner. The guard swapped his officer's overcoat for a thin waterproof cape but Lowry then escaped and acquired a German helmet to complete his disguise. After noting troop movements and battery positions, he headed for his own lines and went straight to Fifth Army headquarters to report what he had seen.

Meanwhile, the 2nd Middlesex got cut off and many ended up behind the French lines. Lieutenant Colonel Page was pleased to welcome them back a couple of days later, believing they had been captured.

24th Division, Vrély and Warvillers back into Reserve

The first German attack drove the 12th Sherwoods and the 8th Queen's out of Vrély on the left. The next one captured Warvillers from 72 Brigade Battalion on the right, forcing the 13th Middlesex to redeploy to stay in touch. Major General Daly ordered a general retirement during the afternoon, while heavy rain blinded the Germans. The whole division withdrew through Carey's Force and into reserve.

XVIII Corps

30th and 20th (Light) Divisions, Arvillers

Lieutenant General Maxse's two battered divisions were placed under French control but the relief took longer than expected because they were dealing with two French divisions. The Germans attacked before it was complete and both the 30th and 20th Divisions were driven back from Arvillers and through the French troops around Le Quesnel and Hangest. Captain Tait and the 12th Rifle Brigade stopped the Germans cutting off large numbers of men as the whole line fell back another four miles to Mézières and La Neuville.

28 March Summary

The British and Dominion soldiers had stopped the German attacks for now but there would be others. CIGS General Wilson told Haig that the War Cabinet had just agreed every fit trained man would be sent to France. The move would not increase the size of the BEF but it would bring it back up to strength. Haig had been asking Pétain to relieve Fifth Army as soon as possible but the arrangements were postponed following the retreat around Montdidier. Instead, Rawlinson was told his tired troops had to hold on between the Somme and the Avre because the French divisions were needed to shore up First Army's line.

The Germans, meanwhile, knew Operation Mars had failed. Seventeenth Army had not widened the breach in Third Army's line and it had only had limited success elsewhere. 'Before Bucquoy and Hébuterne the blood of Below's divisions had flowed in torrents; enormous sacrifices had been made in vain.' Hurried planning had meant that parts of the bombardment had missed the British trenches while the creeping barrage had been poor. The failure meant Eighteenth Army would be no longer looking to drive the French back towards Paris, instead it would help Second Army capture Amiens.

Ludendorff would stop Mars and cancel Operation Valkyrie, Sixth Army's attack north of Arras. Instead, Sixth Army was to prepare Operation Georgette (a scaled down version of George). It would attack across the Lys plain and drive towards the rail centre of Hazebrouck, eighteen miles behind First Army's front. That would cut the main supply route to most of the BEF and threaten the Ypres Salient. General Ferdinand von Quast was told to be ready to attack in just over a week.

Chapter 17

The Power of Attack was Exhausted

29 March

After a rainy night, Foch and Haig, and their chiefs of staff, Weygand and Lawrence, met in Abbeville to discuss future operations. It was time 'to restore order everywhere and remedy the dispersion of the troops which has been the natural consequence of the haste with which they have been engaged'. In the meantime, the generals had to make sure that there were enough reinforcements and ammunition to hold on. The British Fifth Army had to make sure the Germans did not reach Amiens while the French First and Third Armies had to push them back north and east of Montdidier.

At the front, it was the quietest day since the offensive had begun. Third Army's left had stabilised while most of its right was behind the Ancre. Fifth Army still had to hold on in front of Amiens. Two divisional commanders, Major Generals Edward Feetham and Malcolm, would be hit by shrapnel during the day; Feetham died of his injuries.

Fifth Army, 29 March
XIX Corps
<u>16th (Irish) and 1st Cavalry Divisions, River Somme to the Amiens Road</u>
Composite brigade battalions of 16th Division held the river bank while dismounted troopers of 1st Cavalry Division were deployed north of the Amiens road. The Germans captured a trench near Hamel so a squadron of the 11th Hussars cantered up and dismounted. They fixed bayonets and the Germans ran as the bold troopers advanced.

<u>61st (2nd South Midland) Division, North of Aubercourt</u>
Major General Mackenzie's men had been 'fighting by day, marching and digging by night, without ever getting a proper meal and without being able to take off their boots or get any rest'. They were only 'holding a thin line of posts 10 miles in front of Amiens with no supports of any kind. Had the Germans attacked during the next three days, Amiens was theirs.' Four Canadian motor machine gun teams were sent forward with orders to fire

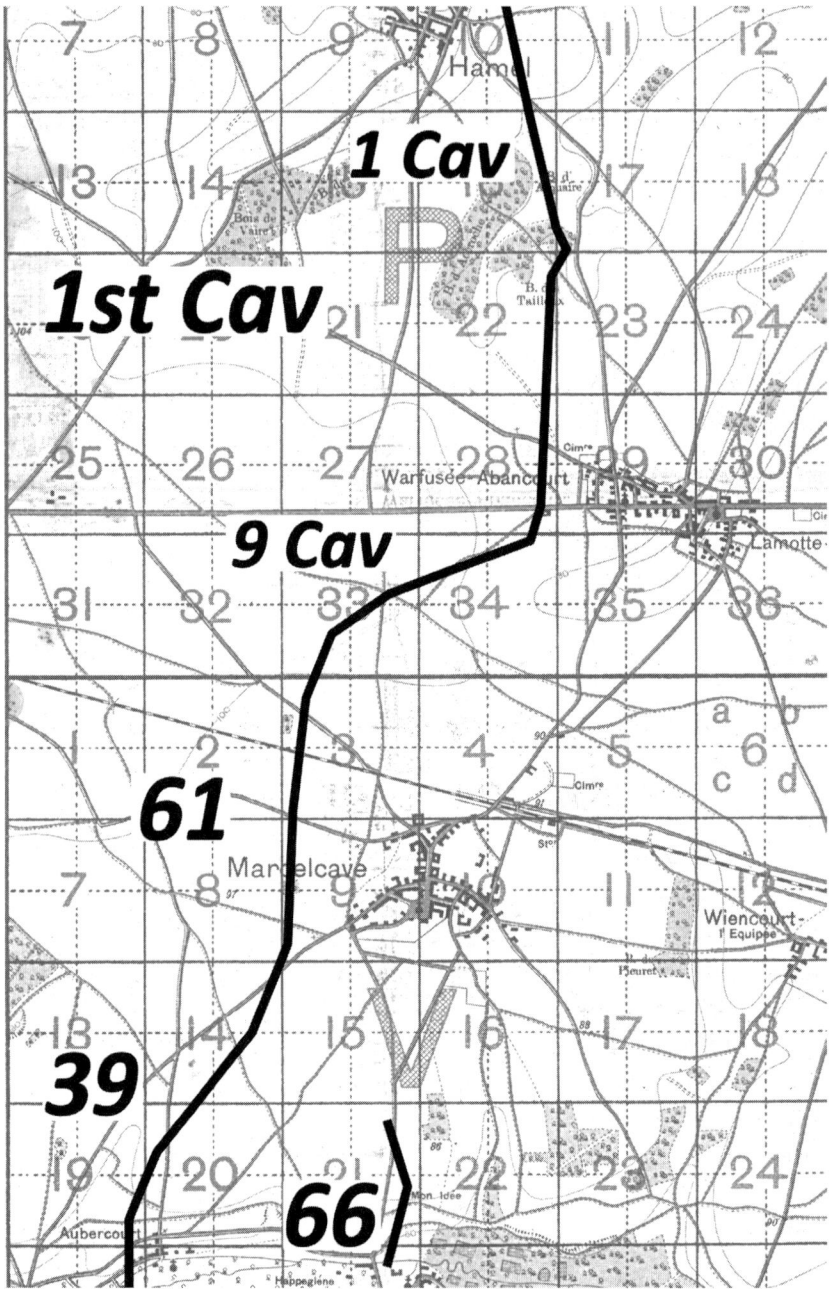

29 March XIX Corps North: The thin line of men between the Somme and the Amiens road held on.

as much ammunition as they could spare, to make the Germans think they faced a lot of men. The ruse worked, they held on and later received the message, 'Well done again, Sixty One,' from Maxse.

39th Division, Aubercourt
Major General Feetham's depleted command was driven back from Aubercourt, on the north side of the Luce stream, after the French retired to Démuin on the opposite bank.

20th (Light) Division, South Bank of the Luce
Major General Douglas Smith's men were in support south of the River Luce but an attack drove the French back through the 25th Entrenching Battalion and Brigadier General Cochrane's 61 Brigade. Brigadier Generals Hyslop and Duncan organised a counter-attack against the enemy flank around Mézières but 59 and 60 Brigade Battalions fell back after all their officers were hit. The Germans drove the French all the way back to Moreuil Wood and Lieutenant Colonel Thomson had to cancel a second counter-attack by the 150 Brigade Battalion when a general withdrawal was ordered.

29 March Summary
The day may have been quiet but there was still the question of the reserves to address. Foch welcomed the news that General Pershing had placed his four American divisions 'absolutely at his disposal'. But Foch thought it was too dangerous to relieve the British troops while the Germans were still strong south of the Somme. He did not want his troops to be fed into the battle piecemeal either because he wanted to assemble a large counter-attack force. He wanted the British to hold on and defend the south bank of the Luce 'to the last extremity'. Foch also told Pétain to send all the British troops of III Corps, still holding on south of the Oise (mainly 58th Division), to Fifth Army.

During the early hours, OHL ordered Seventeenth Army to abandon the Mars attack around Arras. General von Below had to withdraw all the spare infantry and artillery while the rest of the batteries continued firing registration shots to make it look like another attack was imminent. Meanwhile, General von Marwitz was urged to attack around Albert and push across the Ancre before it was too late.

Ludendorff told Eighteenth Army to continue pushing towards Amiens. British, Anzac and French reserves were heading towards the area and General von Hutier's message to his corps commanders said, 'The enemy for the moment has only inferior or beaten troops opposite

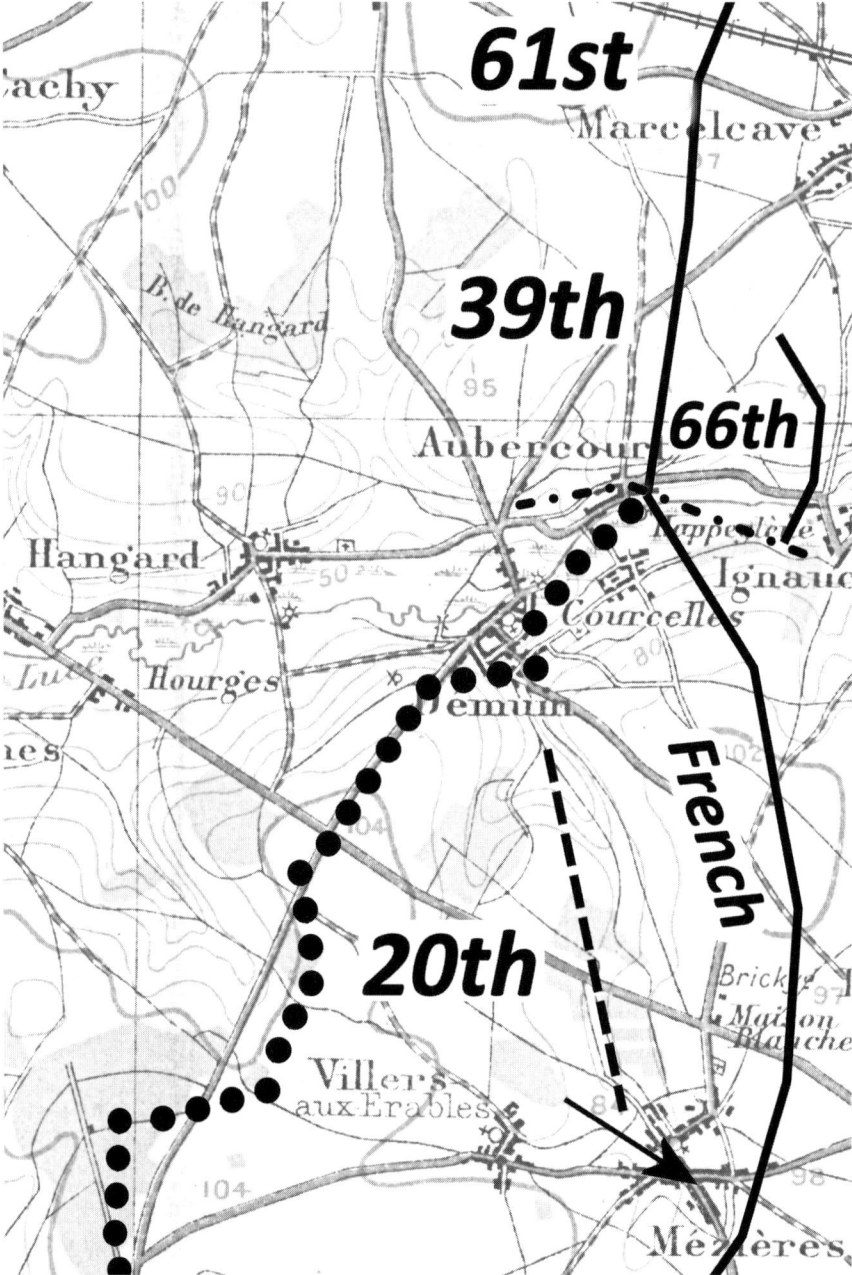

29 March XIX Corps South: XIX Corps' right was driven back along the south side of the Luce stream.

us. Reinforcements are said to be approaching him via St Just and Compiegne. They must not be permitted to engage according to plan. The army will attack to-morrow with all possible force.' Despite all the remonstrations, little offensive action would be or could be carried out for several days.

Ludendorff's instructions to his army commanders read, 'Amiens is now the objective; to secure that place all the efforts of this and the following days will be directed; the attacks near Montdidier and eastward of that town are only diversions designed to detain enemy forces.' The question was, could Second Army reach the important railway centre now that fresh Australians and New Zealand troops were deploying alongside the weary British ones?

Third Army, 30 March
VI Corps
Guards Division, Along the Cojeul Stream
The Germans wanted to advance onto the high ground around the Cojeul stream, so they assembled behind a smoke screen while *Minenwerfers* shelled the 3 Guards Brigade. Planes dropped bombs and then the 1st Welsh Guards and 1st Grenadier Guards had to 'resist the heaviest attack made upon it since the division went into the line'. Wave after wave were 'raked by the fiercest machine-gun, Lewis gun and rifle fire, while the gunners, working on their SOS lines, poured shells into them with relentless persistency'. Bombers later followed a sunken track from Hamelincourt but failed to drive the 2nd Grenadier Guards back and one prisoner 'admitted that the assaulting battalions had been practically annihilated in the attack'.

IV Corps
New Zealand Division, East of Colincamps
The 4th Rifles, 2nd Auckland and 1st Wellington captured a trench on Hawthorn Ridge with good observation over the German position around Serre.

3rd Australian Division, Between the Ancre and the Somme
Lieutenant General William Birdwood opened Australian Corps headquarters as 4th Australian Division prepared to take over from 35th Division along the Ancre. Meanwhile, there were small attacks against Major General Monash's men on the north bank of the Somme. Both 10 and 11 Australian Brigades fought back, 'nibbling' at the German line, probing and looking to take prisoners.

Fifth Army, 30 March
XIX Corps
General Rawlinson was concerned about the whole of XIX Corps front but he was particularly worried about the Moreuil Wood area. Lieutenant General Watts' right flank would be compromised if the French were driven back across the River Avre.

Carey's Force, South Bank of the Somme
The 5th Dragoon Guards restored the line near Hamel with the help of 16th Division's engineers and pioneers during the afternoon. The 15th and 19th Hussars stopped the Germans advancing along the Amiens road during the late afternoon.

66th and 39th Division, Démuin and Aubercourt
The loss of Démuin meant the Germans were able to enfilade 66th Division's Composite Battalion, forcing the Lancashire men to fall back towards Hangard, Bois de Hangard and Lancer Wood. Counter-attacks were made and Lieutenant Colonel Little's composite battalion recaptured Démuin with help from Major Chesney's company of the 6th Lancashire Fusiliers. Several attempts were made to take the high ground overlooking the village but neither one led by Colonel Saint of the Cambridgeshire Regiment, one led by the brigade majors of the 116 and 117 Brigades, nor one by Brigadier General Armytage with 117 Brigade achieved anything.

Lieutenant Colonel Little was forced to withdraw from Démuin and Captain Leask was killed leading the rearguard. Brigadier General Williams wanted to make another try and while 198 Composite Brigade advanced over one mile in pouring rain, Captain Potter was forced to order a withdrawal in the face of heavy machine-gun fire.

Lieutenant General Watts wanted 9th Australian Brigade to retake Aubercourt on the north bank of the Avre, to try and break the German position. So Brigadier General Rosenthal instructed 33rd Australian Battalion to advance from Cachy while Captain Wakelin's company of the 9th Royal Scots covered their left flank. Lieutenant Colonel Fane's 12th Lancers entered Lancer Wood on the left flank in lines of squadrons. The Australians could not reach their objective but they had stopped the Germans advancing any further.

20th (Light) Division, Rifle Wood and Little Wood
The French had abandoned Mézières and the Germans infiltrated Moreuil wood in the early morning mist. Lieutenant Colonel Welch was killed as the 6th Shropshires were driven out of Villers-aux-Érables so Brigadier

General Hyslop was told to counter-attack with 59 Brigade. Both the 12th KRRC and 12th Rifle Brigade received their orders late and while Captain Pemberton and Lieutenant King cleared the village, they had to withdraw due to heavy losses. Both Rifle Wood and Little Wood were abandoned as the division fell back and it needed help from Captain Pollock's 150 Composite Battalion to retake them.

2nd Cavalry Division, Moreuil Wood

Major General Thomas Pitman was instructed to secure Moreuil wood so the Canadian Cavalry Brigade saddled up only to meet French troops withdrawing across the Avre at Castel. The French general told Brigadier General Seely that his men were retiring because a large number of Germans were heading their way.

The Canadians continued to head for Moreuil wood and soon came under fire so Lieutenant Colonel MacDonald instructed two squadrons of Lord Strathcona's Horse to dismount and advance on foot. Acting Captain Gordon Flowerdew was mortally wounded leading three troops in a charge towards a battery at the north-east corner of the wood; he would be posthumously awarded the Victoria Cross. His men rallied on the dismounted troops, including those led by Lieutenant Harvey, VC, (awarded in 1917).

Lieutenant Colonel Straubenzie simultaneously made the Royal Canadian Dragoons charge against the south-west and north-west corners of Moreuil wood while the Fort Garry Horse and a squadron of Lieutenant Colonel Darley's 4th Hussars helped clear the north part of the wood. The 4th Hussars, 16th Lancers and 5th Lancers cleared the rest of the wood with 2nd West Yorkshires' help but the Germans soon recaptured the south end.

8th Division, Moreuil Wood

Major General Heneker was instructed to man the Avre bridges between Castel and Moreuil, in case the Germans captured Moreuil Wood. Major Griffin would end up restoring the line west of the wood with the 'very wet and weary' men of the 2nd Berkshires and the 2nd East Lancashires.

30 March Summary

His Majesty King George V had arrived in France on 28 March and he visited Haig's GHQ in Montreuil-sur-Mer the following morning. The commander-in chief reported that the worst was over but he also made several complaints. The BEF was 100,000 men weaker than it had been twelve months earlier but he was forced to hold an extra twenty miles of front. The collapse of the Russians meant there were three times as many

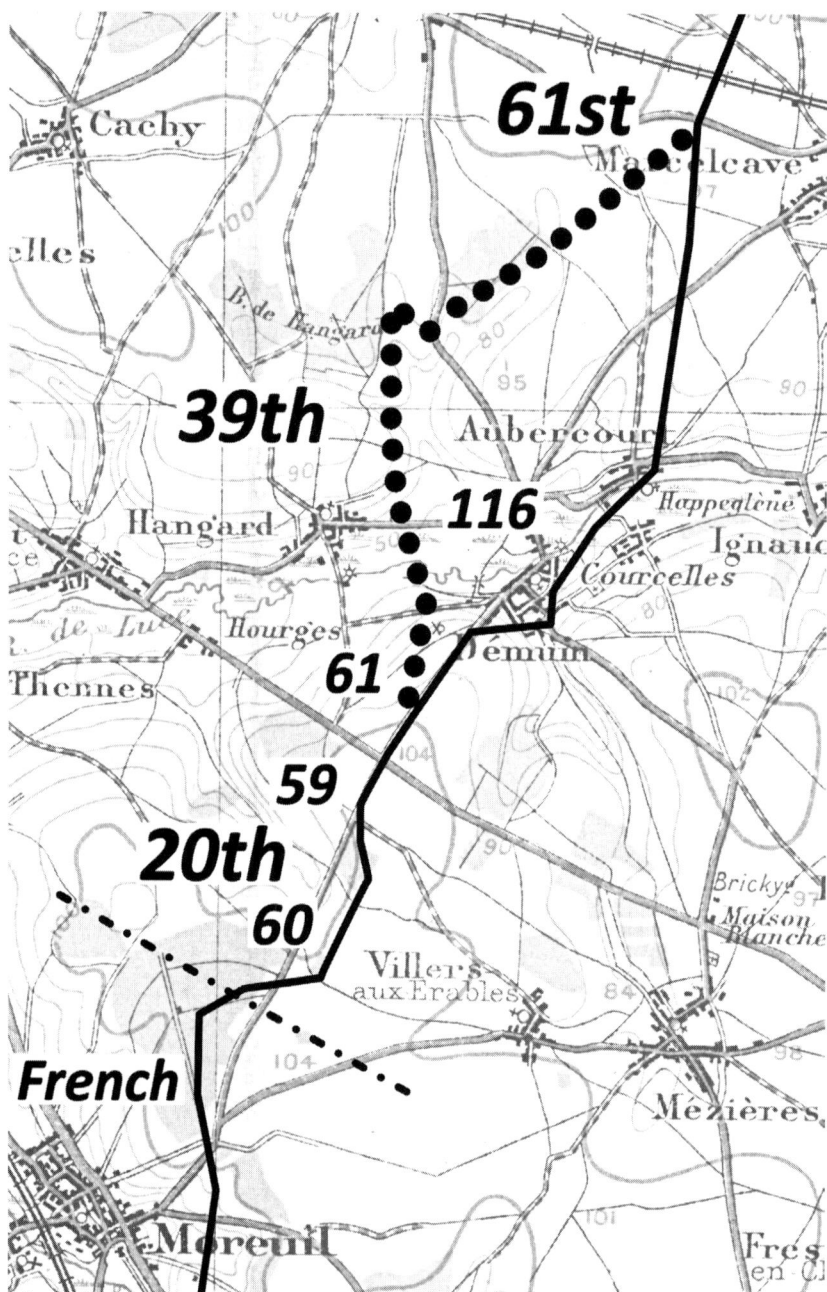

30 March: XIX Corps' right was threatened when Moreuil Wood was lost but a cavalry charge restored the situation.

Germans facing the British than there were in the spring of 1917. He also pointed out that the French Armies had still not fully recovered from the mutinies while it would be some time before the Americans were ready to make offensive action.

The King then visited Major General John Salmond at the Royal Flying Corps headquarters in St Omer and General Julian Byng's Third Army headquarters in Beauquesne, near Doullens. He would head home on 30 March and send a congratulatory message to GHQ. Haig would issue it to the troops as a Special Order of the Day:

> *My short visit to the battle front gave me an exceptional opportunity of seeing you and some of your generals engaged in the fierce battle still raging, and I thus obtained personal testimony to the indomitable courage and unflinching tenacity with which my splendid troops have withstood the supreme effort of the greater part of the enemy's fighting power. I was also fortunate enough to see some units recently withdrawn from the front line, and listened with wonder as officers and men narrated the thrilling incidents of a week's stubborn fighting.*

President Woodrow Wilson had also sent an optimistic message to Haig: 'May I express to you my warm admiration of the splendid steadfastness and valour with which your troops have withstood the German onslaught and the perfect confidence that all Americans feel that you will win a secure and final victory.'

Haig visited General Rawlinson to see how the handover between Fifth and Fourth Army staffs was progressing at Dury. He also contacted Clémenceau to ask if French troops could take over Moreuil Wood and Rifle Wood and Foch agreed they would. They all agreed Ludendorff's plan to reach Amiens was failing and one German observer reported, 'the power of attack was exhausted. Spirits sank to zero. The division suffered a reverse the like of which it had not yet experienced.'

XIX Corps, 31 March
The day was cold and wet but there was little activity on the north bank of the Somme. One trench raid by the 4 Australian Brigade captured the German plans for reorganising their front.

<u>8th and 20th (Light) Division, Moreuil Wood</u>
The only attack of the day was aimed at 8th Division's position in Moreuil Wood. The 2nd Devons were pushed out of the north side of the wood

but Captain Burke's men held on until the 1st Worcesters formed a flank covering the south half. The 5th Lancers then galloped forward and held onto the north-west corner of the wood until the 11th Durhams (Pioneers) and the 6th Shropshires arrived. The Germans now poured enfilade fire into 20th Division's brigade battalions to the north, forcing them to abandon Little Wood and Rifle Wood.

The 6th Dragoon Guards reinforced 3 Cavalry Brigade on the south bank of the Luce while the 4, 5 and Canadian Cavalry Brigades deployed along the river. Major General Heneker also sent Brigadier General Coffin's 25 Brigade to block the route to the River Avre. Major Griffin would lead the counter-attack by 200 men of the 2nd Royal Berkshires and 2nd East Lancashires which cleared Moreuil Wood.

1 to 3 April

The attempt to drive XIX Corps away from the French was the last German attack for some time. Ludendorff decided his men needed three days rest before making the next attempt to reach Amiens. But all was not well behind the German lines as one observer noted: 'the attack was a miscarriage such as the division had not seen before. Spirits sank low. Was this the end? Was the offensive beyond our strength?'

The French prepared to take over the line between Hangard and Moreuil but General Watts wanted to improve the situation north of Moreuil Wood before they did. Major General Pitman sent 1,000 dismounted troopers of the 2nd Cavalry Division through Rifle Wood under cover of a machine-gun barrage and the 5 Cavalry Brigade then cantered forward to secure the ground. French troops took over Rifle Wood and Moreuil Wood and Fifth Army finally returned to the BEF at midnight.

Conferences

Haig told Clémenceau he thought the BEF still faced the biggest threat and he desperately wanted the French to attack. Pétain confirmed the French would 'launch an attack as early as possible', just as soon as they had organised their logistics. Moves were also underway to relieve the Moreuil Wood area, so all the British troops could concentrate around Villers-Bretonneux. Foch's General Directive No 2 called for the British Third and Fourth Armies to attack either side of the Somme. Meanwhile, the French would advance towards Montdidier.

The question was, would the Germans attack the British at Villers-Bretonneux or the French around Montdidier? There were also signs they could attack in the Ypres Salient or across the Lys plain but the BEF was running out of reserves. Around one third of the BEF's divisions had just

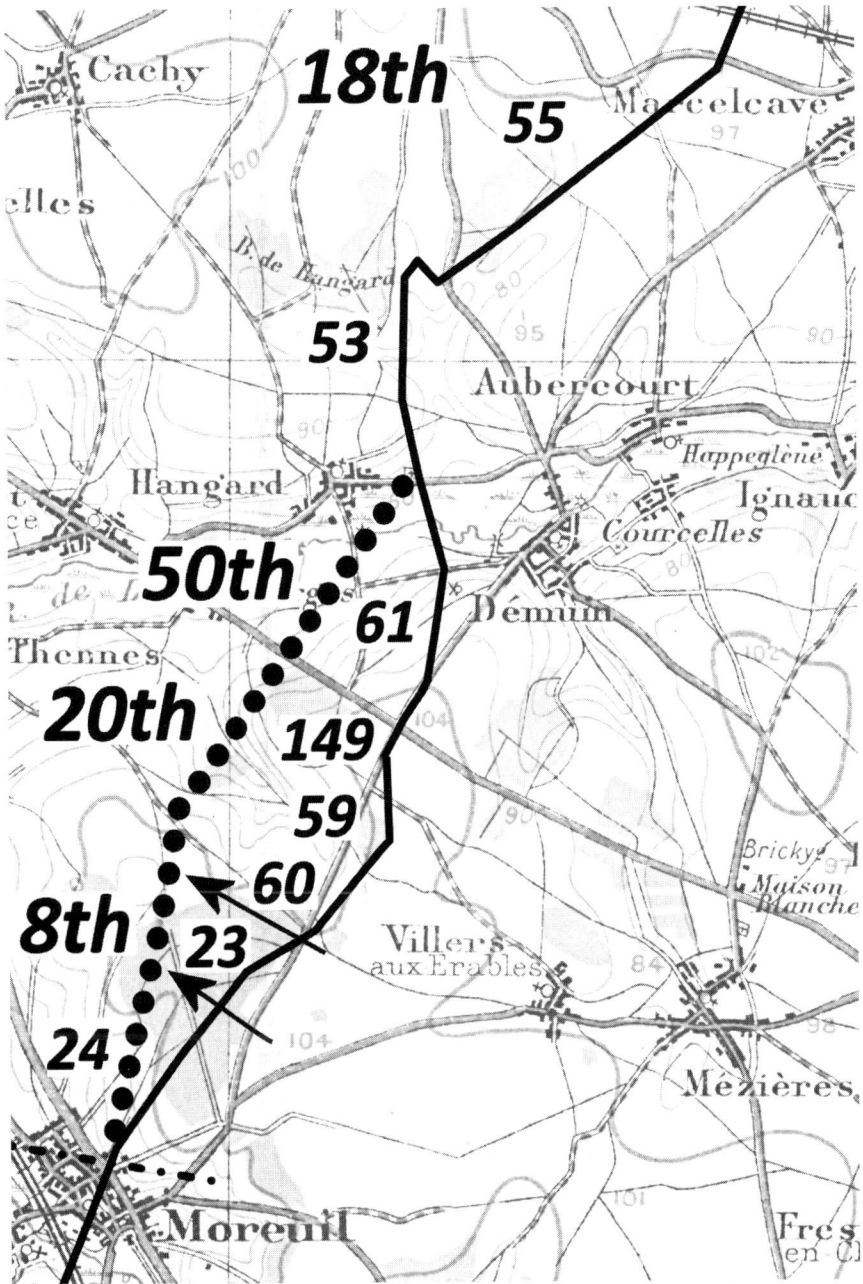

31 March, XIX Corps' South: A final attempt to clear the woods on XIX Corps' right ended in failure, so the Germans regrouped for three days.

received replacements to replace casualties, while another third were awaiting theirs. Haig placed what few reserves he had around Arras, ready to move north or south. He had also warned General Plumer to prepare to evacuate the Ypres Salient.

Foch aired his grievances at the Inter-Allied Conference at Beauvais on 3 April. He thought the powers bestowed on him at the Doullens conference had left him with 'responsibility without proportionate authority'. It was difficult to get anything done and he was having to 'persuade instead of directing'. The French, British and American representatives agreed that Foch had to control strategy but each commander-in-chief had to remain in tactical control of his troops. They could also appeal to their government if they thought their army was being compromised by Foch's decisions.

There was also a call to rationalise the distribution of planes along the whole Western Front. Currently it was believed that the German Air Force had twenty-five per cent more planes than the newly renamed Royal Air Force. Meanwhile, the French air force outnumbered the German by a massive eight to one across their sector.

The Question of Gough

Haig put Gough's case to Lloyd George on 3 April but the Prime Minister was dissatisfied with Fifth Army's performance. The failure to develop the Battle Zone meant there was no time to man the Green Line, even though Gough had not had enough men to develop it. It had taken the Germans three days to push Third Army beyond the Green Line and even then, only from part of it. Fifth Army's rapid retirement to the Somme and Crozat Canals meant units lost heavily as they moved. The fact that Fifth Army had only held the canal line for a few hours meant that the French had had no time to deploy properly. That had in turn sparked a rapid retirement and a huge loss of territory which Lloyd George had to explain to the French.

Lord Derby, Secretary of State for War, told Haig that public opinion was against Gough. The newspapers were not interested in the difficulties of holding such a long sector with so few men, their headlines only reported the woeful story of Fifth Army's rapid retreat. Haig's offer to take the blame and resign was ignored. Instead Gough was ordered to England where Lord Milner, Secretary of State for War, told him his career would be 'considered as opportunities occur'. There would be no enquiry.

Fourth Army, 4 April

The soldiers endured rain and mist as the Somme chalk turned into thick mud under the constant churning of shells, wheels and boots. But for many, it was the first time they had eaten hot food, rested their sore feet and slept properly since the battle began.

The plan was for Second Army to push the British Fourth Army towards Amiens while Eighteenth Army forced the First French army away from its ally. There was no secret about the plans because prisoners confidently let their captors know what was coming. The ground seized on 4 April would allow the heavy howitzers to shell Amiens and the resultant panic would make it difficult to supply the British troops. The main push towards the city would be made the following day.

XIX Corps

Lieutenant General Watts had two divisions south of the Somme. Both had been in action during the early days of the battle and they had only just received a few drafts while in reserve. All the battalions were still understrength and there were hardly any experienced officers or NCOs to show the new arrivals what to do. The same applied to the infantry in support, four miles behind. The only consolation was the 3rd Cavalry Division was in reserve.

14th (Light) Division, North of the Amiens Road

Major General Cyriac Skinner had only been with the division three days when it went into line north of the Amiens road. The survivors were still tired after their exertions between 21 and 23 March while the new arrivals were anxious about their first battle. The division began taking over the line late on 3 April, leaving no time to check the ground or organise the trenches to their liking.

The first attacks drove the 7th and 8th Rifle Brigades back down the Amiens road onto the 7th KRRC around Bois d'Accroche. Brigadier General Winser welcomed reinforcements from the 9th Scottish Rifles but 41 Brigade was still driven back. The Germans then turned behind 42 Brigade and the 9th KRRC covered the 9th Rifle Brigade and 5th Oxford and Bucks as they fell back. Brigadier General Forster kept his headquarters in Hamel as long as possible, so as not to cause alarm, only to be captured along with two of his staff; Forster was then hit by a stray bullet.

9th Australian Brigade, South of the Amiens Road and Villers-Bretonneux

Some German troops turned south from 14th Division's area against 35th Australian Battalion's flank. Lieutenant Colonel Goddard's men fell back through Villers-Bretonneux to Bois l'Abbé so Brigadier General Rosenthal sent 33rd Australian Battalion to fill the gap across the Amiens road. The original plan was for Lieutenant Colonel Morhead to counter-attack with 6th Cavalry Brigade. However, the Australians were under such pressure that Brigadier General Seymour had to tell his troopers to dismount and reinforce the line.

The Germans kept pushing so Brigadier General Rosenthal made 35th Australian Battalion responsible for the Villers-Bretonneux area. He sent the 34th Australian Battalion north-west of the village and the 36th Australian Battalion to the south side. Meanwhile, XIX Corps sent five Canadian motor machine gun batteries and six armoured cars forward to help 9th Australian Brigade hold on.

Lieutenant Colonel Milne's 36th Australian Battalion counter-attacked south of the village with a company of the 35th Australian Battalion on the left and the 7th Queen's on the right. Their combined efforts drove the enemy back and the 6th London Regiment reinforced the 7th Queen's right flank. A second attack by part of 33rd Australian Battalion was reinforced by a squadron of the 17th Lancers cantering up on its left flank. A Canadian motor machine-gun battery silenced the enemy machine guns while Goddard sent the 34th Australian Battalion forward to fill the gap in the Australian line. He made all three battalions crawl forward to find better positions during the night.

18th (Eastern) Division, South of the Amiens Road

Major General Lee's men stopped the attacks around Lancer Wood until the 35th Australian Battalion fell back through Villers-Bretonneux. Brigadier General Wood's men struggled because the mud was clogging up their weapons and Germans surged forward as the rate of fire slackened along 55 Brigade's front. Both the 7th Buffs and 8th East Surreys were pushed back on the 7th Queen's, allowing the enemy to occupy the north end of Lancer Wood and turn the 7th Queen's Own's flank. Brigadier General Higginson sent Lieutenant Colonel Dewing's 8th Berkshires forward to hold 53 Brigade's line. Both the Queen's Own and the Berkshires suffered heavy casualties as they fell back onto the 10th Essex and Major Tosetti was killed silencing the machine gun trained on the escaping men. The loss of Lancer Wood meant the 6th Northants had to wheel through Hangard Wood on 54 Brigade's front. However, Brigadier General Sadleir-Jackson made sure they held their flank around Hangard village, alongside the French.

The French and the Germans, 4 April

The French First Army advanced east of Moreuil but 'the attack which had begun so well, was broken and in spite of valour, it could not be got going

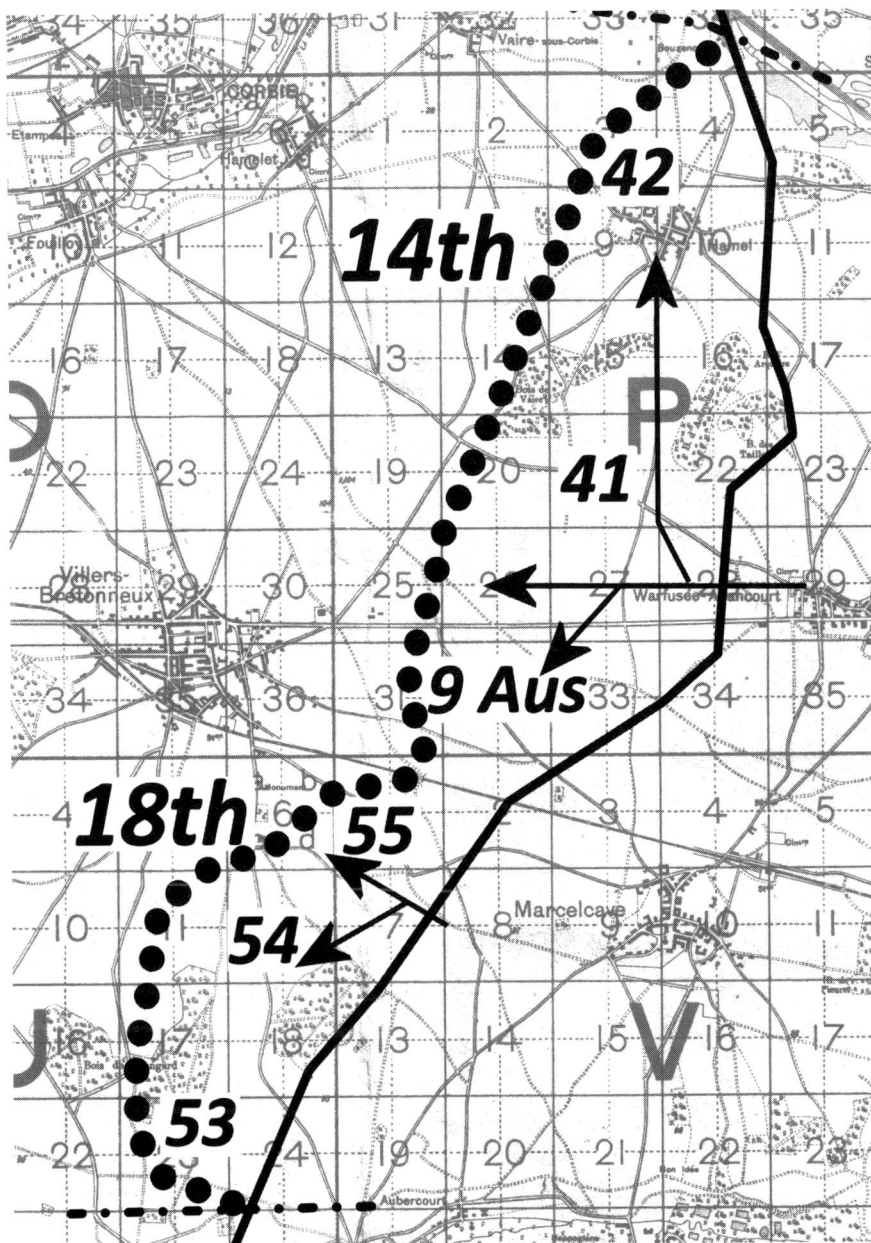

4 April XIX Corps: The 14th Division had not time to organise itself before it was driven back but a rapid counter-attack made sure Villers-Bretonneux stayed in Australian hands.

again.' A counter-attack drove the French back another two miles, bringing Eighteenth Army ever closer to the important railway and the River Noye south of Amiens; but not close enough. The order to continue the attack on 5 April was given before the Crown Prince reported his men had not reached the Noye because it had been difficult getting supplies across the River Avre.

The Final Attack; 5 April

Seventeenth and Second Armies widened the scope of the attack to hit Third Army north of the Somme once again. Or at least that was the plan. The German soldier was as tired as his British counterpart, only now it was his turn to suffer from a lack of ammunition and food. The British logistics chain was shorter now, while the German supply wagons were having to cross the devastated areas.

Prisoners and deserters warned that an attack was due and everyone 'stood to' when gas shells started hitting the battery positions. The front line was hit at dawn but the bombardment was a shadow of that fired on the morning of 21 March. The attack only involved a few assault teams trudging forward through the rain and mist because of the ammunition shortage.

IV Corps

42nd (East Lancashire) Division, Bucquoy

The Germans attacked 125 Brigade's position around Bucquoy during the morning, some moving over the top and others bombing along trenches. Lieutenant Colonel Brewis's 1/7th Lancashire Fusiliers held their ground north-east of the village but two companies of the 1/8th Lancashire Fusiliers were wiped out to the south-east. A wounded Lieutenant Ivers held up the attack until Lieutenant Colonel Clive moved the 1/5th Lancashire Fusiliers forward. Lieutenant Colonel Davies was killed organising the counter-attack but Major Castle made sure the Lancashire Fusiliers went forward and Brigadier General Fargus was pleased to hear that Bucquoy had been retaken.

37th Division and 4 Australian Brigade, Rossignol Wood and Hébuterne

Major General Hugh Bruce-Williams was instructed to recapture Rossignol Wood and the divisions either side staged false attacks (called Chinese Attacks) to draw attention away from 63 Brigade. Nine out of the ten tanks of the 10th Battalion slated to support the advance ditched crossing the rough ground. The 8th Somersets were late because they waited for the tanks, so they lost the barrage and were soon pinned

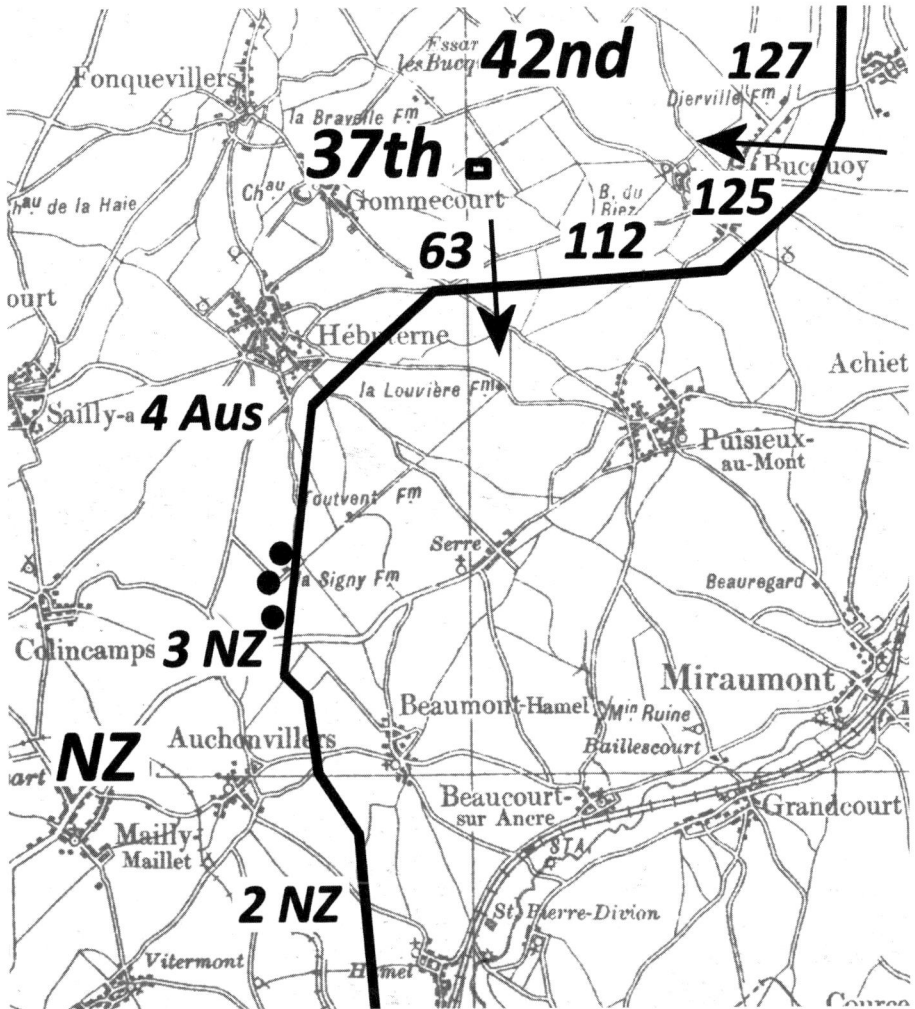

5 April IV Corps: Bucquoy was lost and recaptured but it was impossible to recapture Rossignol Wood.

down. Second Lieutenants Moody and Askey were killed leading the 8th Lincolns but they too ended up unable to advance further than a sunken road; they retired when they ran out of grenades. The 15th Australian Battalion captured the Poplars but they too withdrew after seeing the Lincolns retire.

The temporary loss of Bucquoy meant Lieutenant Colonel Smith's 13th Royal Fusiliers had to cover 111 Brigade's exposed flank for a time.

New Zealand Division, West of Colincamps
The 3 New Zealand Brigade were subjected to a number of attacks and the 4th Rifle Brigade were eventually driven out of La Signy Farm.

V Corps

63rd (Royal Naval) Division, North Part of Aveluy Wood
Major Walker's 7th Royal Fusiliers were overrun in Aveluy Wood and while Captain Tealby formed a new line, the Germans advanced through 190 Brigade's position towards Mesnil during the night. Major Clutterbuck and Captain Newling led the 1st and 2nd Royal Marines forward the following morning and they re-established contact with the 4th Bedfords and the 24th London Regiment.

47th (2nd London) Division, South Part of Aveluy Wood
The Londoners were hit by volleys of rifle grenades as small groups of Germans advanced through Aveluy Wood. A couple of machine gun teams got behind the 1/23rd London Regiment but they held on until the Germans withdrew. The 1/24th London Regiment had to form a flank when the 7th Royal Fusiliers lost the north end of the wood so Major Marshall took the divisional pioneers forward. They suffered heavy casualties when they advanced the following morning because the barrage missed the German machine-gun teams who had grouped together on one flank.

12th (Eastern) Division, Facing Albert
Major General Scott's men stopped the first attack out of Albert. Captain West was wounded when the 5th Berkshires were driven back, so the 9th Royal Fusiliers bombed down the line from the flank, recovering part of Major Bartley-Deniss' trench. Lieutenants Collins' and Howe's companies of the 7th Sussex helped recover the rest in a hastily organised night attack.

VII Corps

4th Australian Division, Along the Ancre at Dernancourt
The enemy crept through the hedges surrounding Dernancourt against 12 Australian Brigade's line of outposts laid along the railway embankment. The veteran Lieutenant Colonel Leane went as far as to say the bombardment was 'the heaviest since Pozières' on the Somme back in the summer of 1916. The artillery did not see the SOS signals in the mist so the Germans broke through 47th Australian Battalion on the railway curve, allowing them to

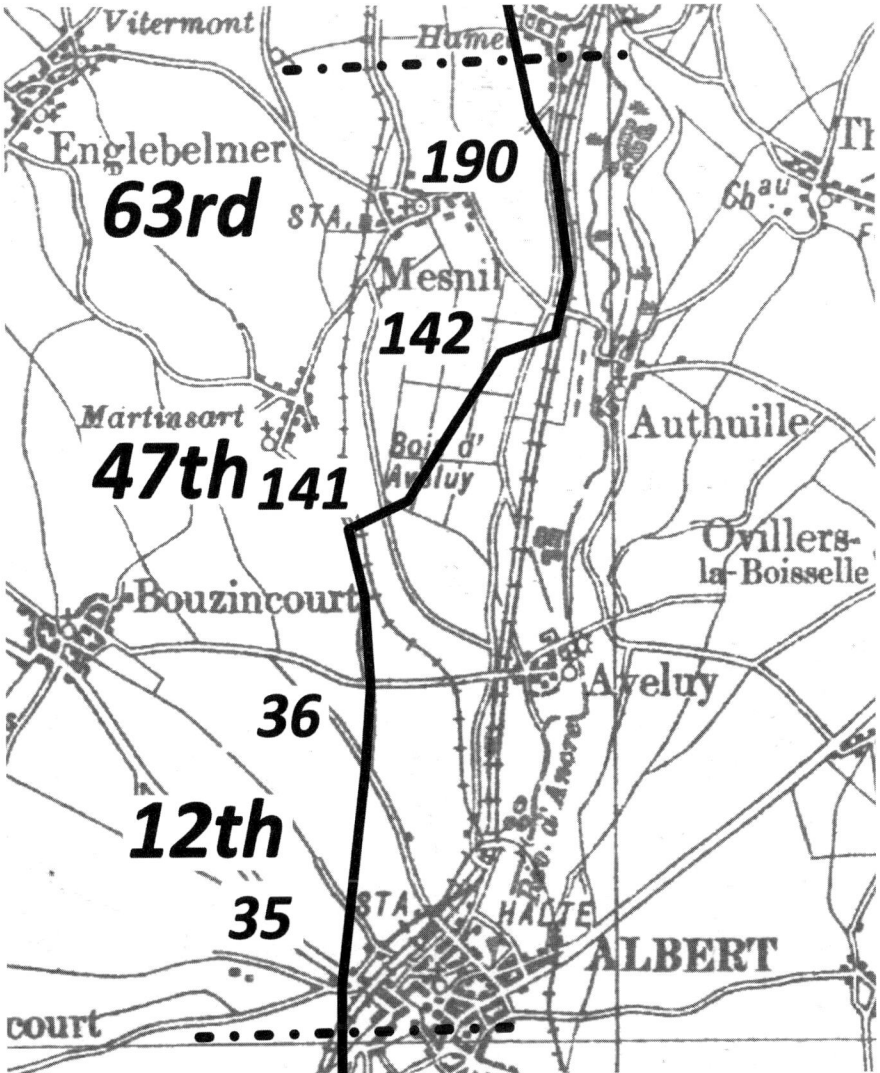

5 April V Corps: Trenches were lost and recaptured along V Corps' line but the Germans could not expand their bridgehead across the Ancre.

enfilade the full length of the embankment. The companies on Lieutenant Colonel Imlay's flanks stopped them going further until reinforcements occupied Pioneer Trench.

For a time it looked as if 52nd Battalion's flank would be rolled up but Captain Kennedy's men held on until Major General Sinclair-MacLagan

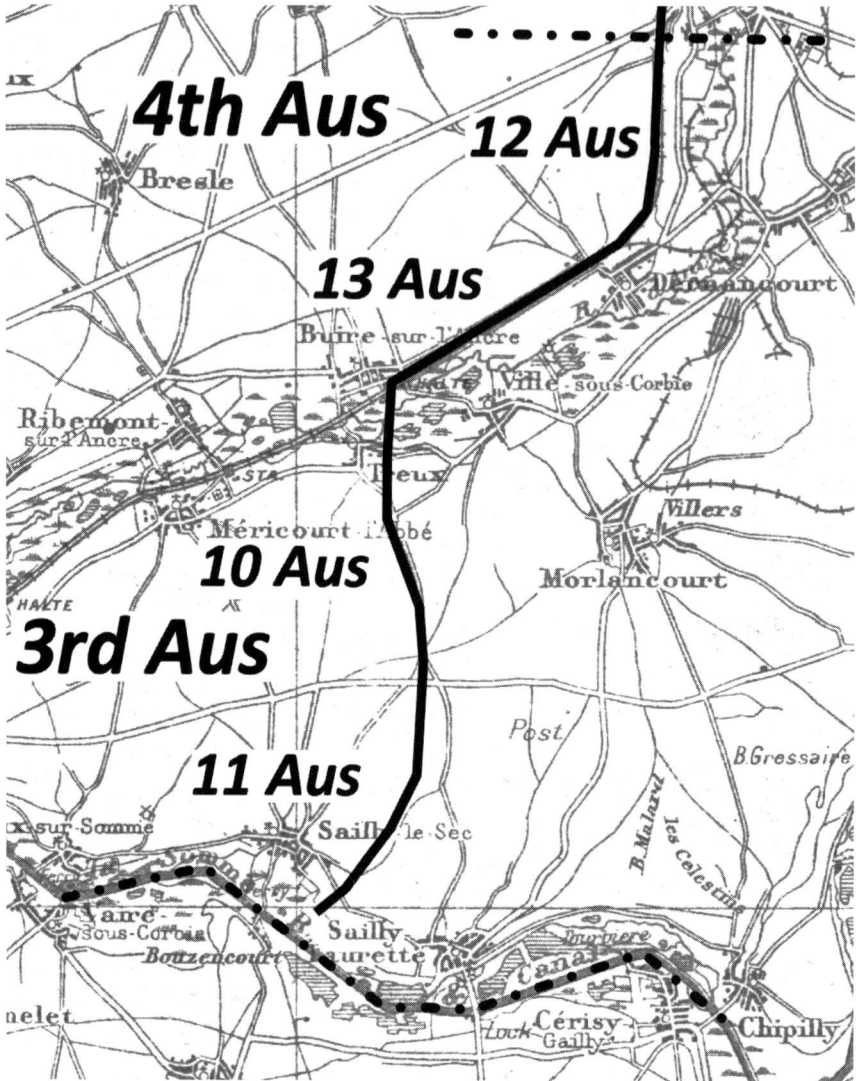

5 April VII Corps: An attack penetrated 4th Australian Division's line at Dernancourt but it was restored by a counter-attack.

organised a late afternoon counter-attack. The barrage crashed down and then four battalions advanced 'in one line or throng' six minutes later. There were heavy losses and while a final charge forced the Germans to fall back, the tanks which were supposed to reinforce the position turned up too late to help.

3rd Australian Division
The 39th Australian Battalion stopped an attack against Treux, east of the Ancre.

XIX Corps
Attempts to drive the 15 Australian Brigade back along the south bank of the Somme failed. Another attack against 6 Cavalry Brigade north of the Amiens road was also stopped. The 6th Northants lost a trench north of Hangard but 18th Division recovered it.

The Germans
Hopes for a big push on Amiens had resulted in a few localised attacks, so Ludendorff suspended all operations. It was now time to look to Operation Georgette, which would be launched across the Lys Plain on 9 April.

Chapter 18

Conclusions

A Shortage of Men

The BEF was short of 100,000 men by the end of 1917 because the casualties from the campaigns at Arras, in Flanders and then Cambrai had not been replaced. Lloyd George sent General Jan Smuts to investigate at the end of January 1918 and his report had both good and bad news: 'I am satisfied that the morale of the army is good… There is no question that the men are tired. This applies more especially to the infantry…' But the War Cabinet still refused to send the men needed to bring the BEF up to strength, so Haig was forced to reorganise it. All that could be done was to reduce most divisions from twelve battalions down to nine, disbanding and merging many battalions.

The Russian Revolution meant that the Allies could soon face a big attack and it would take place before the American Expeditionary Force was established on the Western Front. For the first time in three years it looked as though the British soldier was going to have to prove himself on the defensive. But battalions were understrength, men were tired and officers were inexperienced because most were replacements.

While German divisions moved from the Eastern Front to the Western Front, Haig was forced to send divisions to Italy. The BEF was also forced to take over additional frontage from the French, further reducing its reserves. Meanwhile the new Supreme War Council was asking for a General Reserve to be created from divisions that did not exist. It seems the politicians were out of touch with the military situation, leaving the generals to do the best they could with what limited resources they had.

Improving the Defences

Haig correctly assumed the Germans would attack the BEF and he gave the order to improve the defences a few days after Cambrai ended. The shortage of men meant the engineers, labour battalions and other construction units had to rely on the infantry to carry out the manual work. But they had to spend most of their time maintaining the logistics chain, leaving them little time to improve the defences. It also left them little time for training or resting.

Most of the work was done on the Forward Zone, even though it was often where a battle had ended or in front of the Hindenburg Line. Nowhere was ground given up, even when it was an unfavourable position. Units had been warned that there could be no retreat, while experience told the British soldier that it was usually impossible to hold the front line during an offensive. Those in the outpost line knew they had little chance of surviving the bombardment or escaping the infantry attack that followed.

The defensive plan relied on the line of strong points in the Forward Zone brought about by the shortage of manpower. However, communications between strongpoints were faulty and the bombardment often cut them completely. Some officers objected to this 'blob system of defence, as it had been called in derision before the War... Some even went so far as to call the policy suicidal.' One veteran of 1914 said, 'It don't suit us. The British army fights in line and won't do any good in these bird cages.' Work on the Battle Zone was varied while hardly anything had been done to the Rear Zone which was often just a half-dug, half-wired trench. The lack of men left divisions with few reserves to counter-attack, so many strongpoints were surrounded and left to fight on until they ran out of ammunition.

The manpower situation had led to the BEF's Forward Zone being strong while those behind were weak. This was the reverse of the German model and it would cost Third Army and Fifth Army dearly. A lot of their men were lost in the first few hours, leaving divisions short of tactical reserves to fight back with. The BEF's general situation meant there was a shortage of strategic reserves to shore up the line.

The Opening Attack and the Defence

The attack was not a surprise when it came; in fact many were relieved it did start where and when it was anticipated. It had been possible to get the tens of thousands of infantry to the front during night marches, while the artillery relied on map fire to hit targets rather than registering them. However, it was impossible to disguise all the other preparations needed for such a large offensive.

The use of the German artillery was unconventional but effective. The rapid fire of the field guns was used to smother the British artillery with gas, neutralising many batteries before zero hour. Trench mortars were used to hit the front line, and they too fired quickly. It had been possible to register many before zero hour and they were far more accurate than conventional artillery. This left the heavy guns free to disrupt the command and communications network.

The preliminary bombardment was less powerful than expected but it had been well thought out and achieved three important things. It supressed the British artillery; it disrupted Third Army and Fifth Army's communications; and it shattered their front-line defences. This meant headquarters had little news for a long time, making it difficult to make informed tactical decisions. It also left the gunners without up-to-date information on targets. The mist meant that machine gunners could not see targets while the artillery could not see the infantry's SOS signals through the fog and smoke. The combination of all these factors meant that many defence schemes were compromised.

The Germans also suffered coordination problems resulting in the assault being carried out at different times, but the practised infiltration and outflanking tactics often worked well in the mist. Advanced groups used maps to locate strongpoints and avoided them, driving deep into the British rear. Parties of storm troopers followed compass bearings through the gaps and headed for the Battle Zone. The final groups dealt with the strongpoints and other centres of resistance with machine guns, flame projectors, trench mortars, field guns and the occasional tank. The advance moved fast in many areas but some strongpoints held out far longer than expected while some groups became disorientated in the mist.

The nature of the battle changed when the fog cleared. Many German units were caught moving in dense formations, resulting in heavy casualties. Meanwhile, many British units found themselves trapped because the enemy was across their line of retreat. Clear skies meant pilots could take to the skies and many German planes helped the infantry by strafing to pin down enemy troops. The British pilots could see many targets but communications were so badly disrupted that the gunners could not be contacted in time.

The destruction of communications before zero hour and the subsequent inability to re-establish them during the retreat meant artillery was often unable to help the infantry. Many times during the battle, the field artillery had to cooperate with the nearest infantry units, firing at targets delivered by hand by mounted messengers, often over open sights. The heavy artillery often could not help because they were far behind the front and out of touch with the fighting. They were reduced to firing at map targets, such as likely troop assembly points, road junctions and other bottlenecks. The heavier guns were sometimes a liability because of a lack of tractors to move them along the congested roads and many batteries had to be abandoned.

A Late Response to the Manpower Crisis

Lloyd George eventually chaired a meeting concerning reinforcements for France on 23 March. The War Cabinet decided against introducing conscription in Ireland where there was a political situation. Haig refused to take Indian troops back in France because they had suffered too much sickness in the wet, cold European climate. The immediate solution was to send all the men in training and all the trained men working in reserved occupations to France; everyone on leave would also be recalled to their units. It meant the Admiralty had to find shipping so double the number of men could be moved across the English Channel. Around 113,000 would reach France in just two weeks, more than offsetting the number of casualties suffered during the Somme offensive. The situation was improved by recalling divisions and heavy guns from Italy and Salonika.

Haig's Defensive Strategy

By 23 March, Haig had formulated a strategy based on the evolving situation. The BEF was facing a massive attack which had driven it from its three defensive zones. It was now facing a battle in the open and had to break contact as soon as possible, to give it time to establish a new defensive line.

GHQ's operations chief, Major General Davidson, went to Third Army headquarters to explain the BEF had run out of reserve divisions. Haig was asking First Army and Second Army to provide more but it would take several days to withdraw them from the line and move them south.

Haig's Chief of the General Staff, Lieutenant General Lawrence, was sent to Fifth Army with the same message about reserves. But there would be no reserves for Gough, he had to fight on until the French had assembled enough divisions to take over his position south of the River Somme. Haig and Lawrence also visited Byng to tell him their plan for stopping the German onslaught. Third Army's left flank had to hold on around Arras but he was to withdraw his centre back to the old 1916 front line and his right to the River Ancre.

The old Somme battlefield presented a logistics nightmare because six months of shellfire had destroyed any landmarks. The few roads were packed with traffic 'crawling at a snail's pace' and those who dared venture off it faced a maze of decaying trenches, shell holes and entanglements. Some artillery teams became lost trying to navigate a route and ended up having to retrace their steps. Haig wanted to retreat across the devastated area, so it was behind the German front and their problem.

The Germans were convinced Third Army was in full retreat when it started moving fast and in some places they were right. Byng's plan involved a rapid, and sometimes chaotic, withdrawal, but on the whole the British soldier performed admirably during the retreat. Third Army escaped virtually intact but divisions had been split up and many men had become separated from their officers. There was also a huge gap between Hébuterne and Beaumont Hamel, made worse by the premature demolition of the bridge at Miraumont. However, the British logistics chain was getting shorter and easier to control while German supplies were now having to be carried across the devastated areas. The German infantry threw caution to the wind as they tried to catch up with Third Army, giving the British gunners plenty of lucrative targets. But some batteries were unable to shoot at them because dumps were running out of ammunition while wagons were struggling to deliver shells.

The French Response

The French were slow to reinforce the southern flank of the breakthrough. For several days Pétain was convinced Operation Michael was only a preliminary attack and that the main one would fall elsewhere against the French line. This was partly due to the German diversionary tactics and partly due to the French reluctance to believe that Fifth Army's situation was as bad as it was. Gough was supposed to hold on until the French had deployed enough troops to counter-attack Eighteenth Army's flank. The failure to hold the Somme and Crozat Canals resulted in the deployment area being lost and French divisions being engaged piecemeal.

The French chose to send their infantry forward alone and while it was a tactically sound decision, it caused problems. Artillery needed special trains to move their guns and horses, or they had to travel by road. The British infantry had suffered many casualties as they fell back but their artillery had not. The plan was for the British to withdraw through the French infantry while the British artillery continued to give support, relying on its established logistics chain. The idea did reduce the amount of traffic on the roads but coordinating the actions of the infantry and artillery on a fluid front was difficult enough without the added language problem.

Later German Tactics

At times the Germans 'skilfully carried out' their advance. Their 'front was covered by large patrols, each carrying one or two light machine guns. The use of light signals by these patrols was most remarkable. They signalled each stage by sending up a Very light, resulting in light signals going up as far as the eye could reach.' Flares were used to tell the Germans gunners how far the infantry had advanced. Pre-determined signals told them when a barrage was needed and the infantry would advance after a pre-agreed length of time. Patrols were used to probe the British line and they fired flares to indicate they had found a gap. The main body of troops would then head straight for it.

Infantry sometimes ditched their rifles so they could carry machine gun ammunition. Stretcher bearers were also seen carrying ammunition boxes forward before taking wounded back.

At times German officers sent their men forward without identifying where the British line was. Time and again waves and columns of troops advanced only to be scattered by rifle, machine gun and artillery fire. Some German commanders became over-confident and made their infantry advance without artillery support. They were often caught in the open by rearguards resulting in heavy casualties.

The British tried to remove or destroy surplus food and ammunition, to prevent it falling into enemy hands. However, enough was left to make the German soldiers think they had been lied to. For long enough they had been told the U-boats had been sinking supply ships heading for Britain, bringing its armies to starvation levels. The Germans enjoyed feasting on the abandoned stores of food and drink, only to become downhearted when they realised the implications of their findings. The Allies were not starving.

Managing the Retreat

Officers had no experience in controlling fluid battles and they often fell back as soon as they saw the enemy moving past their flanks. Communications during such a fast-moving battle were difficult and it was difficult to anticipate how long it would take orders to reach the front line; it was even harder to guess what the enemy would do. Headquarters had to keep moving and cars could not get along the congested roads. It was often left to mounted staff officers to taken messages to the brigade and battalion commanders while they had to rely on their runners to get the message to the company commanders.

There were few defensive positions en route and the men had to dig where they stopped with the tools they had to hand; sometimes with their hands. They had few sandbags, no wire and little time to build any defensive position. The retreat exhausted the British soldiers but their morale was still good, especially when they started fighting back rather than falling back. But while the front line was holding, the rear area was crowded with stragglers who drifted towards villages where they joined the first officer they found. Stragglers' posts were set up on 25 March to gather them together but they could have been established earlier and there could have been more of them.

Ambulances found it hard to evacuate the wounded along the busy roads and the Royal Army Medical Corps personnel found it increasingly difficult to work when the casualty clearing stations started moving back. Road control during the retreat became virtually non-existent while the thousands of refugees, many of them elderly or young, only added to the traffic chaos. One solution was to create cross-country tracks controlled by traffic police which only military traffic could use.

Soldiers often fed themselves, foraging food from abandoned canteens and stores, but it was difficult to find water, particularly when moving across the old Somme battlefield. The Army Service Corps did its best to stock up dumps with ammunition of all calibres but the lorry drivers found it difficult to find both the railheads and the front line because they were moving so fast.

All across Third Army and Fifth Army, the men repeatedly did what their officers asked of them; they carried out their orders and then marched having had little food or water. They had little sleep but persevered time and again under the most trying of circumstances. They were determined to hold on and their tough defensive stance illustrated what could have been achieved if more men had been available to improve the Battle and Rear Area Zones.

Index